POWER AND LEADERSHIP
IN INTERNATIONAL BARGAINING

Shibley Telhami

Power and Leadership in International Bargaining

THE PATH TO THE CAMP DAVID ACCORDS

COLUMBIA UNIVERSITY PRESS
New York

COLUMBIA UNIVERSITY PRESS
NEW YORK   OXFORD
Copyright © 1990 Columbia University Press
All rights reserved

Library of Congress Cataloging-in-Publication Data
Telhami, Shibley.
Power and leadership in international bargaining :
the path to the Camp David accords / Shibley Telhami.
p.   cm.
Includes bibliographical references.
ISBN 978-0-231-07214-4
ISBN 978-0-231-07215-1 (pbk.)
1. Israel-Arab War, 1973 — Peace.   2. Egypt — Foreign relations —
Israel.   3. Israel — Foreign relations — Egypt.   4. Diplomatic
negotiations in international disputes.   5. Middle East — Politics
and government — 1945—   I. Title.   II. Title: Camp David accords.
DS128.183.T44   1990
327.6205694 — dc20   90-30836
CIP

Casebound editions of Columbia University Press books are Smyth-sewn
and printed on permanent and durable acid-free paper

Printed in the United States of America

To My Parents
Zeki and Terese Telhami

Contents

Preface   vii

Part I: The Puzzle and the Approach

1. Overview   3
2. A Framework for the Study of Cases in International Politics   18

Part II: International Politics and the Preferences of Israel and Egypt

3. The Superpowers and the Preferences of States   45
4. Regional Politics and the Preferences of Egypt   84
5. International Politics and the Preferences of Israel   107

Part III: Specifying the Parameters of Bargaining: Domestic and International Preferences at Camp David

6. Preferences, Perceptions, and the Structure of Bargaining   127

Part IV: Bargaining Performance: An Evaluation

7. Bargaining Performance: A Case in Comparative Foreign Policy   157
8. Conclusion   196

Documentary Appendix   205
Notes   241
Bibliography   261
Index   273

Preface

*A*NYONE GROWING up in the Middle East in the last four decades is bound to be obsessed with issues of war and peace. So persistent the state of war seems, so hopeless the future, so remote the answers, that one turns to the philosophical to find answers and hopes beyond the material world; one searches the belief-systems of Middle Eastern cultures for explanations not found elsewhere. I myself, once dedicated to the study of pure mathematics, turned to the study of philosophy and Middle Eastern religions that appeared to dominate the belief systems, to motivate the behavior of states, and perhaps even to perpetuate conflict. After a full year of research in Israel and Egypt, observing and studying the link between religion and politics, theology and belief systems, I was convinced that the links are superficial, the answers largely political and economic, and the conditions of the apparently cursed region hardly unique. My obsession led me to the study of politics.

The surprising events that followed my research visit to the region fueled my interest further. I had become the first Israeli citizen ever admitted to Egypt at a time when Israel and Egypt were in a state of war. Israeli officials seemed perplexed. Yet, exactly one year later, the president of Egypt stunned the world by visiting Jerusalem to declare "No more war." Can one man change history? Can war be stopped magically through simple political decisions? Is the answer to be found in "good" governments? In benign superpowers? In changing perceptions? Surely all these variables count somewhat, but how do we decide their relative significance? How do we go about finding an answer?

With these general theoretical questions, I set out to study a very remarkable case in Middle East history, a study that intensified my obsession with war and peace. My answers, although they offer no more hope about the state of affairs in the Middle East than I had had before, were in important respects liberating for me. The key to this personal freedom was in my conclusions which affirm the Middle East is not so unusual and that unique and enduring cultural and religious traits are not responsible for its misery. There is a certain solace in this for those among Middle Easterners who had grown so desperate about their own state of affairs in contrast to an apparently "normal" outside world that they questioned their own normality. With this issue out of the way, I settled into my new role as a professional political scientist to raise the general questions about war and peace and other issues of international relations. The Middle East became my primary laboratory, although personal interest is ever present, and the Camp David accords became a central case study for my general theoretical interests.

My later study of the Camp David accords took me to Egypt, Israel, the West Bank, Jordan, and the Soviet Union. I conducted several interviews with key Camp David negotiators from the United States, Egypt, and Israel, and I examined extensive literature related to the case in Hebrew, Arabic, and English. Many among those interviewed were extremely generous with their time, some providing me with several extensive sessions. I am grateful to all those who were kind enough to share their thoughts and information with me. I am especially thankful to Minister Ezer Weizman, Minister Shimon Peres (now Finance Minister), to Ministers Ibrahim Kamel and Butrus Ghali, to Ambassador Tahseen Bashir, to Undersecretary of State Harold Saunders, to Dr. William Quandt, and to Dr. Aleksandr Kislov.

My theoretical study benefitted from many individuals too numerous to name. Several, however, had substantial influence on my thinking. I have learned more about the study of international relations from Kenneth Waltz than from any other person; his classic *Man, the State and War* left an enduring impact; his suggestions were always insightful; his encouragement and personal concern always inspiring. Benson Mates influenced me in ways of which he cannot be aware; a logician of impeccable standards, he nonetheless wisely counseled me *against* the excessive application of rigorous logical standards to the study of politics; his personal friendship and obvious interest have been uplifting. John Harsanyi has provided me with the kind of intellectual synthesis that I sought; his mastery of philosophy, mathematics, and social science made his generous advice indispensable. George Lenczowski has been a dedicated teacher and friend; his knowledge of Middle East diplomacy and his remarkable intellectual memory have assisted me time and again; his personal concern was always felt.

I have also benefitted a great deal from the comments of and interaction with several friends and colleagues. In particular, I should mention Gregory Gause and Barry Preisler, and my dedicated assistants: Linda Saghi, Sharon Shible, and Thomas Holloway. Many merits in this work are owed to them and many unmentioned others; the shortcomings are my responsibility alone.

POWER AND LEADERSHIP
IN INTERNATIONAL BARGAINING

I

The Puzzle and the Approach

1

Overview

CONSIDER THIS puzzle: after decades of conflict and four devastating wars, and from seemingly irreconcilable positions, Egypt and Israel signed the historic Camp David accords in the fall of 1978. The behavior of Egypt is particularly perplexing. As the leader of the Pan-Arabist movement, Egypt had appeared most committed to its relations with other Arab states and had been Israel's most avowed enemy. Yet, in a sudden shift that surprised political experts and the public alike, Anwar Sadat's Egypt reversed its historical pattern at the cost of isolating itself from the Arab world. And although Egypt's behavior is central to an explanation of the startling accords, the degree of Israeli concessions and the central role that the United States played also require examination.

The empirical component of this work addresses two questions. First, why did Egypt and Israel move to sign a bilateral peace agreement at the expense of Egypt's relations with the Arab world? Second, what explains the specific terms of the Camp David accords?[1] The theoretical component develops a framework that can be employed not only for Camp David, but also in other cases of international relations, since the framework yields general hypotheses that apply beyond the case at hand.

In this work, I infuse international relations theory with empirical events, and demonstrate the compatibility of bargaining theory and realist theory while indicating the empirical relevance of both. I also make two unconventional arguments about the Camp David accords. The first is that Egypt's move to sign a bilateral peace agreement with Israel even at the expense of its relations with the rest of the Arab world resulted from major changes in the *distribution of military and economic power*, both globally and regionally—not from leadership change and internal economic crises; in this sense, realist theory is extremely relevant to the empirical events considered. The second conclusion is that many of the specific terms of the agreements concluded at Camp David were determined by actual bargaining strategies and tactics, which were a function of leadership and system of government. Specifically, I argue that *centralized* systems of government ("strong states") are *less* conducive to optimal bargaining than decentralized governments ("weak states") are, and that Egypt's highly centralized government weakened Egyptian bargaining. In addition, I argue that, given the suitability of some personality traits (and the unsuitability of others) to optimal bargaining, President Sadat's personality was especially unsuited to good bargaining.

Since blending theory and empirical cases is highly unusual, especially in the field of Middle East politics, there will be some inevitable over-simplification of both theory and facts, some shortcomings, and a peculiar style; but my hope is that despite these, the overall attempt and the resulting conclusions will make them worthwhile.

As puzzling as many political events may be, the problem, as James Kurth put it, is not "that there are no answers but that there are too many answers."[2] Although the Egyptian initiative leading to the Camp David accords surprised most analysts, post facto explanations abound. Explanatory variables have ranged from Sadat's personality and culture to domestic economic difficulties and superpower politics. While most of these explanations can be rejected on simple grounds of inconsistency and lack of empirical fit, serious methodological questions have to be answered before an alternative explanatory framework can be proposed.

Which of these variables — leaders' personalities, domestic politics, bargaining processes, regional conflict, superpower competition, or arbitrary combination—are most appropriate for explaining the Camp David accords? If several variables are relevant, what is the relative weight of each and how can we assess this relativity without encountering the serious problem of "overlap" or "collinearity?"[3] Answering these questions requires the development of a consistent and generalizable framework of analysis that will also guard against ad hoc explanations.

The Camp David accords provide an unusually appropriate empirical case for demonstrating the relative explanatory power of competing variables in shaping state behavior. At the level of superpower and regional relations, the outcome of the Camp David process promised to substantially affect superpower interests in the Middle East, to increase or decrease the chances of war, and to alter the shape of regional politics. In addition, the bargaining process was so well-defined, so clearly isolated, and so intensely continuous, involving the highest levels of government, particularly in its final stages, that it should provide a clear insight into the effect of the art of negotiating on the agreements. Moreover, the striking contrasts among the domestic systems of government in Egypt, Israel, and the United States should shed some light on the relative effects of these systems on the bargaining process. Finally, if personalities ever play a major role in international affairs, then surely the personalities of Anwar Sadat and Menachem Begin, especially in the context of their respective systems of government, should be expected to show their unmistakable marks on the events leading to the accords at Camp David.

The Theoretical Task

The development of a methodological framework for the study of international relations, especially those involving formal bargaining, is a central task of this work, and it is undertaken in the next chapter. I will limit myself here to a brief articulation of some of the framework's components.

The method is designed to avoid three persistent problems facing theorists of international relations: the level of analysis problem;[4] the confusion of positive, abstractive, and prescriptive theories;[5] and ad hoc theorizing. The method relies on the general form of bargaining theory for organizing variables and theory types in a consistent fashion and on a research program that should minimize ad hoc explanation.

This framework requires the systematic identification of the preferences of the states represented at Camp David.[6] Since the method of identifying these preferences relies on the specification of historical patterns of behavior, the task leads to further generalizable propositions about the foreign policies of Egypt, Israel, and the United States that are tested not only in the case of Camp David but also across time. Some important patterns of inter-Arab relations and Arab-Israeli relations are identified to provide a general understanding of interstate relations in the Middle East.

The framework also requires the development of a general method for assessing both bargaining performance and bargaining outcomes. This task leads to general hypotheses about optimal bargaining behavior, and to additional propositions which explain the degree of fit between actual and optimal bargaining behavior in specific situations. The Camp David accords provide a good opportunity to demonstrate the utility of these general propositions.

THE CAMP DAVID PROCESS

Before examining some common explanations and providing a systematic alternative, it is useful to review the unfolding of the historical process that led to the Camp David accords.

The Camp David accords were a remarkable event in Middle East politics. Indeed, the Egyptian initiative surprised not only political experts and policy makers worldwide, but also the Israeli and Arab peoples. Few political scientists, later quick to advance explanations, had anticipated this seemingly sudden change in Egyptian policy. In the fall of 1976, a year before Sadat's visit to Jerusalem, one Israeli political analyst did see my own admittance to Egypt for a research project—I was the first Israeli so admitted—as a sign of changing policy, but I had not agreed with him at the time nor did I expect the dramatic changes to come.[7] Most Israeli leaders were also taken by surprise. In June 1977, Labor Party leader Shimon Peres predicted that a new war was likely to break out within a few months.[8] Nothing could have been further from the truth. When Sadat finally visited Jerusalem, Israelis danced in the streets in near euphoria, shock waves rattled the Arab world, and the international community watched in disbelief.

The surprise was understandable. Ever since the creation of the state of Israel, Egypt had been its most avowed regional enemy, and major wars had been fought by the two nations in 1948, 1956, 1967, and 1973. A generation of Egyptians had grown up knowing Israel as the "illegitimate, temporary, Zionist entity" which had displaced the Palestinians and taken control of Arab land by force, and that "whatever is taken by force can only be returned through the use of force."[9] For two decades, Egypt had also been the leader of the Arab world and the primary advocate of Pan-Arabism and Arab unity. The same generation of Egyptians that had grown to think of Israel as the main enemy with whom no compromise could be tolerated also came to think of their homeland as the "United Arab Republic," suppressing its distinct Egyptian character even when this united republic had only one firm member. They grew used to hearing radio broadcasts from Cairo as the "Voice of the Arabs." It is understandable, therefore, that most were surprised when Sadat announced, in the fall of 1977, the political initiative that entailed a commitment to conclude peace with Israel even at the expense of Egypt's relations with the rest of the Arab world.

Yet, the "Camp David process" had begun as early as 1970, encompassing the 1973 Arab-Israeli war and the Egyptian shift from alliance with one superpower to another. Egypt had already been inclined toward a peaceful agreement with Israel, in 1970, and had sought American mediation only to be turned down. The 1973 war was essentially the first step toward a favorable, negotiated agreement. Although the war did not result in an overwhelming Egyptian military victory, it succeeded in increasing superpower interest in a settlement to the conflict, and it improved Egypt's bargaining position.

Immediately following the war, Egyptian and Israeli military officials met, for the first time since 1949, to negotiate agreements on "the disengagement of forces," mediated by the American Secretary of State Henry Kissinger. The new stage of negotiations moved to Geneva, where Israel, Egypt, Syria, and representatives of the Palestinians were to meet under the auspices of the Soviet Union and the United States, in an attempt to conclude a comprehensive settlement to the Arab-Israeli conflict.

The Geneva talks quickly stalled, ostensibly over Palestinian representation. Israel sought to prevent the inclusion of the Palestine Liberation Organization, while the Arabs insisted on it on grounds that the PLO was the "sole legitimate representative" of the Palestinian people. Aside from the Syrian-Israeli and Egyptian-Israeli disengagement agreements (which were in reality separate bilateral agreements mediated by the United States), little was accomplished on the longstanding issues. As the regional threat of war declined, the probability of another oil embargo diminished, and as Israel increased its military edge over its Arab neighbors, there seemed little hope or incentive for progress. Egypt appeared paralyzed by events beyond its control, having appeared to have lost its position of leadership in the Arab world to the new oil-rich movers and shakers. Israel elected a new, more extreme government (composed largely of Menachem Begin's Likud) that was apparently less willing to compromise. Finally, the United States voted out the Ford-Kissinger team with whom the Egyptians had developed a strong working relationship.

At this point, Sadat seized the political initiative by his visit to Jerusalem. As his speech to the Israeli Knesset demonstrated, however, Sadat continued to insist on the same Arab demands for a comprehensive settlement that Egypt had advanced in Geneva. Even as the Egyptians entered the formal negotiations at Camp David, the position remained largely intact as Egypt's official opening position. For its part, Israel made it clear, almost immediately after Sadat's visit, that it was interested only in a bilateral agreement with Egypt, with perhaps some symbolic gestures regarding the West Bank and Gaza. So great was the gap between the Israeli and the Egyptian positions that at several points between Sadat's visit and the formal negotiations at Camp David hopes for an agreement dimmed greatly, and the Egyptians threatened to call off their initiative. President Jimmy Carter, in a desperate attempt to revive the peace prospects and to prevent the collapse of the historic initiative, arranged the intense bargaining conference at Camp David. For thirteen remarkable days in September 1978, leaders and negotiators from Israel, Egypt, and the United States met at Camp David in one of the most striking negotiating efforts in international diplomacy. Although the eyes of the world were focused on these historic events, the negotiators themselves were fully isolated from the outside world and were intensely focused on the Arab-Israeli conflict.

Whatever the declared positions of Egypt and Israel as they entered the negotiations, the two agreements concluded at Camp David were in effect bilateral, pertaining largely to Egyptian-Israeli relations. One agreement committed Israel to full withdrawal from the occupied Sinai in exchange for a peace treaty with Egypt and the establishment of diplomatic relations between the two countries. The other established a "framework" for making further progress on the West Bank and Gaza. It was agreed that negotiations would follow to establish Palestinian "autonomy" on the West Bank and Gaza for a five-year transition period, during which further negotiations would eventually determine the final settlement of outstanding issues.

The two agreements were separate; that is, there was no link between the fulfillment of their terms. The first agreement brought tangible results, but the second remained entirely symbolic. Since there was no deadline for concluding the negotiations on Palestinian autonomy, the status quo could be maintained indefinitely without violation of the letter of the agreements. "Autonomy" was imprecisely defined, thus allowing for widely different interpretations. Israel retained the right to veto any specific settlement at the end of the five year transition period, thus reserving the capacity to maintain the status quo. The practical issue of Jewish settlements on the West Bank and Gaza was ambiguously treated. Israel apparently secured the right to build new settlements, and therefore the capacity to change any final agreement by changing the facts "on the ground." Finally, the Palestinians were not given sufficient incentive to participate in any autonomy talks. The accords did not recognize their right to self determination and, although the text of the accords referred to the Palestinians as the "Palestinian people," a letter from President Carter to Prime Minister Begin that accompanied the agreements acknowledged that "in each paragraph of the Agreed Framework document the expressions 'Palestinians' or 'Palestinian people' are being and will be construed and understood by you as "Palestinian Arabs."[10]

In short, the Camp David accords were little more than bilateral agreements between Egypt and Israel. However, because the accords signaled a major departure from Egypt's previously declared position toward Israel, as well as a breach in the unified Arab political front, they require explanation.

COMMON EXPLANATIONS

The most prevalent explanation of Egypt's change of policy is related to Egypt's immediate economic crisis of 1976–1977, just prior to Sadat's initiative. Food riots by tens of thousands of Egyptians threatened Sadat's government and prevented it from making necessary cuts in the massive governmental food subsidies. According to this explanation, Sadat's initiative was largely intended to save his regime (or the longer-term Egyptian economy) by gaining badly needed financial aid from the United States and by reducing the disproportionately large military budget.[11]

There can be no doubt that Egypt experienced major economic problems and that, like any other government, Sadat must have been seriously concerned about the riots. But a direct causal link between these factors and the Camp David accords is unlikely. The riots were neither the first nor the worst that Egypt had experienced since 1952, and there is no reason to doubt that, like others, this crisis could have been resolved by less dramatic means. More importantly, Egypt had the option of receiving aid from other Arab states instead of relying on the United States, since several Arab states had offered to replace American aid and to finance Egypt's military.[12] Finally, it seems unlikely that Sadat would seek to preserve his power in the face of domestic strife by undertaking such a highly controversial step as his mission to Jerusalem. Put differently, while Egypt's economic difficulties constitute a relevant variable, they do not sufficiently explain the dramatic change in foreign policy.

A second possible explanation is pseudo-Marxist, linking Sadat's initiative to his "open door" (*infitah*) economic policy which was launched in 1974.[13] The new economic structure in Egypt was designed to liberalize the economy, remove many governmental controls, increase reliance on the market, and—perhaps most importantly—to attract foreign capital. This new policy, the argument goes, unleashed a business class in Egypt which was as determined as it was influential. This class reasoned that no major inflow of foreign capital could be attracted in the face of continuing conflict between Israel and Egypt, since stability is essential for investment. As a result, the Egyptian government was manipulated into Camp David by this new class.

I will not here raise questions about the logic of the causal link in this argument. Rather, I shall focus on one simple fact concerning the vision of those in Egypt who strongly advocated the open-door policy. Most proponents of this policy saw the source of capital as the oil-rich Arab states. In the words of one advocate, speaking to the Egyptian parliament, "capital is abundant around us and surplus in the oil states is $50 billion . . . we need your approval."[14] Another added that "we must welcome Arab and foreign support."[15] It is improbable that this group would encourage a policy that would clearly cut off Egypt from this major source of capital.[16]

A third possible explanation links Egypt's behavior during Sadat's presidency to the personal and cultural characteristics of Sadat himself. Attributes such as Sadat's apparent inclination toward Western technology and civilization, cultural characteristics such as Sadat's obsession with "honor," and personality characteristics such as his penchant for drama, are said to be responsible for Egypt's behavior.[17] Aside from the serious theoretical difficulties involved in linking leaders' personalities to state behavior, there are specific reasons to discount such an argument in this particular case. Whatever his personal preferences may have been, Sadat initially favored closer ties with the Soviet Union. He had reversed his predecessor's policy by signing a friendship treaty with Moscow, and he criticized those Arab countries that had improved relations with the United States. Only after it became clear that Egypt's interests were not well served by such an alignment did Sadat change course. Links between other personality and cultural characteristics and Egypt's behavior seem far-fetched. Raphael Israeli, for example, emphasizing Sadat's apparent obsession with personal and national "honor," argued that "Sadat's honor was restored by the [1973] war, which enabled him to negotiate and ultimately make peace with Israel."[18] Appearances aside, Sadat had attempted to avoid the war by making gestures toward the United States, but these gestures were not taken seriously by Secretary of State Kissinger, who saw no urgency in responding to Sadat. Moreover, Sadat persisted in his initiative even when most of his fellow Arabs, including many of his own countrymen, accused him of having no honor and of selling out to Israel and the United States.

There are of course other explanations that have merit, for example the central role that Egypt's relations with the United States played in Egypt's decision to proceed in the path to the Camp David Accords.[19] But here too, the general global context of theses relations, and the links between regional and global variables are not systematically articulated.

Although I have argued that common explanations for the Camp David accords are inadequate, it does not follow from this that the variables employed in these explanations, such as the leader's personality and domestic politics, are entirely irrelevant. But any systematic explanation must be not only consistent, but also capable of assessing the relative explanatory power of each variable within a general framework. The presentation of a systematic and comprehensive explanation that employs such a framework constitutes the rest of this book.

Summary of Empirical Findings

EXPLAINING THE MOVE TOWARD PEACE

The employment of the proposed framework in the Camp David case results in some general hypotheses and surprising conclusions. One of the interesting findings about Camp David is that a single variable, the *distribution of military and economic power* among states, explains a great deal about the inclinations of Israel and Egypt that led to the accords.

At the level of superpower relations, I argue that incremental changes in the balance of military power between the United States and the Soviet Union, both in general and in the Middle East region, have had a measurable impact on the preferences of states in the region. Specifically, as rough strategic parity between the United States and the Soviet Union was attained in the late 1960s, Egypt was forced to make choices between alignment and semi-nonalignment. The inclination to choose one superpower over the other was necessary largely because of the changing character of superpower relations and changes in the regional distribution of power. Ideology, personal preferences, and domestic politics in Egypt appear to have played less significant roles.

At the regional level, I argue that changes in the distribution of military and economic capabilities in the Middle East from 1950 to 1980 altered Egyptian preferences, so that Arabism was no longer useful to Egypt as a means of attaining regional independence and leadership. In the 1950s Egypt's dominant economic and military position in the Arab world made Arabism, and its central symbolic issue of Palestine, useful for enhancing Egypt's influence both regionally and internationally. By the 1970s, however, things had changed dramatically. The commitment to Arabism and to Palestine, given regional changes in the distribution of military and economic power, led to a decline in Egypt's regional influence and made Egypt increasingly dependent on other Arab states. Although historically Egypt had sought to lead the Arab world, this enduring objective ultimately (and ironically) entailed the abandonment of Pan-Arabism in favor of a bilateral agreement with Israel. Through strategic alliance with the United States, Egypt would attain more regional independence and would attempt to block Israeli regional hegemony by competing with Israel for American support. This strategy could, paradoxically, return Egypt to leadership of the Arab world. Leadership, Egypt came to realize, is based on independence and relative power, not on rhetoric.

By itself, this conclusion is telling. The major shifts in Egypt's foreign policy represented by Sadat's initiative appear largely the result of international variables, not domestic and personal factors as many analysts were inclined to conclude. However, while international changes do explain the broad foreign policy inclinations of Egypt, they do not sufficiently account for particular events, such as the terms of the final agreements with Israel. The specific terms of these agreements, some of which have significant implications, can be explained only by lower-level variables.

International variables also explain many of Israel's preferences. Whether or not one assumes that Israel has expansionist designs, Israeli preferences can be derived from the more limited assumption of security interests in the context of a hostile environment and limited resources. Through the employment of a formal model, the "chain store paradox," I argue that these assumptions lead to predictive hypotheses. In particular, two general hypotheses are shown to hold throughout the short history of Israel: the consolidation of close relations with the United States while preventing other regional actors from competing for these relations; and the separation of Egypt from the rest of the Arab world. These two objectives are enduring components of Israeli foreign policy and account for much of its behavior. The Egyptian initiative of 1978 thus posed a serious dilemma for Israel. It promised the attainment of Israel's regional objective at the risk of undermining Israel's more important international objective. Israel's behavior at Camp David was designed largely to protect its relations with the United States and, beyond that, to maximize its chances of attaining the regional objective. However, as with Egypt, the international dynamic in itself does not explain the specific terms of the accords, and recourse to lower-level hypotheses is necessary.

But this international dynamic leads to an interesting conclusion about the Camp David negotiations: the most important immediate objectives of Israel and Egypt at the negotiations pertained *not* to their mutual relations but to the strategic competition between them for alliance with the United States. President Carter noted that Prime Minister Begin told him at Camp David that there had to be two agreements, "the most important was between the United States and Israel, and the other, of secondary importance, but obviously also crucial, was between Israel and Egypt. The most important one would have to come first. He wanted the whole world to know that there were no serious differences between Israel and the United States."[20]

The Egyptians, too, perceived the relationship with the United States to be of central importance. Butrus Ghali, Egypt's Minister of State for Foreign Affairs, saw the Egyptian competition with Israel for alliance with the United States as the "most important leverage" that Egypt held in the negotiations, and the "secret weapon that Israel feared most."[21] In the end it was the threat of losing this competition that may have compelled Sadat to change his plans to abandon the negotiations.[22]

The active American role in the Camp David accords derives from two independent and enduring components of American policy in the Middle East. The first is the strategic objective of minimizing Soviet influence and securing the flow of oil to the West; the second, deriving from domestic politics in the United States, is the commitment to the survival and well-being of Israel. While these preferences sometimes coincide, there is an inherent tension between them that can be reduced only by ameliorating the Arab-Israeli conflict. The Carter administration's strong desire for a settlement of the conflict stemmed primarily from its awareness of this inherent and costly tension in American policy, especially after the Arab oil embargo.

EXPLAINING THE SPECIFIC TERMS OF THE CAMP DAVID ACCORDS

An assessment of the terms of final agreements reached at Camp David is accomplished by using a basic bargaining framework that allows the use of positive, prescriptive, and abstractive theories without overlap.

This bargaining framework requires the identification of the preferences of the three Camp David negotiators. This is accomplished hierarchically, by identifying first their international preferences and second their domestic preferences across time.[23] In the case of the United States, for example, it was found that while international preferences recommended a role as full participant in the negotiations, domestic preferences pulled in the direction of mediation. Given American priorities, domestic preferences ultimately dominated.

As far as Egypt and Israel were concerned, international changes in the distribution of military and economic power made some kind of agreement between Egypt and Israel preferable to no agreement, though a relatively broad range of agreements was possible. The prediction of a specific agreement from this range, while it could have significance for the future, seems impossible if one relies strictly on derived preferences at the international level. How, then, does one evaluate the specific agreements that were reached? More generally, how does one evaluate the outcome of international bargaining?

I argue that comparing the actual outcome to the opening bargaining positions of the actors is a poor method of evaluation, and that derived preferences are, in themselves, insufficient for predicting a specific outcome. Instead, I propose to assess the bargaining behavior of actors as it deviates from the recommendations of prescriptive bargaining theory. While prescriptive bargaining theory cannot predict determinate solutions, it does recommend optimal strategies (i.e., those that maximize an actor's chance of attaining his preferences). Accordingly, several general strategies recommended by prescriptive bargaining theory are outlined and compared with the actual behavior of the actors.

This analysis shows that of the three participants in the Camp David negotiations, Israel's behavior coincided most with optimal bargaining strategy, Egypt's least, with American behavior somewhere in between. The task is to explain why one state behaved optimally while others did not. Two principal variables are used: the states' systems of government and the leaders' personalities. After making the general theoretical argument that centralized systems of government are less conducive to optimal bargaining than decentralized ones, I argue that the Israeli system of government was more conducive to optimal bargaining than either the Egyptian or the American systems. And, on the basis of specific personality criteria that are introduced, I argue that Begin's personality was more conducive to optimal bargaining than Sadat's or Carter's. Significantly, differences in personality characteristics were largely responsible for the outcome of the issue of Jewish settlements on the West Bank,[24] while differences in the system of government were largely responsible for the lack of firmer linkage between the agreement on Egyptian-Israeli peace on the one hand, and the agreement on Palestinian autonomy on the other. It is important to note that the evaluation, as summarized above, pertains to the achievement of *given* national preferences, not the formation of those preferences. For example, it may be argued that, while the Israeli system of government is conducive to the *attainment* of national preferences, it may not be conducive to the formation of "good" national preferences that maximize Israel's long-term security. Policy formation lies outside the scope of this work, as it involves the selection of some independent "good" that states "ought" to pursue.[25]

Prescriptive bargaining theory can tell us only that an actor is likely to maximize his chances for a favorable outcome if he pursues an optimal strategy. It does not inform us about *which* specific objectives would have been likely. Thus, in the case of Camp David, better bargaining by Egypt would have led to a more favorable outcome. The nature of this outcome, however, cannot be specified on the basis of prescriptive theory alone.

Through analysis of the actors' preferences and their relative power I specify several issues which may be called "bargaining issues," that is, issues over which the exact outcome could only be determined through bargaining. Two primary bargaining issues, which could affect the future of Arab-Israeli relations, are a) linkage between normalization of Israeli-Egyptian relations and Palestinian autonomy, and b) the Jewish settlements on the West Bank and Gaza. On both issues the outcome was decidedly in favor of Israeli preferences, thus begging the question of whether Egypt could have attained more. Prescriptive theory informs us that Egypt did not try hard enough, that it did not sufficiently test the limits of Israeli compromise, but it does not tell us what might have occurred if Egypt had tried its best. It may have been the case, as at least one top Egyptian negotiator believed, that not much more could have been achieved.

In order to evaluate the specific outcome I have used abstractive bargaining theory. Although it is speculative, because it has not been established as positive theory, abstractive theory has the capacity to predict determinate solutions. However, even if one accepts the axioms of abstractive bargaining theory, its empirical application is limited because the actual preferences of actors cannot be easily translated into mathematically manipulable terms. The assessment of the specific outcome that emerges from less-formal analysis is that, given better bargaining tactics Egypt would have achieved a better agreement in terms of the two main bargaining issues. Specifically, the failure to attain concrete links between the two Camp David agreements is due to inferior Egyptian bargaining, which stemmed largely from a system of government that is not conducive to optimal bargaining. The failure to conclude a more binding agreement on settlement building in the West Bank and Gaza resulted from the superiority of Begin's bargaining style to that of Carter and Sadat.

Since these conclusions about Camp David derive from general hypotheses that appear to explain historical trends in Egyptian and Israeli foreign policies, some tentative conclusions will be drawn about their expected behavior in the future.

In the concluding chapter, I argue that if these assumptions hold, and if the other aspects of the overall Arab-Israeli conflict remain unresolved, the future of Israeli-Egyptian relations looks bleak and the chances of additional regional conflict are high. Egypt has little incentive to improve relations with Israel, and many incentives to return to the Arab fold. But Egypt's ability to regain influence in the Arab world, as its recent success indicates, will be contingent on what leverage it can deliver to the Arabs vis a vis Israel. The old leverage was military power; the new leverage may be diplomatic success. Short of the latter, the future of Israeli-Egyptian relations is unpromising.

APPENDIX 1

"AL-ANBAA," DECEMBER 1976

Translated by the author from Arabic

An Approval and Its Meaning

THE EGYPTIAN authorities' approval to permit the Arab-Israeli university student Shibley Zeki Telhami to enter Egypt for the purpose of completing his higher education came, perhaps, to point out a change in the traditional Egyptian policy and its exchange for a new, open policy towards those carrying Israeli passports. The truth of the matter is that Mr. Telhami entered Egypt with American documents, but the Egyptians were told in advance that this student was an Israeli (Christian) Arab, and that he had secured the approval of the Israeli government prior to his departure. This fact did not prevent the Egyptians from deciding to act as his host for the purpose of preparing a study at Al-Azhar University. We have said that this step may point out some change in Egyptian policy, for we still remember the days, not too long ago, when the Egyptians refused to allow the "Peace Pilot," Ebi Natan, to enter Egypt. The difference between the two is very clear and to the advantage of the "Peace Pilot" . . . It seems that we have forgotten a point of great importance, that Sadat's Egypt differs from Nasser's Egypt.

2

A Framework for the Study of Cases in International Politics

Introduction: Defining the Methodological Problems

MY OBJECTIVE in this chapter is to develop a general and systematic method for the study of cases in international relations that is especially suitable for studying the specific questions raised about the Camp David accords. In particular, I will propose a method that reconciles realist theory of international relations with bargaining theory, while employing variables at several levels of analysis. This method is intended to overcome two serious methodological problems confronting the student of international relations—problems which stand in the way of the consistent employment of variables at different levels of analysis and thus inhibit the reconciliation of bargaining theory and realist theory.

The first of the two problems is the general tendency to confuse theory types; this inclination often leads to mistaken assessments of the theoretical assumptions employed. The second is the almost inevitable "overlap," or collinearity, of theories at different levels of analysis, which makes the arbitrary combination of variables at different levels a serious flaw. Although this problem can be sidestepped by focusing on variables at one level while ignoring the others, such an approach can leave a great deal unexplained. Moreover, in many cases of interstate relations, we rarely have the large data bases that can help minimize this problem statistically.

My aim is to define the nature of these problems by setting forth some new categories and to develop a conceptually consistent framework that avoids them. First, in distinguishing among theories according to their intended purpose, I propose a new category, *abstractive theories*, in addition to the commonly recognized positive and prescriptive types of theory, and show how confusion of these types often leads to mistaken evaluations of theoretical assumptions. Second, I explore the implications of two recognized methodological problems for the theorist of international relations, collinearity and the "cross-level" fallacy, and offer some propositions for avoiding both problems. Third, I defend the "nesting" approach to the level of analysis problem, going beyond the heuristic argument while identifying a serious limitation of this approach. Fourth, I propose a bargaining framework for studying cases in international relations which overcomes the limitations of the nesting approach and also makes constructive use of the three theory types while avoiding the stated methodological problems.

The arguments on which this approach is based are general ones that should hold for many cases in international relations other than Camp David. The rest of this book will be a demonstration of the utility of this approach in the concrete case of Camp David, where I hope it will yield a better explanation of the accords than has been provided by competing approaches, and where the approach's utility in deriving hypotheses about the behavior of states in general becomes apparent.

Section A: A Typology of Theories by Intended Purpose

Scholars understandably tend to lose sight of some fundamental differences among several types of theories and, therefore, theoretical assumptions. For example, and especially in international relations, one may merge prescription with description: consider the often confusing treatment of the concept of "national interest."

A *descriptive* theory would employ national interest as an analytical assumption that is neither good nor bad, but one that can best explain the way states behave; a *prescriptive* theory would posit national interest as a "good" to be pursued whether or not it coincides with what states in fact tend to pursue. The two concepts are obviously different and rarely coincide; yet there is a tendency to blur this distinction and proceed as though both concepts are one and the same.[1]

I shall propose a typology of theories of behavior based on the theories' intended purpose, and evaluate the implications of the theoretical assumptions of each type. In the process, I hope to show how the lack of separation among them can create serious problems, and how the proposed framework can make constructive use of all three types without entanglement.

Furthermore, the articulation of a third category, *abstractive* theories, is needed for a better assessment of prevalent theories in the social sciences. Although positive theories are the primary concern of the social sciences, prescriptive and abstractive theories can also be employed in a useful fashion, so long as the difference between them remains clear. But to develop a framework that maintains the analytical separation of these types requires a clear definition of each, identifying the logic of the theoretical assumptions in every case.

Before proceeding to define each type, it is worth noting a potential objection to this differentiation: in practice, one can seldom make a clear distinction between prescription and description, between the "ought" and the "is." While this is certainly the case, I do not find this a serious objection to the *analytical* separation of the two. The relevant criterion is, in the end, which method (separating the two concepts or not separating them) is more useful for the ends of the social sciences; it is strictly a pragmatic criterion. In this respect, I find the objection little more useful than the defendable philosophical proposition that "everything is causally interconnected."

POSITIVE THEORIES

Positive theories are intended to explain and predict. The criterion for evaluating the acceptability of such a theory is strictly pragmatic: the relative explanatory and predictive power of the theory, empirically evaluated, compared with competing theories.

My working definition of positive theories is generally consistent with the work of Imre Lakatos. Since I have considered this issue at length elsewhere,[2] I will limit myself to three points of immediate relevance. First, theories are neither deductive nor inductive; the *form* of positive theories are deductive in the sense that the hypotheses derive logically from the axioms, but the *acceptability* of a given theory is determined empirically, by comparing its explanatory and predictive power with those of competing theories. Both deductive form and empirical testing are necessary. Second, theories are not evaluated in a vacuum, lest we engage in *ad hoc* explanations; they are evaluated in the context of a research program (or paradigm). That is, acceptable theories must be consistent with a given network of other acceptable theories. This point is particularly important for my framework, since a research program must be offered at the outset.

Third, the theoretical assumptions of positive theories are strictly axiomatic; they are neither true nor false. Yet their acceptability is not taken for granted simply because they may be intuitively sensible or theoretically elegant; it is empirically evaluated. The empirical tests do not apply to the axioms themselves, however, but to the hypotheses derived from them.[3]

This point is also important in the present work, since some may raise questions about the derived preferences of Egypt and Israel, and about their assumed "rationality." So long as these assumptions are reasonable, their acceptability depends strictly on the empirical testing of the hypotheses derived from them, in comparison to competing hypotheses. The reasonableness of the axioms is determined by the extent to which they conform to other axioms of the assumed research program, especially those of the "core" theory.

PRESCRIPTIVE THEORIES

By *prescriptive* theories, I mean theories whose purpose is to *recommend* behavior. Prescriptive theories are distinguished from "normative" theories in that the former recommend means to given ends, while the latter recommend the ends themselves. I preclude "normative" theories from my categories because, when they are analyzed rigorously, most turn out to recommend means; when they do not, they turn out to be simply statements of conviction, not "theories." Consider some normative theories that posit ends as good-in-themselves. Plato's concept of freedom articulated in the *Republic*, for example, is derived almost tautologically from the concept of harmony, which is taken for granted as a good-in-itself. Similarly, Soren Kierkegaard recommends the pursuit of inner freedom by defining it in a way that coincides with his definition of the human self.

Theories of justice in political philosophy often follow a similar logic. But most of these theories, when pursued rigorously, tend ultimately to advocate means, not ends, or are reduced to statements of conviction. The reason for this inevitable reduction of theories that attempt to prescribe ends is that no philosopher has been able to show how the "ought" can be derived from the "is." Although many philosophers have attempted such derivation,[4] the consensus among philosophers remains that the task is inherently impossible. Consequently, the prescription of the ends of human action is independent from the way the world is; prescription of ends is a value judgement and can be accepted or rejected only on the basis of personal convictions.

Prescriptive theories, recommending *means* to given ends, are prevalent in social science. These theories take for granted the ends of the particular agent, but set out to derive the optimal means for attaining them. To do so, however, prescriptive theory needs to rely on positive theory. If one assumes, for example, that the primary objective of American foreign policy is the containment of the Soviet Union, prescriptive theory could recommend the optimal means to this end. But in order to do so, the theorist must be in a position to explain and predict Soviet behavior as well as the behavior of other states, and for that purpose, positive theory is needed.

The primary difference between prescriptive and positive theories is that the theoretical assumptions pertaining to the pursued ends are necessarily contingent in prescriptive theory; they take the form of "if . . ., then. . . ." Thus, while the ends are taken for granted within the theory, the recommendation of means in the real world must be done without losing sight of the contingency of the ends. Prescriptive bargaining theory is a good example of this, and, employed carefully, can yield constructive results.

ABSTRACTIVE THEORIES

Abstractive theories are the least understood of the theories of behavior, despite the recent proliferation of formal game theories and bargaining theories. They neither explain nor recommend behavior; their purpose is largely intellectual, hypothetical, and exploratory. They are useful not only as intellectual exercises, but also in their ability to open new frontiers for potentially positive theories. For example, sometimes our theoretical assumptions about behavior in given social situations will be insufficient to lead (theoretically) to specific predictions ("solutions"); they may simply lead to a more limited range of outcomes. This is what John Harsanyi calls an "indeterminacy problem" or "bargaining problem."[5] The specific outcome of the situation can be determined only "by explicit or implicit bargaining among the players." Clearly, however, positive theories that provide determinate solutions (predictions) are desirable, for, as Harsanyi put it, "only a theory providing determinate solutions can suggest reasonably specific, empirically testable hypotheses."[6] In their absence, an abstractive theory could be devised by imposing additional *speculative* theoretical assumptions, with the primary purpose of providing "determinate" outcomes. But the resulting theories are clearly not descriptive but purely abstractive; they cannot simply be accepted as positive theories. Their utility lies in their ability to provide a starting point for future positive theories. Much of the literature in game theory and mathematical economics is abstractive.

Aside from providing specific determinate solutions in areas where positive theories can predict only limited ranges of outcome, abstractive theories are also useful for the development of a "stock" of tentative hypotheses that have theoretical relevance in areas of interest to behavioral scientists; this helps inspire new ways of testing, and when those are developed it helps provide immediate theoretical implications for further testing. It is sometimes assumed that, since deduction is logically trivial, it is simple; yet, mathematicians spend lifetimes deducing new hypotheses from old axioms. The point is that much work is required to derive appropriate hypotheses, and having a stock of such hypotheses available for eventual testing could be very helpful.

What then is the "status" of abstractive theories? Assuming, for example, that two abstractive theories possess equal theoretical predictive power, are they equally acceptable in the absence of empirical means of testing? One measure of relative acceptability—relevance for given empirical situations—is the "reasonableness" of axioms. An axiom of an abstractive theory is *unreasonable* if it contradicts axioms of an accepted positive theory (or paradigm); it is *highly reasonable* if it coincides with, or may be deduced from, an axiom of an accepted positive theory; and *somewhat reasonable* if, given auxiliary hypotheses, it can be consistent with assumed axioms. An abstractive theory containing unreasonable axioms is unacceptable. The more highly reasonable axioms an abstractive theory contains, and the fewer somewhat reasonable ones it assumes, the more acceptable it is.

Empirically, abstractive theories can often be used constructively as preliminary models in exploratory research which is intended to eventually produce positive theories. Later I will propose a procedure for utilizing positive, prescriptive, and abstractive theories for the constructive interpretation of empirical events.

THEORETICAL ASSUMPTIONS: AN EXAMPLE

It should be evident that the primary difference among the three types of theories proposed is the nature of the theoretical assumptions, or axioms, in each. In positive theories, the acceptability of the assumptions depends on the relative empirical utility of the hypotheses derived from them. In prescriptive theory, the assumptions are contingent, but the contingent hypotheses derived from them must also meet the criteria of positive theory. The assumptions of abstractive theory, on the other hand, are strictly speculative and tentative. A helpful illustration can be given in terms of the often-confusing assumption of "rationality."

The acceptability of the assumption of rationality in theories of behavior depends on the type of theory in question; objections to the use of this assumption are often based on the failure to distinguish between types. In the case of positive theories, the assumption of rationality is strictly axiomatic. The acceptance of the theoretical assumptions is based solely on their predictive and explanatory utility, *not* on the "empirical" verifiability of the assumptions themselves.

In prescriptive theory, the assumption of rationality rests on grounds other than the explanatory or predictive success of theory itself; it does not refer to the real world, and is by definition contingent. The form of such theories is usually like this: *if* agent A seeks end E, *then* the optimal means to achieve E is M; a "rational" agent seeking E would pursue M. This is simply a theoretical concept that says nothing about rationality (or its lack) among actors in the real world. The problem is that prescriptive theories are sometimes applied as if they were positive theories, resulting in mistaken inferences. For example, a theorist may argue as, Robert Axelrod does in *The Evolution of Cooperation*, that *if* states want to cooperate in this anarchic world, *then* they should pursue a set of prescribed strategies. It is a mistake, however, to infer from this that states in the real world do not pursue the prescribed strategies because they are "irrational." The fact is that states may not seek cooperation as their primary end; the "if" in prescriptive theory may not hold in the real world. And the fact that states may have ends that dominate cooperation has nothing to do with rationality, so long as these ends are consistent.[7]

The assumption of rationality in abstractive theories is simply speculative, for the purpose of providing "determinate solutions" in theory. Much of the formal literature in mathematical economics and game theory is of this sort. Its predictive utility is, by definition, limited. In situations where no positive theories are available, abstractive theories can provide speculative predictions. Often in the field of social science, however, the distinction between abstractive and positive theories is blurred, and consequently there is a tendency to associate the "rational actor" theories with *abstractive* theories, and to treat abstractive theories as if they were positive. Axelrod's work provides a good example of the potential problems entailed in blurring the distinction: his central questions and inferences are positive, but his method is abstractive.[8] As he sets out to determine whether cooperation can emerge in a world of egoists without central authority, he relies on an abstractive model, the 'iterated prisoner's dilemma,' that in some (and only some) aspects resembles certain situations in international relations. According to the formal model, cooperation tends to evolve over time, as most actors tend to employ a strategy of reciprocation. To infer from this result that reciprocation is likely to evolve among states is erroneous; even the slightest difference between the abstractive model and the real world could lead to major differences in inferential result.

The objection to the assumption of rationality is sometimes an objection to the indiscriminate use of this assumption; that is, to its a priori acceptance without empirical testing. This is a particularly legitimate criticism, but in the end it reduces itself to stating that abstractive theories are not positive theories.

There is a more common and more intuitively acceptable point about the assumption of "rationality" in theories of behavior. Any change in behavior, Harsanyi argued, "must be ultimately explained in terms of personal incentives for some people to change their behavior."[9] From the philosophical point of view, however, this reduction need not take place, although it is certainly intuitively helpful. A theory explaining the behavior of states, for example, need not be reduced to show how individuals within a state carry out a predicted policy. As Robert Jervis pointed out, "theory and explanation need not fill the link between cause and effect. Indeed, this is impossible. One can always ask for the links between the links."[10] The only time that such reduction of explanation must take place is when there appears to be a contradiction between the assumptions of the given theory and those of another accepted theory explaining behavior at the level of the individual.

Despite the different assumptions in positive, prescriptive, and abstractive theories, all three types can be employed constructively in the social sciences—so long as the logical separation is maintained.

Section B: Levels of Analysis

Before proceeding to offer a framework that maintains the separation among theory types, another serious problem must be considered: level of analysis. For many years, theorists of international relations have identified several levels of analysis for the systematic study of international politics. Kenneth Waltz has specified three levels, David Singer has defined two, and several other theorists have proposed still different levels. Even though distinctions among levels have become common, the nature of the difficulties has remained unclear. Some political scientists wonder, therefore, whether these distinctions are necessary. It has been argued, for example, that levels of analysis simply provide a convenient way to categorize existing theories, and that theorists should not be discouraged from combining variables at different levels.[11] Others have argued that theories at different levels of analysis, even when they contradict each other, may all hold. This only indicates, so the argument goes, that "truth is dialectic."[12] I will argue in this section that the distinction between levels of analysis is fundamentally important for systematic theorizing, and that the arbitrary combination of variables at different levels is likely to lead to faulty theory and illogical inferences.

The problem is not simply one of deciding at what level to abstract. Two serious problems arise at any level of abstraction. The first is the commonly recognized problem of inference from one level of analysis to another, or the "cross-level" fallacy. The second problem, more serious and less well understood, arises from the arbitrary combination of variables that are causally related; this is the problem of collinearity. Although not limited to variables at different levels, it is almost inevitable in such a case.

THE PROBLEM OF COLLINEARITY

The problem of collinearity has been recognized for some time by students of statistical method. The problem arises when a theory employs more than one explanatory variable, even when these are at the same level of analysis. Inferences derived from such a theory hold if and only if the explanatory variables are completely independent of each other; that is, if and only if no one variable is a function of the others. Take, for example, the one hypothesizing voting behavior as a function of the voter's religion and socioeconomic status. Suppose further that both social class and religion are strongly related to voting behavior. The problem is that both "independent" variables, religion and social class, may also be related to each other. Consequently, treating them as independent variables in the same equation may lead to mistaken inferences about the dependent variable.

The problem of collinearity is even more serious when the independent variables are at different levels of analysis.[13] In such cases it is more likely that the independent variables are related to each other. For example, if one wishes to explain state behavior as a function of several independent variables at different levels (say, leader personality, national ideology, type of government, international system, etc.), one is likely to encounter the problem of collinearity. How much of a leader's personality is due to ideology, or to the nature of the system of government? By the time a politician becomes the prime minister of Great Britain, for instance, he or she is likely to be fully socialized into his or her respective party and political system. A centralized system of government demands a different type of personality from that required by a decentralized one. The international environment or the domestic state of affairs may be such that at a given moment the national mood in a democratic society opts for a leader possessing a given type of personality; the election of a Carter or a Reagan or a Bush may not be a coincidence. It may be the case, for example, that presidential personality correlates well with certain aspects of American foreign policy. Jimmy Carter's personal commitment to moral issues may be responsible for his administration's emphasis on human rights. But it is also possible, indeed likely, that the post-Watergate, post-Vietnam domestic mood led the United States to elect him as president precisely because of these particular aspects of his personality. Similarly, the domestic mood in the United States could be at least partly caused by international events such as the failure in Vietnam and the rise of detente with the Soviet Union. The upshot of all this is not that the personality of the leader is an illegitimate variable, or even an insignificant one; rather, there is likely to be a causal relation between the several explanatory variables at different levels of analysis that makes inferences about the dependent variable inaccurate.

The problem of collinearity is particularly significant for theorists of international politics. In case of perfect collinearity, i.e., when one variable is a linear combination of other variables, the problem is beyond statistical resolution. The problem of partial collinearity can, in theory, be minimized statistically if the analyst has access to hundreds of cases. One can, for example, determine the extent of collinearity, drop or add some variables, and so forth. But given the limitations of the cases encountered by the student of international relations, there is simply no way around the problem other than through conceptual separation of variables. I shall propose a method to accomplish this separation later in the present chapter.

CROSS-LEVEL FALLACIES

Ever since W. S. Robinson wrote his influential article about devising inferences from ecological correlations,[14] what has been termed the "ecological" fallacy and its inverse, the "individual" fallacy, have been thoroughly considered by many social scientists. Even though Robinson's pessimism has been shown to be less than justified and some of his conclusions have been challenged by many social scientists,[15] a consensus remains that the ecological fallacy poses practical dilemmas for the social researcher. Hayward Alker has identified several other types of cross-level fallacies.[16] The most relevant for the level of analysis problem is the "individual" fallacy (the inverse of the ecological fallacy), which generalizes from individual behavior to collective relationships. A good hypothetical example of the cross-level fallacy that is relevant to international relations is provided by James Lee Ray.[17]

There are related substantive problems of inference that often arise in political explanations. If one argues, for example, that Egypt pursued Pan-Arabism in the Nasser era because it was useful for Egyptian national objectives (an explanation at the level of the state), one cannot infer from this that Egyptian leaders deliberately calculated that Pan-Arabism is useful, or even that the Egyptian leaders were not individually sincere in their commitment to Pan-Arabism (which would be an inference at the individual level). The explanation means only that Egyptian national objectives seemed to dominate the behavior of the state regardless of individual sentiments. Similarly, from the argument that the Soviet ruling elite is committed to the communist ideology which seeks the eventual disappearance of the system of nation-states, one cannot automatically infer that the Soviet state behaves in a manner conducive to achieving this objective.

Given this restriction on cross-level inference, there is a puzzling methodological question that is worth noting. If all we need in order to accept some theoretical assumptions about the behavior of states, aside from their reasonability, is their relative power in explaining state behavior, why are we inclined to test the deliberations and statements of individual policy makers in the process of confirmation? Indeed, I have tended to do the same in this work.

The answer is, I believe, straightforward. While individual-level evidence can neither confirm nor disconfirm hypotheses at the level of the state, its total absence is puzzling, prompting a need to reexamine one's assumptions. The reason is that, while policy makers may rationalize policies in many ways, if these policies are consistent and durable, one would expect that, somewhere, at some time in the process of policy deliberations, someone would articulate motives that coincide with the appropriate assumptions. Therefore, the existence of some evidence at the *individual* level is a further requirement for the "reasonability" of the ascribed preferences of *states*. But such evidence is not a substitute for an empirical evaluation of the behavior of a state across time.

AVOIDING THE LEVEL OF ANALYSIS PROBLEM

From the discussion above, two hypotheses follow automatically, and a significant third needs further elaboration. The first hypothesis, which follows from the cross-level fallacy, is that from a theory at one level of analysis one cannot derive inferences at another level. The second, derived from the problem of collinearity, is that a single theory cannot arbitrarily employ variables at different levels of analysis. The third is that theories at different levels of analysis may be conflictive; their consistency must be shown if they are to be accepted as being complementary rather than competitive. Theories are nonconflictive if and only if their assumed environments do not overlap. This last point is as central as it is difficult to demonstrate.

An example is in order. Take theories that employ social class as an explanatory variable for international (or more accurately, global) relations. Such theories cannot logically employ *states* as variables, even in a complementary way, because the global environment of "social class" overlaps with the global environments of "states". (Unless one refers simply to social class within given states, which would shrink the environment.) The only way to avoid this problem of overlap is to posit a perfect fit between class and states: for example, if a set of states (like capitalist states) provided one class, while other sets of states provided other classes. In this case, however, it seems obvious that class would merely describe some pattern of relations among states, which would not differentiate this approach from a realist one.

The implication here is that an approach employing social class as an explanatory variable for global relations is strictly incompatible with an approach that employs the state as a unit of analysis; both approaches cannot be members of the same research program.

The hierarchical procedure proposed below applies only when given theories are compatible as members of the same research program, and theories at different levels of analysis can be compatible only if the assumed environments of the independent variables do not overlap. Indeed, a research program which is adequate for explaining behavior is likely to include theories at different levels of analysis. Most theorists of international politics agree that the inclusion of such variables is necessary, although they may disagree on how to accomplish the task of determining the relative importance of each variable in a consistent fashion.

To be sure, the issue of the relative weight of pertinent variables cannot be settled a priori, and is likely to vary from one empirical situation to another, even though an aggregate hierarchy of relevance may be possible. What is required, however, is an already established procedure for determining the relative weight of variables.

Section C: The Nesting Procedure

In the absence of the kind of data required to minimize this problem statistically, one way to avoid the problem of collinearity is to establish logical separation among the relevant variables. The primary objective is to prevent the overlap of variables at different levels. One way to achieve this is to separate the environments completely.

This can be done by arranging the theories hierarchically according to their level of generality. Then, since we lack the ability to control some variables while testing the weight of others, we must start the procedure by testing the relevant variable at the highest level of generality. The reason for this is not simply economy and convenience; it is the logical way to proceed if these levels are all members of the same research program. This point needs further clarification.

Consider the following: if theories are strictly competitive, then the need to arrange them in a complementary fashion does not arise. This latter need arises only if the theories are compatible, i.e., if they belong to the same research program. An example of this is to agree that system-level variables, as well as certain domestic variables, play a significant role in determining state behavior. In this case the need to assess the relative importance of each set of variables arises. Since it is already agreed that both levels count, the question is which level counts independently. If a theory at the highest level of generality holds, as assumed a priori,[18] then it must hold independently of the others. The mere abstraction at that level holds the lower levels constant. Once the relative importance of the variables at the highest level is established for the specific empirical case, we can then proceed downward to the next level in a procedure that some have called "nesting."[19]

It should be stressed that the order of this hierarchical procedure holds only if the given theories at the different levels of analysis are accepted a priori as complementary and are therefore part of the same research program. It does not hold as a procedure to test *competing* research programs whose "cores" are at different levels of analysis. This point may account for some confusion about the logic of this hierarchical procedure.

It should also be noted that starting with the highest level does not mean that it is necessarily the dominant one; rather, it means that if it applies then it is likely to dominate. For example, theorists may agree that when the security of a state is seriously threatened, security is likely to dominate all other variables in determining the behavior of that state, but the security of states may not always be seriously threatened, and consequently other variables may then count more. Nevertheless, we start the procedure by examining the issue of security in the specific case to be studied, then move to the next variable, and so on.

NESTING AND INTERNATIONAL RELATIONS

Most theorists of international relations agree that in order to explain the relations of states, several causal variables at different levels of analysis are necessary. It is generally agreed that variables such as superpower competition, the domestic system, leader personality, and psychological variables seem to count, both in the aggregate determination of patterns of interstate relations and in individual cases. Many good and plausible theories have been advanced about which variables within each category seem relevant. Where theorists disagree is on the issue of determining the relative importance of these variables, in both aggregate and specific cases, and on what procedure to employ in the task of determining relative importance. Moreover, these theories may be in direct conflict with each other, so that we cannot accept them all a priori. Although some political scientists have argued that all these theories could hold simultaneously *even if* they conflict with each other, because truth is "dialectic," such arguments cannot be of positive use to social science.[20] It can easily be shown that if two contradictory propositions hold, then every conceivable proposition can be derived from them, making them irrelevant for the task of explanation and prediction.

What one needs is a network of theories that are consistent with each other—i.e., a research program, and a procedure to assure the requirement of consistency. For that task we need a starting point, a "core" theory, to which we can relate the other theories. The best starting place is an acceptable theory at the highest level of generality. In international relations, the highest level of analysis from which useful theories have been proposed is the level of "international structure," by which is meant the durable characteristics of the environment of states, most notably the lack of a single central authority to regulate state behavior.

What determines the level of generality is not the unit of analysis itself but the general population, or environment, of the units. For example, a global population of individual people is as general as a global environment of states or classes. Thus, the issue of the starting point cannot be determined a priori. If, however, as noted earlier, one posits a general theory of international relations that sets class or the individual (across the global environment) as the unit of analysis, one must explain global relations (such as war) *without* reference to the state. In that case, these theories must serve as cores for different research programs that are incompatible with a research program employing states as units of analysis.

INTERNATIONAL STRUCTURE AS A CORE LEVEL

Starting an international relations research program at the level of the international structure is appropriate for a simple reason: it is the highest level of generality at which useful and verifiable hypotheses about the behavior of states have been proposed; and there is a near consensus among theorists of international relations that at least one international characteristic, anarchy (the lack of central authority), has important implications for the behavior of states (although there is considerable disagreement about the relative weight of this variable, compared with others). Since the choice of core does not bear on the empirical question about the relative weight of variables, the prevalent disagreements do not pose a threat to this procedure.

Many theorists of international relations, from Thucydides to Morgenthau, have made significant contributions in pursuit of the implications of international anarchy in international relations. No one, however, has pursued these implications more rigorously and systematically than Kenneth Waltz.[21]

Elsewhere, I have considered the objections to Waltz's theoretical propositions at length.[22] A summary of the general propositions is pertinent, however, since their relevance in explaining the Camp David accords will be examined in this work. From the simple assumption that states seek, at a minimum, self-preservation in the context of a self-help anarchic environment, several general propositions could be inferred. First, when a state's security is at stake this consideration dominates all others in determining that state's behavior. Second, states, when they are threatened, tend to attempt balancing the threatening power, alone if they can or with others if necessary. Third, the relative military and economic power of states is a critical determinant of the states' behavior; the more powerful states are more likely to achieve their objectives. Fourth, a change in the distribution of military and economic power is likely to result in corresponding new alignments among states. Fifth, to the extent that superpowers are the most powerful states, their relations, their power in relation to each other, their competition, and their foreign policies can affect the behavior of smaller states in dominant ways; a regional superiority of power by one state could be negated by superpower involvement. Sixth, the number of superpowers, and the incremental differences in their power, is significant in determining the behavior of states.

The strongest objections to Waltz's propositions are that they are too general, that they fail to predict most international events, and that they ignore many other determinants of state behavior. Although these criticisms are largely correct, objections on these grounds miss the value of a general theory. Precisely because the theory is at a high level of generality, because the assumed characteristics are minimal and exceptionally durable, because no other single theory at the same general level can explain more, and because the predicted effects—the balancing tendency of states, the inclination of states to become independent to the extent possible, and the causal importance of relative power—are verifiably dominant in the behavior of states, the theory provides a good starting point (or core) for a more general research program. It is of course true that other theories at lower levels are needed to explain more specific behavior, but starting with this level as the core of a series of theories provides a reference point to guarantee the consistency of the complementary theories.

In studying international relations, the student can distinguish several levels at which potentially useful variables can be found. In principle one can distinguish an infinite number of levels, although for any level to be of practical use it must have specifiable and durable characteristics (a structure), which substantially limits the practical possibilities. The choice of appropriate levels varies from one issue-area to another, but cannot vary from one specific issue to another within the general issue-area lest we engage in ad hoc theorizing. At any rate, the proposed set of theories at the specified levels, arranged in a consistent way, can be deemed appropriate until an alternative set of consistent theories at different levels can be shown predictively superior. This is a particularly important point, since I claim neither that the levels that I identify are the only relevant ones nor that they are inherently the best ones. The proposed framework is one way to accomplish the necessary tasks of any research program.

Once the appropriate levels are specified, they must be organized hierarchically, starting with the international structural level. One example of this hierarchical ("nesting") arrangement is provided by Vinod Aggarwal in his study of the international trade in textiles.[23] Aggarwal distinguishes three appropriate levels for his study: the overall international strategic system, the overall international trading system, and the textile system. These levels are arranged hierarchically in that order. Aggarwal then proceeds to derive the effect of one level on the next.

A SERIOUS LIMITATION OF NESTING

Although Aggarwal points out that domestic structures and individual-level variables can also be of interest, he refrains from identifying them systematically as additional levels in his nested set. Whatever his reasons for excluding these levels, Aggarwal could not just include them in this simple nesting arrangement, for there are some fundamental problems that must be overcome first.

Herein lies the problem: in international relations we are most often interested in explaining the *outcomes* of interaction among states, not simply the *decisions* of individual states. This poses a problem in terms of including state-level characteristics as explanatory variables for such outcomes. Although it makes sense to establish a causal relation between the international structure and a given outcome of state interaction (since at any given time there is only one international structure), it is problematic to specify domestic structures as a cause of this outcome, for at any given time several structures interact. Domestic structure can more easily be specified as being a cause of a given state's decision, but both the state's decision and the outcome also depend on the behavior of the other states involved in the issue. Yet there can be little doubt that domestic variables sometimes play a dominant role in international politics. The need, therefore, remains strong to devise a procedure to systematically assess their relative importance. I shall argue that the framework proposed below, based on bargaining theory, can be employed to resolve this problem. The framework is useful not only in avoiding the level of analysis problem but also in constructively and consistently utilizing the three types of theories described above. The hierarchical levels that I will employ in studying Middle East politics will include the overall international level, the regional (Middle Eastern) level, the domestic level, and the individual level.

Section D: The Promise of the Bargaining Framework

The framework of bargaining theory is ideal for overcoming several conceptual and practical problems. First, the framework deals with both the outcomes of interaction among actors (in this case states),[24] and the individual preferences of each actor. This permits the inclusion of state and individual-level variables in the nesting procedure, when applied to the identification of preferences. Second, the framework of bargaining theory incorporates the "distribution of power" element of realist theory (the conflict point), while allowing for tactical moves that may be independent from this distribution (the rationality postulates). Third, the framework is conducive to making good use of all three theory types: the identification of preferences requires positive theories; prescriptive theories are employed as reference points against which actual bargaining behavior can be measured; and abstractive theories help determine a speculative outcome, given optimal bargaining by all actors.

The format of bargaining theory lends itself to the study of international issues even if no formal bargaining takes place; much of the relations of states are a type of bargaining and involve improving positions for implicit or explicit bargaining. Even war is often a step toward improving a state's "bargaining" position; when Egypt launched a war against Israel in 1973, its aims were largely in this direction.[25] As Glenn Snyder and Paul Diesing put it, bargaining theory is central because its constituent elements correspond to what are widely regarded as the most important elements in international behavior— e.g., power, interests, conflict, and cooperation—and because it is directly relevant to what we are presumably most interested in theorizing about (it being a theory about the interaction of entities in a condition of interdependence), the interactions between sovereign states.[26]

Yet formal bargaining theory, especially when it yields determinate solutions, is generally abstractive. This entails obvious difficulties in its automatic application to empirical situations.[27] But the form of this generalized formal theory is especially suited to organizing positive, prescriptive, and abstractive theory constructively, while avoiding many of the methodological problems outlined earlier.

Several characteristics of this model should become apparent from an examination of figure 2.1. First, both X and Y are better off reaching agreement than not. But the parameters indicating this fact are all "structural." The utility function of each actor, and the costs for each in not reaching an agreement (represented by point O), must be established a priori: realist theory is thus essential in establishing these parameters before examining the dynamics of the bargaining game. Second, the bargaining game eventually centers on the efficient boundary, where it becomes a zero-sum game. After all, if the interests don't become conflictive at some point there is no need for bargaining. This point is sometimes overlooked; while both actors are better off reaching an agreement than not, there are many possible acceptable agreements; in the real bargaining space, one actor's gain is another's loss. Third, the bargaining space represents consistent sets of preferences for both players; this is the minimal requirement for an assumption of rationality. Fourth, even if both the bargaining set and the O point can be specified, they are insufficient to lead to a determinate solution without additional assumptions about the expected behavior of X and Y; all we can predict is that the agreement will fall on the efficient boundary. This is what James Kurth referred to, in substantive situations, as "a priori underdetermination." Fifth, specifying both the bargaining space and the O point in empirical situations is not only difficult but also requires explanations of change in the preferences of players: how is it that the players suddenly find it better for both to reach an agreement? Sixth, in empirical situations, there is always a

FIGURE 2.1. Formal Bargaining Model

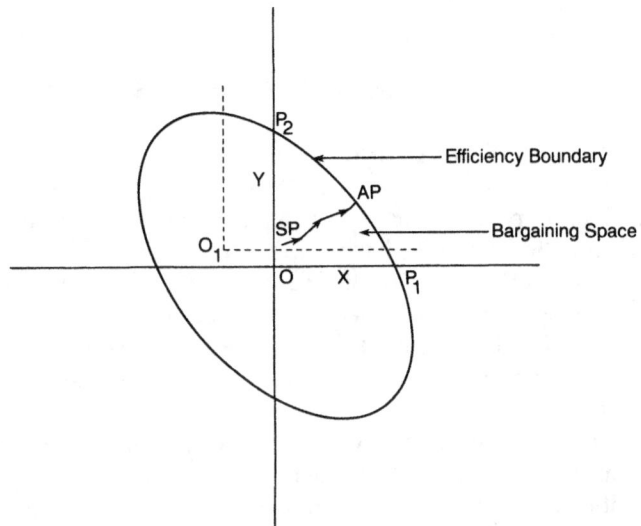

FORMAL BARGAINING MODEL

The formal utility model for a two-person bargaining theory takes the following general two-dimensional form. The space within the figure is the total bargaining space; X and Y represent the players. Moving east increases the utility of X; moving north increases the utility of Y. Point O, the "threat payoff" point, represents the payoffs to both players if no agreement is reached. The northeastern quadrant represents the practical bargaining space, since any point within that space is better than O for both players. The boundary within that quadrant represents the efficient boundary, since for any point within the space, another point with equal or better payoffs for both players can be found on that boundary. Point P1 represents the minimally acceptable outcome for Y, and P2 the minimally acceptable outcome for X. The point SP represents a typical starting point for bargaining, AP a typical agreement point, and the line between them typical moves in the bargaining process.

certain degree of uncertainty about the real preferences and power of the other player. Consequently, player Y, for example, may attempt to project point O as being point O' because this would further limit the efficient boundary in his favor. As a result the bargaining process, given uncertainty, can alter the bargaining set; the point O can be partly a function of the bargaining strategies. This feature can be captured theoretically in formal bargaining theory.[28]

In briefly describing the general formal model of bargaining, I have so far avoided introducing alternative abstractive assumptions about the "rational" behavior of the players, leaving the model largely underdetermined; I shall rectify this in chapter 7 when speculating about what might have happened at Camp David. For now, I will outline my proposed procedure for studying international issues in general, and the Camp David accords in particular.

Section E: Methodology

OUTLINING THE PROPOSED METHOD

A. Employ positive theory, through the nesting procedure, to determine the following "bargaining set:"
   1. The preferences (utility function) of each player.
   2. The costs of not reaching an agreement and, consequently, the minimally acceptable outcome for each actor.
B. Employ prescriptive theory to determine optimal bargaining strategy.
C. Employ positive theory to account for deviation of players from optimal strategies; devise general hypotheses about variables conducive to optimal bargaining behavior.
D. Employ abstractive bargaining theory to speculate on likely outcome given optimal behavior.
E. Evaluate the relative relevance of variables at different levels in accounting for the actual outcome.

ELABORATION FOR THE CASE OF CAMP DAVID

Although the procedure outlined above applies to relations among states even in the absence of formal bargaining, it is clearly easier to demonstrate in formal bargaining situations. Even then, however, the procedure entails analysis that goes far beyond the bargaining itself. Since much of the task depends on defining the "bargaining set," which provides the parameters for the expected outcome, the process begins much earlier. In this regard, the Camp David accords provide an excellent case for demonstrating the utility of the method.

Before outlining the application of this method to the Camp David case, it is worth noting several aspects that minimize the chance of ad hoc explanation. First, the preferences ascribed to Egypt and Israel at Camp David are shown to hold across time; i.e., they explain much of the consistent foreign policy patterns of both states. Second, the proposed explanations are consistent with a widely accepted research program, employing variables that explain the behavior of other states.

In this respect, the puzzling accords, at least as far as Egyptian behavior is concerned, are shown to conform to a pattern; ad hoc variables, such as unusual leadership, are ruled out. Third, some general hypotheses about the bargaining behavior of states are tentatively tested in the cases of Egypt, Israel, and the United States.

The application of this method to the Camp David accords will proceed as follows:

Identifying Preferences. Identifying the preferences of Israel and Egypt, is central for the task at hand. The procedure first identifies the international preferences of each, then the domestically motivated ones. The identification is accomplished by relying on positive theory. It proceeds by (a) axiomatically ascribing specific preferences to each actor; (b) showing that these assumptions are reasonable by revealing their compatibility with the general assumptions of the core theory; and (c) testing these assumptions empirically by showing how they explain the behavior of each actor, not only in the case of Camp David but also across time. This latter point is worth noting, since the application of the method in a time-series fashion increases the validity of the results in terms of other cases.

For example, one central assumption pertains to Egypt's regional preferences. It is argued that Egypt has, ever since the 19th century, consistently sought to lead (or dominate) the Arab world. But to accept this assumption, one needs to show that it is "reasonable," especially given that the core assumptions claim only that states, at a minimum, seek security; and to show empirically that this assumption explains historic Egyptian foreign policy better than competing assumptions.

Once identified, states' preferences are arranged hierarchically at the following levels: overall international politics, regional Middle Eastern politics, domestic politics, and the level of individual leaders. Before I define these levels more clearly, it is worth emphasizing that at this stage we are still dealing with the specification of preferences, not outcomes. Because of this, the inclusion of domestic and individual levels does not pose problems. It is also worth noting here that the crucial variables of *realist* international relations theory would be captured at this stage of identifying preferences.

Levels Employed. By overall international politics, I simply mean the behavior of the superpowers, and the fundamental implications of international anarchy for the behavior of states. Attention is set on those discernible patterns of superpower behavior that derive from (a) their relations with each other in the context of anarchy, and (b) those systematic and durable aspects of their foreign policies, independent of their relations with each other. This last point needs elaboration.

While there can be little doubt that, when major issues of security and economics are at stake, the competition between the superpowers can dominate their behavior, this may not be the case when the issue at stake is less than critical. But an issue that is of marginal importance to a superpower may be critical to smaller states. Consequently, it is essential in studying regional politics to examine the patterns of the superpowers' foreign policies in the given region, including their domestic foundations. It is impossible, for example, to study American relations with the Middle East without taking into account America's basic commitment to the state of Israel. Several consistent hypotheses will be advanced about the effect of superpower competition and foreign policies on the preferences of Egypt and Israel.

By regional politics I simply mean the patterns of inter-Arab and Israeli-Arab relations. While other regional factors (such as Iranian-Arab relations) could be added, the variables chosen exhibit sufficient regularity on their own and seem to explain a great deal. In chapters 4 and 5 I advance several simple hypotheses about these patterns that are consistent with the hypotheses at the international level.

Internal variables will include only two components: the system of government and leaders' personalities. While here, too, one can include many other variables, I have chosen those which can be generalized to other cases that also seem to explain a great deal. However, in every case that a proposed hypothesis is tested successfully, the following question is asked: Are there additional unique variables that cast doubt on the success of the hypothesis? In each case some possible alternative explanations employing such unique variables are considered. The ultimate test, of course, is to provide an alternative research program, or alternative hypotheses at other levels of analysis that pretend to explain more than the ones here proposed.

Change in the international preferences of each state will be measured as a function of one primary variable: the changing distribution of power both at the level of the superpowers and at the regional level. Since this variable derives directly from the core propositions of the proposed research program, its reasonability is guaranteed, but its utility needs empirical confirmation. This latter task takes up a great deal of this work, since one central question involves the change in Egyptian preferences by 1977 which involved a reversal of Egyptian policy toward Israel and the Arab world.

Once the preferences of Egypt and Israel and their minimally acceptable agreement points are established, the bargaining set is complete. Although American preferences will also be discussed, I will treat the actual bargaining as a bilateral Egyptian-Israeli event; for although the United States played a role in the negotiations, this role was in the end that of a mediator in bilateral negotiations.

The positive establishment of the preferences of Egypt and Israel, and their minimally acceptable outcome, in itself provides an explanation for much of the Camp David accords. Analysis of the bargaining set, however, will show that at the outset of the negotiations there were a range of possible outcomes, any of which would have been preferable to no agreement for both sides. A central question remains, therefore: what explains the actual outcome?

Use of Prescriptive Bargaining Theory. Following the next step in the proposed procedure, prescriptive bargaining theory is employed to determine which strategies were available to maximize each side's chances of attaining its preferences. The prescriptive propositions are derived from some basic assumptions about the structure of the bargaining situation without much reference to empirical detail; since prescriptive theory is by definition contingent, the propositions will be used strictly as reference points for evaluating the bargaining behavior of both sides and explaining it. The bargaining strategies of Israel and Egypt will be analyzed to measure the degree to which they appeared to conform to, or deviate from, optimal bargaining behavior as determined by prescriptive theory. Once this task is accomplished, several general hypotheses will be proposed to explain the deviation from optimal bargaining. In particular, hypotheses will be proposed which link the system of government and the personalities of individual leaders to optimal bargaining; these hypotheses will derive from positive theory and will be expected to apply in other cases.

Use of Abstractive Theories. As pointed out earlier, neither the prescriptive propositions nor the basic assumptions about the bargaining set are sufficient for the prediction of a specific bargaining outcome. To the extent that informed speculation is useful both as a reference point and as a first step in the establishment of better positive theories, an abstractive solution is desirable. This can be accomplished with the addition of a speculative assumption of "rationality." I will examine such a solution to the general bargaining game and attempt to derive from it what the outcome of the Camp David accords could have been had both sides followed their optimal strategies. Such a derivation is, of course, merely speculative.

The final step in the procedure is to establish the relative weight of several variables in determining the outcome of the Camp David process. In particular, how much of the outcome is explained by the bargaining set itself, and how much by the actual bargaining process? Of the variables that determined the bargaining set, which ones counted more: those at the overall international, regional, or domestic level? Of the variables that seem to explain the deviation from optimal bargaining in the bargaining process itself, which are more relevant: system of government, personality of the leader, or some unique variables that do not lend themselves to useful generalizing?

Following the procedure outlined above, I identify the impact of global and regional politics on the preferences of Egypt and Israel, employing realist theory of international relations in chapters 3–5. In chapter 6, I summarize the international component in the preferences of each actor, and relate it to domestic constraints. In addition, I consider the issue of misperception and its impact on the method employed. In chapter 7, I employ prescriptive bargaining theory, given the specified preferences of the actors, in order to evaluate the bargaining performance of each actor. Finally, abstractive bargaining theory is employed to evaluate possible outcomes, given optimal bargaining strategies by the actors.

II

International Politics and the Preferences of Israel and Egypt

3

The Superpowers and the Preferences of States

WHAT IS the primary determinant of change in the policies of the superpowers in the Middle East, and how do these policies affect the preferences of states in that region? These two questions constitute a general starting point for identifying the preferences of Egypt and Israel within the context of the research program I have proposed.

In this chapter I posit superpower competition in the Middle East as a function of the incremental changes in the distribution of military and economic power among them.[1] Since this variable is a central one in terms of the research program, its reasonability should be evident. Its acceptability, however, will depend largely on the degree to which it explains major shifts in superpower policies in the region since World War II.

Next, I show how incremental changes in the distribution of power between the Soviet Union and the United States have affected the preferences of states in the Middle East, especially those of Israel and Egypt. This latter case is particularly important in light of Egypt's puzzling shift from alliance with the Soviet Union to the United States in the 1970s. I argue that, by the late 1960s, increased strategic and regional parity between the Soviet Union and the United States compelled states that were engaged in regional conflicts to seek closer alliances with the superpowers; nonalignment was no longer an option. As a result a major shift occurred in Egyptian policy toward the superpowers—a shift from semi-nonalignment to alignment.[2] The subsequent alteration from one superpower to another was a function of the shift toward closer alignment, in the context of Egypt's regional objectives. On the other hand, close Israeli-American relations are considered to be important components of both Israeli and American foreign policies.[3] The strength of these relations is shown to be a function of the degree of strategic parity between the Soviet Union and the United States.

Bipolarity and Superpower Competition in the Middle East

In a recent work on Middle East politics, noted historian of the Middle East L. Carl Brown confessed that:

> Like most of my generation of academics specializing in Middle Eastern Studies, I rejected the old scholarly and diplomatic tradition that regarded the Middle East as an arena of great power confrontation. . . . When, however, I witnessed a major Middle East political leader start a risky war against a militarily stronger opponent, not so much in hope of victory but to provoke international intervention that might result in eventual gains for his country, I came to accept explicitly what I had long sensed implicitly: Middle Eastern political leaders have been taking similar actions for almost two centuries.[4]

What Brown eventually observed has been long recognized by regional actors. Concerned with imbalance in regional conflict, disadvantaged actors seek superpower commitments to remedy their inferiority. The history of the conflict in Lebanon demonstrates that even domestic groups entangled in civil war have the ability to attract superpower intervention. Describing Egypt's strategy after the defeat by Israel in

1967, Egyptian journalist and former presidential advisor Mohammed Haykal wrote:

> As a result of the 67 war, the balance at the local level tilted strongly in favor of the Israelis, so the only option to Egypt was to lift the conflict onto the higher, international level, where the balance was more equal, until the time when Egypt was in a position to match Israel's strength with her own.[5]

Understandably, however, many Middle East specialists, concerned about a long-prevailing Western tendency to explain Middle East politics strictly as a function of superpower competition, had gone to the other extreme of ignoring the substantial impact of the superpowers on regional politics. Today, few analysts discount the major role that big powers play; the key question, however, is the extent of this role. Is there a systematic way to assess the relative relevance of superpower influence in the Middle East?

Employing the distribution of power as the primary variable in explaining changes in superpower policies, I advance the following propositions: both the United States and the Soviet Union became more directly involved in the Middle East in the late 1960s and early 1970s than at any other period since World War II; the terms of their competition had dramatically changed as a result of increased parity. Non-status quo states could no longer receive automatic superpower support without closer, more formal alliances. As a consequence, Egypt came to believe in the need for a closer, more formal alliance with either superpower in order to achieve Egyptian objectives. This new need stemmed largely from the new strategic parity between the superpowers. Sadat's moves toward the United States were not automatic, and were preceded first by an attempt to forge a closer alliance with the Soviet Union, reversing his predecessor's policies. But *economic* disparity between the superpowers limited Soviet capacity and willingness to aid Egypt;[6] and change in the regional distribution of power modified Egypt's regional objectives.[7] Both of these variables account for the ultimate Egyptian switch from the Soviet Union to the United States.

The key explanatory variables in this analysis are the incremental change in the distribution of miliary and economic power between the two superpowers; specifically, the extent of parity (or disparity) between them at both the strategic and regional levels. Realist literature has generally focussed on the implications of the distribution of power

FIGURE 3.1. Superpower Inclinations Toward the Third World Given Relative Economic and Military Capabilities

MILITARY CAPABILITIES

	Relatively Strong	Relatively Weak
Economic Capabilities: Relatively Strong	**1** • Demanding of allies • Erosion of influence not tolerated even if opponent does not directly gain Examples: US either/or policy in 50s USSR in late 60s	**2** • Accomodating stance; offer help to other states without too many demands • Be satisfied with erosion of opponent's power, even without direct gains Example: USSR mid-50s to early 60s
Economic Capabilities: Relatively Weak	**3** • Careful and selective commitments • Some erosion of influence tolerated Example: USSR in 70s and 80s[1]	**4** • Minimal means of influence • Focus on home front buildup • Subordination of regional issues; do what is needed for internal strength and projection of power Example: USSR mid-40s to mid-50s

1. It is worth noting that the interpretation of Soviet policy in the context of détente is seen here as a function of relative economic disparity. In this sense, Soviet inclination toward détente with the United States is, itself, viewed as a dependent variable. This, of course, does not mean that détente itself, aside from economic disparity, does not account for *some* deviations from these expected policies.

for the stability of the international system[8] or the stability of international regimes.[9] But the literature has not sufficiently separated economic power from military power, and regional power from global power; and it has not suggested particular policy implications for various parts of the world.

Figures 3.1 and 3.2 summarize the proposed hypotheses about expected superpower tendencies given the distribution of both economic and military power between the superpowers, at the global level and

FIGURE 3.2. Superpower Inclinations Toward the Third World Given Relative Global and Regional Strength

	RELATIVE GLOBAL STRENGTH	
	Relatively Strong	**Relatively Weak**
Relative Regional Strength: Relatively Strong	**1** • Demanding of allies • Seek formal relations Examples: USSR in late 60s US in 50s, late 70s and 80s	**2** • Possessive control of allies Fear of erosion of power Example: Britiain in mid-50s[1]
Relative Regional Strength: Relatively Weak	**3** • Selective alliances • Not too demanding of allies to make up for regional weakness Example: US in late 60s, early 70s[2]	**4** • Satisfied with erosion of opponent's influence • Generous, non-selective aid to potential defectors from opponent's camp • Not too demanding of friends Example: USSR in mid-50s to mid-60s

1. Britain was no longer a superpower but still had ambitions at that point.
2. Although the U.S. possessed strategic parity with the Soviet Union in the late 1960s, it had some regional disadvantages emanating from increased Soviet presence in the Middle East, and from the planned withdrawal of British troops from the Persian Gulf. As a result, the U.S. was less demanding of its allies, especially given its limited options in light of the prevailing domestic mood which, following the Vietnam experience, opposed military intervention.

in the Middle East. These explanatory variables are clearly consistent with structural-realist assumptions; but to make a case for their empirical explanatory power requires an outline of their historical impact on Soviet-American competition in the Middle East since World War II. The historical patterns of Soviet and American policies in the Middle East correspond to the tendencies anticipated by figures 3.1 and 3.2. The task of the rest of this chapter will be to trace those patterns.

THE EVOLUTION OF AMERICAN POLICY IN THE MIDDLE EAST

A brief review of American policy in the Middle East reveals how shifts in American policy correspond to changes in the distribution of economic and military power, both globally and regionally, as indicated in figures 3.1 and 3.2. Specifically, in the 1950s to the mid-1960s, the U.S. (the West) held global and regional advantages over the Soviet Union, which explains the either/or American policies (see cell 1, figure 3.1, and cell 1, figure 3.2). By the late sixties, the United States faced regional disadvantages which recommended a new American policy (see cell 3, figure 3.2). But during the late 1970s, the U.S. attained advantages over the Soviet Union both globally and regionally, emanating from the relative economic weakness of the U.S.S.R. (cell 3, figure 3.2).

American priorities and instruments of policy in the Middle East have changed considerably since World War II. To be sure, broad American objectives in the Middle East have been relatively constant; but the relative weight of these objectives, their place among the overall priorities of the American foreign policy, the willingness to act in order to attain them, and the instruments available for their attainment have all changed, reflecting shifts in the distribution of global and regional capabilities.[10]

Specific American objectives in the Middle East have included three enduring components. First, the United States sought the strategic objective of minimizing Soviet influence in the region. Second, there has always been the objective of securing the flow of Middle Eastern oil to the West at reasonable prices and assuring a good share of the trade market in the region; an economic objective that is not easily separable from the strategic one. The third objective involves the enduring and unchangeable commitment to the survival, security, and well-being of the state of Israel; this objective sometimes coincided with the other two but is nonetheless independent of them. Even though these three objectives have always co-existed, it should be at once apparent that aside from the problem of translating them into specific policies, they are potentially contradictory. And even though this inherent tension among American objectives was not equally understood by different U.S. administrations, it often imposed uncomfortable choices for the United States. These choices have evolved as U.S.-Soviet relations in the region have changed.

In the years immediately following the end of World War II, the

European powers which had controlled the region since 1919 continued to dominate the region. Despite the proclamations of independence by former colonies in the Middle East, British and French influence in the newly established governments remained great. Moreover, the British retained direct control of the vitally important Gulf region. Though the United States had little contact with the Middle East and minimal economic dependence on the region, America's European allies, who depended on Middle East oil, were in a position to protect their own interests. As for America's commitment to the survival and security of the state of Israel, that too did not require direct American action. Western Europe provided Israel with the weapons necessary for maintaining a powerful army, a situation that did not change until 1967.

The strategic component of American policy, the objective of minimizing Soviet influence, had little relevance to the Middle East until 1950. The Soviets were mostly preoccupied with Europe and American containment policy, as articulated by George Kennan, was largely Eurocentric. But 1950 brought with it NSC 68 and the Korean War, signaling the globalization of American containment policy. On the face of it, this seemed to have far-reaching implications for the Middle East, but a closer look will reveal that despite the hot rhetoric of the fifties and the persistent perceptions about that period, the regional polarization along global lines was less intense in the fifties than it became in the seventies.

The intuitive expectations about the impact of superpower relations on Middle East politics can vary quite a bit, depending on the specific aspect of superpower relations under consideration. If one compares the rhetoric of the Cold War with that of the period of detente, then one would expect more regional polarization during the Cold War. If, on the other hand, one compares the degree of strategic parity between the superpowers during the two periods, one is inclined to expect the opposite — more regional polarization during détente. A closer examination of American policy in the fifties provides an insight into this question; measuring the relative parity between the superpowers appears to be a better indicator.

The Cold War, to be sure, did not arise in a vacuum, nor did the globalization of containment simply grow out of misperceptions. Even before the Korean War, NSC 68 had been prepared in response to tangible changes in the distribution of military power between the Soviet Union and the United States. In China, the Soviet Union had gained a major international ally at the expense of the United States;

the newly acquired atom bomb gave the Soviet Union the beginnings of strategic parity; Soviet dominance of Eastern Europe enhanced Soviet power; and the apparent Soviet ability to exploit international communism as an instrument of policy added to real Soviet power. But, though these were real advantages for the Soviets, there can be no question that the United States continued to hold a decided edge over the Soviet Union; parity was not at hand and the Soviets clearly recognized this. Rapid incremental changes in the distribution of military power can, of course, be destabilizing, but the *regional* impact of such changes is not the same as that of strategic parity.

The global competition in the 1950s reflected itself in the Middle East through the formation of the Baghdad Pact in 1955. Several things should be noted about the Pact in terms of superpower competition at the time. First, at the time of its inception there was little Soviet penetration in the Middle East. The Egyptian arms deal with Czechoslovakia was consummated later in the year, and only after the United States and Britain had refused to sell arms to Egypt. It was also partly as a *result* of the creation of the Baghdad Pact that the Soviet Union became more aggressively interested in enhancing relations with Egypt. Second, even though the United States played a dominant role in organizing that alliance, the central Western partner in the agreement was Britain, not the United States; the United States had refused to become a member of the pact. Third, the Middle Eastern states that signed the pact—Iraq, Iran, Pakistan and Turkey—were all "northern-tier" states, close to the Soviet Union. All had a substantial British presence and were already partly engaged in regional rivalries; and some (Iran and Iraq) were experiencing a great deal of domestic opposition to governments rooted in the colonial period. These factors raise questions about American motivations during that period.

Examining American concerns, beginning with NSC 68, reveals that in the context of the new global competition with the Soviet Union the United States was as concerned with the erosion of Western global influence as it was with the expansion of Soviet influence (see cell 1, figure 3.1). It was taken for granted that the Middle East was part of the Western sphere, and that any loosening of Western influence represented a loss to the West even if no gains to the Soviets resulted. Thus the independence of Egyptian President Nasser was perceived to be a threat to the West, even though the Soviets simultaneously suspected him of being a CIA plant.[11] The foreign policy inaugurated by Secretary of State John Foster Dulles, which dealt with states that did not commit themselves to an alliance with the West as though they were enemies, fit this pattern (see cell 1, figure 3.1, and cell 1, figure 3.2). In addition, prior to the Suez crisis of 1956, the United States relied heavily on the British to maintain Western influence in the region. Yet British interests in the region did not necessarily coincide with the American objective of containing the Soviet Union. For one thing, British interests were largely economic; for another, the British were the "colonial enemy" in the regional decolonization movement, at a time when the Arab Middle East had little reason to fear the Soviet Union. In effect, the United States entered a polarized Middle East whose two dominant poles were not the Soviet Union and the United States, but a decaying yet defiant British Empire and a rising Egypt; the more the Empire decayed, the more the United States found itself replacing it as the West's regional representative.

The Eisenhower administration was clearly aware of the potential conflict of interests with the British in the Middle East. As early as 1953, it indicated a lack of willingness to be dragged into the Middle East on behalf of British interests.[12] Moreover, Eisenhower perceived the regional importance of Egypt and did not wish to antagonize it by unconditionally supporting British policy. Even though the American government grew to dislike Nasser's neutralism it did not believe that Egypt was a hopeless case.[13] Indeed, it was partly because of this belief that the United States refused to become a member of the Baghdad Pact in 1955; and when Britain joined the Pact the United States appeared surprised and perhaps uncomfortable.[14] The Baghdad Pact turned out to serve British and Iraqi interests in the regional polarization against Egypt, even though the subsequent crisis over Suez substantially undermined the alliance's potential benefits to Britain and Iraq.

As for Nasser's Egypt, the conflict was neither ideological nor global. Aside from the obvious desire for independence (indeed, because of it), Nasser sensed an opportunity to prey on a disintegrating British Empire, and to replace it as regional leader. Even before the Nasser (Nagib) regime came to power in 1952, Egypt was beginning to see its chance to dominate the region at British expense. Despite the new causes of independence and Pan-Arabism, Nasser's tendencies were in many ways not very different from those of Mohammed Ali, whose dynasty Nasser overthrew. Ali, who had governed Egypt more than a century before Nasser came to power, had visions of regional dominance when he sensed the disintegration of the Ottoman Empire. By 1839, this governor of Egypt had dealt the Ottoman army a near-fatal defeat, and appeared to be in a position to permanently dismember the Empire. But the British, concerned about potential Russian expansion if the Ottomans fell, intervened to contain the ambitions of the Egyptians. Ali's dynasty remained, but its influence was vastly diminished.

This helps illustrate that the Soviet-American Cold War was not the *cause* of the regional polarization in the Middle East in the 1950s, and that in fact, the form of that polarization had little to do with Soviet-American rivalry. It also shows that early American entanglement in the region was partly induced by the British and the Iraqis, who had interests quite apart from superpower rivalry. Nonetheless, there can be no doubt that the United States became increasingly involved in Middle East politics, and that the Soviets slowly penetrated the region; the question that remains involves the ways in which this competition affected politics in the region, and how it differed from the conditions of parity in the late 1960s and early 1970s.

By 1956 the only American action in the Middle East was the covert intervention on behalf of the Shah of Iran; this too was advocated by Britain, whose oil companies controlled Iranian oil—control that was threatened by the nationalistic Iranian Prime Minister Musaddegh. But British-French-Israeli collaboration in attacking Egypt in 1956 found the United States directly opposed to, and subsequently more suspicious of, its European allies. The worst fears of the Eisenhower administration were shown to have been justified; the attack made a regional hero of Nasser and increased the immediate potential influence of Egypt by many fold. For the next three years the status quo in the region was threatened more than at any other time since World War II.

Yet in spite of the divergence of interests between Britain and the United States in the Middle East, the United States found itself inheriting the same rules of polarization in the region. Partly because of inexperience in the region, partly because of its preoccupation with the Soviet invasion of Hungary, and partly because of the fit between the existing conditions of polarization and the rigid perceptions of John Foster Dulles, the United States appeared neither willing nor able to make major realignments in the region.

Indeed, the logic of the original polarization of the 1950s continued to dominate American policy in the Middle East (though perhaps to a lesser extent) despite its lack of correspondence with American interests. The eventual division of Middle East states into "radicals" and "moderates," based on the viewpoints of the 1950s, does not appear to best serve American interests; as Appendix 3A clearly indicates, there appears little difference between the foreign economic policies of "radical" and "moderate" Middle Eastern states. Appendix 3B shows that Soviet military presence actually increases when regional polarizations along "radical-moderate" lines increase.

At any rate, following the Suez crisis the United States had little choice but to accept the existing polarization. Ironically, the events at Suez that indicated more than ever the conflict between the interests of the United States and Britain also demonstrated the necessity of accepting the British-sponsored political order in the Middle East. The quick pace of events (the uprisings in Jordan and Lebanon, the overthrow of the monarchy in Iraq, the coming to power of the Baathists in Syria, and the subsequent union between Egypt and Syria) forced the United States into a reactive policy, culminating in the Eisenhower Doctrine[15] in 1957 and the subsequent landing of the U.S. Marines in Lebanon in 1958. Perhaps the most important reason for the lack of American initiative in the region is that, the global competition aside, vital Western interests in the Middle East were not directly threatened, and the United States was not responsible for them. Moreover, despite appearances, subsequent Soviet penetration in the region was more political than military.[16] Not until after the 1973 Arab-Israeli War did the United States have the will, the interest, and the real opportunity to reorder the shape of Middle East politics in a manner more conducive to reducing the inherent tension in American foreign policy toward the region. Henry Kissinger's policy of crisis diffusion, while eliminating the immediate danger, may have wasted that opportunity.

Despite their humiliation in the Middle East as a result of Suez and the subsequent decline of their political influence in the region, the British retained direct control of the sources of oil for more than a decade to come; militarily, the British maintained bases in both the Persian Gulf and Libya. In addition, France remained Israel's primary arms supplier for nearly the same period. In short, the primary American concern was with the potential expansion of Soviet influence; but this potential, as I argue in the next section, was less real than may first appear.

With the coming of the sixties the United States became even less concerned with the Middle East. First, there was the preoccupation with Cuba and the Bay of Pigs, followed by the all-consuming missile crisis and its aftermath. When the rapid escalation of American involvement in Vietnam was added, there was little attention left for the Middle East. Yet the Arab Cold war continued unabated, its roots wholly independent of the global competition.

By the late sixties, however, there were dramatic changes in world politics and, subsequently, in American foreign policy. The United States now found itself directly responsible for all three main Western objectives in the Middle East at a time when both strategic and regional parity with the Soviet Union became facts and when direct military intervention was no longer a desirable tool of American foreign policy (see cell 3, figure 3.2). As a result, the shape and impact of Soviet-American competition in the Middle East changed dramatically. Several events account for these changes.

Many of these changes followed the 1967 Arab-Israeli war, which saw Israel decisively defeat the combined forces of several Arab states, including Egypt. Some, though certainly not all, of these changes were directly linked to that war. The two most notable international outcomes of the 1967 war were the beginning of the end of remaining European influence in the region, and increased Soviet presence. The first European disentanglement occurred immediately after the war, when France stopped arms shipments to Israel (the superior Israeli air force had been largely equipped by the French). This left the United States with the responsibility to fill the gap, which it did even before the Nixon administration took office. The second setback to European influence involved the overthrow of the Libyan monarchy by Muammar al-Qaddafi in 1969, which quickly brought to an end not only the British bases there, but the only American base in the Arab world as well. The third, beginning with 1967, occurred when Britain began its final withdrawal from the Persian Gulf by relinquishing control over Aden; full British withdrawal from the region was completed in December 1971. Consequently, the protection of the oil sources was left squarely on the shoulders of the United States, at the very same time that the United States was being forced to withdraw from its major air base in Libya.

The Arab defeat of 1967 also increased Soviet presence in the Middle East. The destruction of the Egyptian and Syrian armies made both countries militarily dependent on the Soviet Union, and the number of Soviet troops and advisers increased dramatically. So even on this score there seemed to be a need to act in the Middle East.

Yet, as these events were unfolding, America was increasingly suffering from the "Vietnam syndrome," the domestic mood was decidedly against foreign military intervention. It was this situation, Henry

Kissinger later wrote, especially its implications to United States interests in the Middle East, that inclined the Nixon administration toward détente with the Soviet Union; the United States, Kissinger argued, needed time to regroup.[17]

The immediate American solution to the strategic problem in the Middle East was a simple one: instead of relying on direct military intervention as a tool of policy, the United States would depend on militarily strong regional allies. In the Persian Gulf Iran was the logical choice; it was the largest and potentially the most powerful state in the Gulf. Moreover, it was already closely tied to the United States, as well as interested in dominating the Gulf and checking the power of its long-time rival Iraq, which had close links with the Soviet Union. On the Arab-Israeli front, Israel, to whom the United States was fundamentally committed anyway, became a more attractive ally following its lightning victory in 1967. Some analysts had predicted that Arab armies would need as many as 15 years to be in a position to fight again. As a result, American policy under the first Nixon administration was based mainly on the military build-up of both Iran and Israel as guarantors of American interests in the region. Simultaneously, through détente and "linkage," the United States would pressure the Soviet Union to slow the build-up of its clients. Otherwise, the United States would not expend a great deal of effort on Middle Eastern affairs.

By 1970 the United States, alone among the Western allies, became for the first time responsible for all three Western objectives in the Middle East. Perhaps because the role was new, there appeared a lack of awareness that America's objectives were potentially in conflict, and that a policy designed to pursue one objective might be detrimental to the others. It later became apparent, for example, that the Shah's need to finance increased arms purchases made him the strongest proponent of oil price increases in 1974. Furthermore, America's strong support for Israel was responsible for the Arab oil embargo in 1973 and the subsequent dramatic increases in the price of oil, and the arms buildups by America's strategic allies increased regional polarization, which led to increased Soviet influence, and dramatic short term superiority by US allies led to their policy independence from the United States. As Henry Kissinger put it: "I ask [Israeli Prime Minister] Rabin to make concessions and he says he can't because Israel is weak. So I give him more arms, and he says he doesn't need to make concessions because Israel is strong."[18]

It was these tensions that later led the Carter administration to conclude that a coherent American policy in the Middle East, with minimal conflict among American interests there, required a resolution of the Arab-Israeli conflict. As a consequence, President Carter allocated more effort to this issue than any American president before him.

THE EVOLUTION OF SOVIET POLICY IN THE MIDDLE EAST

A quick overview of Soviet policy in the Middle East reveals that their military presence in the region during the 1950s and the early 1960s was in fact minimal; this contrasts sharply with the period 1967–1972, which witnessed the peak of Soviet political and military power in the region. Moreover, the Egyptians' perception of themselves as being almost "nonaligned" before 1967 is relatively accurate. Because of their real inferiority to the United States in the 1950s, the Soviets were willing to provide a great deal of aid to states who would loosen their ties with the West, without demanding much in return (see cell 2, figure 3.1). But by the late sixties, having achieved strategic as well as regional parity, the Soviets were more demanding of their clients; nonalignment was much less acceptable to them (see cell 1, figure 3.1). Soviet clients now had new choices to make.

At the end of World War II, the Soviet Union had little contact with the Arab Middle East. For the first decade after the war it lacked both immediate interests in and the means to penetrate the region. Devastated by a war that killed more than 10 percent of its population and threatened by revived separatist movements within its boundaries, the Soviet Union's immediate objective had to be internal consolidation. The second immediate objective was the tightening of control over newly dominated Eastern Europe. These tasks left little resources or energy for a region like the Middle East, which had been dominated by Western Europe for decades. Both immediate tasks required the Communist government to establish and reinforce its legitimacy (see cell 4, figure 3.1). During the war, even in their ethnically heterogeneous nation Soviet leaders had found Russian nationalism more useful than communist ideology in rallying the population; following the war, ideology had to be stressed uncompromisingly to reestablish legitimacy. In newly controlled Eastern Europe communist ideology had to be stressed in order to establish and justify Soviet dominance. Furthermore, for the first decade after the war the Soviet Union had very limited means of influence in the Middle East; regional Communist parties, minimally effective as they may have been, were one of the few. Consequently both Soviet objectives and means were detrimental to Soviet interests in the Middle East during that period; the Soviets were uncompromising on the issue of communist ideology and, as a result, were not in a position to exploit emerging anti-colonial national movements in the region. Their position was reflected clearly in a 1952 report by Khalid Bakdash, leader of the Syrian Communist Party:

> Our job during the present stage is to muster the broad masses and especially the workers and the peasants . . . To bring this about, the principal orientation of our effort and activity must be toward isolating the nationalist bourgeois and putting an end to its influence among the people. For this bourgeoisie, no matter how much the names of its parties vary, uses its influence to deceive the people and turn it away from the revolutionary struggle; it works also for an understanding with imperialism . . . We must work constantly also to unmask groups and parties claiming to be "socialist," such as the Arab Socialist Party, the Islamic Socialist Front, and Baath Party in Syria, and the Socialist Progressive Party of Jumblatt, etc., in Lebanon . . .[19]

During the late forties and early fifties the Soviet Union would have found it difficult to support "national bourgeoisie groups claiming to be socialist," given its primary tasks both at home and in Eastern Europe. Moreover, the new Soviet alliance with China was similarly cemented on uncompromising ideological grounds; as Chinese leader Mao Zedong put it, "sitting on the fence will not do, nor is there a third road. . . ."[20]

By the mid-fifties, however, both the international and domestic situations had changed for the Soviets, the death of Stalin having provided an opportunity for major policy changes to accommodate the new international situation. The Soviets had successfully consolidated their authority at home and in Eastern Europe, and could now claim to be the other pole in a new bipolar international order. Even though their military and economic power was still inferior to that of the United States, the very real prestige power that the atom bomb and the alliance with China brought gave the appearance of true bipolarity. The new priority in Soviet policy became one of establishing strategic and global parity with the United States. Since the Soviets needed time to bring this about, and since their domestic economic priorities would limit available resources, the Soviets had to rely on new intermediate tactics: projecting more power than was actually at hand, and be satisfied with the erosion of Western influence (see cell 2, figure

3.1). Khrushchev became a master of the game, though this ironically helped to bring about his downfall following the Cuban missile crisis, when bluff proved insufficient. In the meantime, these new tactics seemed to work for nearly a decade, increasing Soviet influence both in the Third World in general and in the Middle East in particular. Nevertheless, the Soviets' position of inferiority vis-a-vis the United States dictated the nature of their relations with the Third World.

By the mid-fifties it was becoming apparent that the post-colonial movements in Asia, Africa and the Middle East had the potential of becoming an important international bloc; the first meeting of leaders from this new movement was held in 1954 in Bandung, Indonesia. It was also becoming clear that the United States, concerned with the erosion of Western influence, would not be supportive of nonalignment. To the extent that most ex-colonial countries had traditionally been in the Western sphere of influence, the Soviet Union stood to gain simply through their independence from the West, without the need to demand alliances; in the context of the new global competition, an American loss was a Soviet gain. It was thus that the Soviet Union inaugurated a new policy toward the "nonaligned states," most notably with Nasser's Egypt.

Soviet ties with Egypt improved rapidly beginning with the arms sale through Czechoslovakia in 1955. During the Suez crisis of 1956, in order to score some costless points, the Soviet Union rhetorically threatened to use its nuclear weapons to compel the Europeans and the Israelis to withdraw (after the highest moments of crisis had passed); when the United States withdrew its offer to finance the Aswan Dam project, the Soviet Union offered to help; and when Egypt sought to rebuild its forces after the Suez war, the Soviets were willing suppliers. Within a few years, similar opportunities were exploited in Syria and Iraq.

Despite the rapid improvement in Soviet-Egyptian relations, one must not lose sight of some basic facts about the nature of this relationship: the Soviet Union, during the first decade of relations with Egypt, provided nearly all the concessions; Egypt was left alone to pursue independent policies. First, the Soviets made a major ideological concession in accepting Arab nationalism even at the expense of local communist parties, who were asked to dissolve themselves and merge with the clearly anti-communist ruling party. Second, the aid provided to Egypt—technical, financial, and military—was of significant magnitude, and on highly favorable terms. Third, Nasser's ambitions to dominate the Arab world were encouraged by the Soviets. Fourth, the Soviets asked for and received very little from Egypt in return; there was no formal treaty of alliance, or direct Soviet military presence. Rather, the Soviets seemed pleased to have simply reduced American global influence, and to have been able to project a perception of Soviet influence.

By the late sixties, however, the Soviets were no longer willing to freely assist any who asked. Several changes account for this new Soviet attitude. First, the Soviets had achieved strategic parity with the United States and their need to project symbolic power diminished (see cell 1, figure 3.1). Second, in the Middle East the Soviets had already achieved a certain degree of regional parity with the United States. Third, the Middle Eastern clients of the Soviet Union, especially Egypt and Syria, had become desperately dependent on Soviet support following the defeat of 1967. Fourth, the loss of China as a Soviet ally and the subsequent improvement in relations between China and the United States made the Soviets seek formalization of relations with their Third World clients, and a military presence where possible.

This changed Soviet attitude had far reaching implications for Soviet relations with Egypt. The Egyptians, anxious to change the regional status quo and (minimally) to regain their occupied territories, found that the old norms of Soviet-Egyptian relations no longer held; Soviet demands increased as the Egyptians' ability to easily obtain Soviet aid decreased. Egypt began to realize that without a close alliance with one of the superpowers, it lacked the ability to change the status quo.

But by the early seventies, economic disparity shifted Soviet priorities, making them less responsive to Egyptian requests for military aid, even as the Egyptians were willing to offer formal political ties and military bases to Soviet Union: Soviet priorities shifted to domestic development, as there was a need for a more efficient use of available resources in light of the large military expenditures of the 1960s. And detente[21] with the United States became a major priority which led initially to a tempering of the regional competition (see cell 3, figure 3.1). Eventually, Soviet reluctance to fully respond to Egyptian requests led to the deterioration of Soviet-Egyptian relations to the benefit of the United States.

SOVIET-AMERICAN COMPETITION IN THE MIDDLE EAST: CONCLUSION

In the 1950s both superpowers had less direct influence and less stake in the Middle East than they came to have in the late 1960s and early 1970s; and because of independent British and French interests in the region the competition was not strictly bipolar. The polarization that emerged in the Middle East was not caused or shaped by the global competition, and coincided more with British interests than with the American objective of minimizing Soviet influence. The Soviets, on the other hand, despite increased influence, had little strategic presence in the Middle East. Their military inferiority to the United States inhibited their ability to demand more from their clients.

By the end of the 1960s and the early 1970s the Soviet Union had achieved its maximum presence in the Middle East. This presence can be measured in terms of three specific indicators: the number of Soviet troops and advisors present, the number and degree of access to military bases, and the number of formal "treaties of friendship" between the Soviet Union and Middle Eastern states. On all three counts Soviet influence reached its pinnacle by 1972 (see appendix 3B). This increase in Soviet influence was due primarily to: (1) the Soviets ability to demand more from their clients as a result of increased parity, and (2) Egypt and Syria's increased dependence on Soviet military aid following their defeat in the 1967 war and the subsequent increase in Israeli power stemming from a new American commitment.

At the same time the Soviet presence was increasing, West European presence in the region was in final decline, and more direct engagement by the United States was on the rise. The Middle East thus became more bipolarized along global lines than it had been at any time since World War II, even as détente was presumably prevailing between the two superpowers. Moreover, this new polarization in the region decreased the utility of nonalignment and gave rise to a new perception (by Egypt in particular) of a decidedly bipolar world.

BIPOLARITY AND THE BEHAVIOR OF EGYPT: FROM SEMI-NEUTRALITY TO ALLIANCE

Having described the ways in which incremental changes in the distribution of power between the Soviet Union and the United States affected their policies in the Middle East, I will now turn to the specific case of Egyptian behavior. In particular, I will show how the changes in Soviet-American relations affected the preferences of Egypt and resulted in a competition for alliance between Israel and Egypt that heavily influenced the Camp David bargaining. More specifically, I will argue that one major change in Egyptian preferences in the early 1970s in relation to the superpowers was from nonalignment to alignment, as a result of increased parity between the United States and the Soviet Union. The switch from alliance with the Soviet Union to the United States was partly a result of strategic parity/economic disparity (see cell 3, figure 3.1), and of the regional preferences of Egypt.

It has been argued above that because of the *objective* disparity of power favoring the United States (the West) in the 1950s and early 1960s, the Soviets were less demanding in their relationship with Egypt, while offering Egypt a great deal of aid; in this sense Egypt was allowed to pursue independent foreign and domestic policies.[22] Egyptian perceptions coincided with this objective picture. Although many in the West saw Egypt as a full Soviet ally during the fifties and sixties, Egyptians continued to view their state as a nonaligned nation; this can easily be seen in the discourse of Egyptian politicians and intellectuals. This Egyptian perception was objectively justified, before 1967, in that the Soviets demanded very little, and were thus viewed in a benign way for the most part. Later, when the Egyptians were forced to alter their policies, they had difficulty forming new perceptions of the Soviet Union.

Near-nonalignment had served Egypt well. At first, it seemed synonymous with anticolonialism, and consequently served Nasser both at home and in the Arab world that he sought to dominate. Moreover, the leadership role that Egypt played in the nonaligned movement gave Egypt the prestige that attracted interest from the superpowers. This in turn made Egypt one of the largest recipients of foreign aid since World War II. A generation of Egyptian elites grew up taking nonalignment for granted, while expecting unconditional and unlimited Soviet support. It was difficult to deal with the inevitable dissonance, therefore, when the Soviets began demanding military bases and formal treaties as a price for their aid to Egypt. When the Soviets became more reluctant to supply the Egyptian army some Egyptians grew perplexed. Even as late as 1978, long after the severing of relations with the Soviet Union, prominent Egyptian intellectuals found it necessary to argue that the Soviets also behaved selfishly. In a front-page commentary in *Al-Ahram*, Egyptian journalist Ali Hamdi al-Jammal wrote:

> The Soviet Union aids the Arabs to a calculated degree not in order that they defeat Israel but in order to establish itself in the Arab area . . . that is because I believed—and still believe—that Moscow's approach to the solution of the Middle East problem does not differ in any way from Washington's approach to this problem.[23]

Similarly, when Egyptian military officers were debating the increase in Soviet demands and the decrease in their willingness to supply weapons to Egypt in 1971, the Egyptian Chief of Staff found it necessary to argue that Soviet concern for their interest was understandable, and that for a relationship between two states to be durable *both* states must benefit from it.[24]

The Soviet Union became increasingly reluctant to sell arms to Egypt even before Nasser's death in 1970. This was partly because of U.S. pressure in the context of détente and the "linkage strategy,"[25] and partly because the Soviets were not particularly interested in changing the status quo in the Middle East. Given that sales of military equipment were their primary means of influence in the area, the Soviets were anxious to maintain Egyptian military dependence on them. As early as 1967, Nasser became incensed with the inadequacy of Soviet military support, and as though he was anticipating Soviet demands in return sent a message to the Kremlin through President Tito of Yugoslavia, "that Israeli occupation of his country would be preferable to the treatment that the Troika were meting out."[26] Later, during the 1968–70 War of Attrition, when the Soviets refused to resupply Egypt with ammunition on the grounds that they did not approve of the war, Nasser became furious.[27] Rhetoric and emotions aside, however, it is difficult to imagine what options Nasser had but to succumb to Soviet pressure. For two decades he had successfully steered an independent course, during which time he had avoided formal alliance with the Soviets and linked himself, seemingly inseparably, to the cause of nonalignment. A dramatic change of course seemed unlikely. Yet it was Nasser, champion of Pan-Arabism and the Palestinian cause, who before his death had accepted the Rogers Plan and watched on the sidelines while King Hussein of Jordan was dealing the Palestine Liberation Organization a crippling blow.

The predicament of alignment was left to Nasser's successor, Anwar Sadat, to resolve; his choices altered the nature of Middle Eastern politics beyond reversal. On coming to power Sadat's perception of Egyptian relations with the superpowers was consistent with the view of Egypt as a nonaligned nation that had been prevalent since the midfifties. Massive Soviet aid to Egypt did not constitute an alliance. But what was beginning to emerge was a genuine belief that nonalignment might not be sufficient to bring about Egyptian objectives. Sadat conveyed both feelings in talks with American Secretary of State William Rogers early in 1971: "I also told Rogers that if the Israeli occupation were imposed on us, or if anyone tried to force us to acquiesce in it, I would rethink about our nonalignment. The Americans know that we are masters in our own country."[28] For Sadat the primary Egyptian objective was clear: the liberation of occupied Egyptian territories. When the Rogers initiative failed it became increasingly clear that a diplomatic solution was not in sight. Sadat became even more convinced that there was no alternative to the military option. Yet Egypt lacked the capability to launch a successful war against Israel and, given Egypt's relations with both superpowers, neither seemed sufficiently committed to helping the Egyptians.

On the other hand Sadat, perhaps more so than Nasser, saw no alternative to the superpowers; to him the world of 1970 was strictly bipolar. As soon as he came to power he made his views on the relative irrelevance of the Third World for Egyptian objectives known to all. His Minister of State for Foreign Affairs, Butrus Ghali, recalled that Sadat considered relations with the Third World to be "insignificant," and that he refused to be "bothered" with such matters, always delegating them to less-prominent aides.[29] Gesturing derogatorily with his hand, Sadat would instruct Ghali or another aide to deal with such matters on their own.[30]

The failure of the American diplomatic initiative and increasing Soviet demands led to Sadat's reassessment of Egyptian nonalignment. His early decisions following that assessment should firmly discredit the proposition that Sadat's later expulsion of Soviet troops from Egypt derived from his personal dislike for the Soviet Union and from his inclinations toward the West. His first choice, necessitated by Egypt's strategic position, was in fact to forge a closer and more formal alliance with the Soviet Union. Indeed, during his first months in office Sadat denounced those Arab states who were improving their relations with the United States. Referring to Algerian president Boumedienne, Sadat concluded: "He has sold himself to the Americans, politically and economically. He has just signed a contract with American companies to supply petroleum and liquified gas for decades to come. His economy will absolutely be tied to America's."[31] As late as May 1972, only two months before Sadat expelled Soviet troops from

Egypt, he proclaimed in an address to the People's Assembly: "I shall take strong measures against people who criticize Egypt's major ally, Russia, rather than Cairo's enemy, the United States."[32]

To be sure, the Soviet Union continued to resist the sale of offensive weapons to Egypt and increased its demands for military facilities. But given its immediate military objective, Egypt had little choice but to try to consolidate relations with the Soviet Union even at the cost of granting the Soviets more influence. As a former chief of staff of the Egyptian armed forces put it: "No other country or group of countries simultaneously could and would have supplied Egypt with the arms in profusion and sophistication needed to combat Israel. . . . Only a superpower could have had the development and manufacturing capacity. Of the Superpowers, only the Soviet Union had the will."[33]

Sadat was apparently willing to do all that was necessary to achieve his goals, including making Egypt a formal ally of the Soviet Union and granting the Soviets major military facilities. As Sadat later wrote, "When the Soviets threatened in 1970 that they would evacuate the SAM missiles unless Soviet experts were permitted to man them, I said: 'Do you want to keep a Soviet presence in Egypt? All right! Just give me the weapons! I don't fear a Soviet presence!' "[34]

Reversing his predecessor's long-held policy of formal nonalignment, within months of coming to power Sadat had agreed to sign a "treaty of friendship and cooperation" with the Soviet Union in the hope that the Soviets would increase their commitment to Egypt. He did so, however, only after he had removed the Soviets' closest allies in the Egyptian government in an internal power struggle. Moreover, to secure the arms he desired, Sadat may have offered the Soviets facilities *beyond* what they had requested. Sadat apparently initiated the proposal that the Soviet fleet use the port facilities at Mersa Matrouh, and that the Egyptians pay for the new arms purchases in hard currency for the first time.[35]

In spite of Sadat's gestures, the Soviets remained reluctant to sell sophisticated arms to Egypt and seemed committed to preventing an Egyptian military initiative. Their demands from Egypt also increased: at Mersa Matrouh, they requested air and ground facilities in addition to naval port access.[36] Delivery of some promised weapons was withheld in a fashion designed to prevent an Egyptian attack against Israeli forces during Sadat's much publicized "year of decision." Other Egyptian requests for arms went unanswered. By the beginning of 1972 it was becoming apparent that the Soviets were not likely to meet the Egyptian requests; Sadat complained to his military officers that "the

Americans are giving Israel complete support, while the Soviets have not yet supplied us with what they promised last October."[37] His defense minister, Sadek, declared that the Soviets "had not supplied us with the weapons and equipment we needed. They were deliberately blocking Egypt's offensive."[38] Subsequent Egyptian attempts to remedy the situation ended in failure.

Egyptian options, however, were very limited; it is perhaps because the Soviets were well aware of this that their expulsion from Egypt took them by surprise. Given Egypt's immediate military objectives, there seemed to be no alternative to the Soviet Union. Yet the Soviets were not about to jeopardize détente with the United States for Egypt's sake, and many Egyptians began to re-examine Soviet objectives in the Middle East. A symposium held at the Center for Political and Strategic Studies at *Al-Ahram* in May 1972 concluded that Egypt:

> should realize that the superpowers accorded very low priority to the Middle East problems and that détente would distract their attention from the Middle East even more. Egypt had to shape its policy so as to force the superpowers to become more involved in solving the conflict in the Middle East.[39]

Sadat himself apparently perceived Soviet objectives along similar lines. A month after expelling Soviet troops from Egypt, Sadat remarked:

> Détente, sealed between the Russians and the Americans in Moscow at the May 20 summit, is now the dominant strategy of the Soviet Union. The cold war between the blocs is over, and détente will work for 20–25 years at least. But détente means that small powers like us will be crushed. The Soviet Union does not want us to go to war.[40]

Once it became certain that the Soviet Union would try to prevent an Egyptian offensive, the foundation of Soviet-Egyptian relations was shaken beyond repair. Aside from military support, the Soviets lacked any effective means of influence in the Middle East; the removal of the military instrument made the Soviets useless to the Egyptians (see appendix 3A and appendix 3B for data on the link between Soviet military support and influence in the Middle East). Moreover, the presence of Soviet troops on Egyptian soil might have complicated Egypt's position in terms of the superpowers in the event of war.

In July 1972, Soviet troops were expelled from Egypt in a move that surprised the international community. Nonetheless the Egyptians, having decided to launch the war even without additional Soviet military support, were still in need of military and political support when war broke out; the treaty of friendship and cooperation with the Soviets was left in force. The Soviets, to preserve their international credibility, would still have to come to Egypt's aid in wartime. The potential confrontation between the Soviet Union and the United States during an Arab-Israeli war would compel both to allocate more energy to the Arab-Israeli conflict. The state of "no war, no peace" that the Egyptians found unacceptable, would be altered.

The period following the 1973 war was one of political negotiations. Having done better than expected in the war and having demonstrated the ability to rally other Arab states behind it, Egypt was in a much improved bargaining position. And since the United States, which was perceived to hold decisive influence in relation to Israel, demonstrated its urgent interest in resolving the conflict now that vital American interests seemed threatened, the Egyptians were willing to throw in their political lot with the United States. Egypt accepted Henry Kissinger's unilateral initiative for the disengagement of forces between Israel and Egypt as a first step in a process that would continue, through the Geneva conference, with the aim of achieving an overall settlement of the Arab-Israeli conflict. But while Kissinger's shuttle diplomacy succeeded in separating the forces in a fashion that reduced the risk of a new surprise war, it also contributed to the eventual stalemate in the negotiations. By defusing the crisis situation through a partial and technical agreement, a historical moment of opportunity for a more lasting settlement may have been lost.

Crises like the one that prevailed immediately after the 1973 war, though dangerous, can also provide unusual opportunities for fundamental structural change. In crises, governments seem to have the capacity to elevate the issue at hand to the top of their priorities, and therefore make the decisions necessary for fundamental change. Once the disengagement agreements were concluded, however, there seemed to be little incentive for substantial progress at Geneva. A frustrating deadlock was inevitable. Although the negotiations leading to the disengagement of forces are not the focus of this work, it is worth noting that many Egyptian officials and intellectuals blame President Sadat for inferior bargaining, which contributed to "wasting" Egypt's leverage.[41] They see decided similarities between Egypt's bargaining behavior at Camp David and the negotiations leading to the disengagement agreements.[42]

While Egypt relied fully on the United States, to the effective exclusion of the Soviet Union, this reliance was a result of the perception that after the 1973 war the conflict with Israel would be largely political. Thus, Sadat did not appear especially concerned that one outcome of the disengagement agreements was to minimize the Egyptian military threat as short-term leverage in the Geneva negotiations. But Egypt was not unaware that its military forces remained an important element for the negotiations in the long term. Indeed, the years 1974 and 1975 witnessed the heaviest military expenditures in Egypt's modern history, reaching a peak of 52 percent of GNP in 1975. While the negotiations were proceeding Egypt could not hope to get an amount of arms from the United States that would serve as leverage in the negotiations with Israel; the Soviet Union remained the only option for military assistance. Thus, while the Egyptians were moving closer to the United States on the political level, they attempted to maintain their military relations with the Soviet Union (as noted earlier, the Egyptian-Soviet Treaty of Friendship was kept intact). Egypt was once again attempting to have the best of both worlds, but given Soviet-American parity, this strategy was bound to fail.

By 1976, Egypt's hope for turning the leverage of the 1973 war into a negotiated settlement through the mediation of the United States had been frustrated. The Geneva talks proceeded at a snail's pace, and Israel improved its strategic position. To increase its diminishing bargaining power, the Egyptian government turned to the Soviet Union, requesting sophisticated weapons that would enhance Egypt's capacity to strike deep inside Israel in case of war. But the Soviets appeared unwilling to assist in a process that would ultimately benefit the United States. Desperate, the Egyptians bypassed Moscow and asked to purchase Soviet weapons from India.[43] When the government of Indira Gandi informed Egypt that because of Soviet opposition, it would not provide the weapons, the Egyptians had to once again consider their options.

Sadat's choice became clear only one day after the Indian refusal, when he announced his decision to void the Egyptian-Soviet treaty. It is not at once obvious why Sadat opted to rely fully on the United States and almost irrevocably sever his relations with the Soviet Union, instead of reversing his steps at that point. A full explanation of this choice is provided in the next chapter's discussion of regional politics. The answer lay primarily in Egypt's regional objectives, given the major changes in the distribution of military and economic power in the Middle East. Having made Egypt fully available for alliance with the United States, Sadat calculated that Egypt's bargaining position in relation to Israel would be significantly enhanced. To be sure, there remained some psychological barriers between the United States and Egypt that prevented any rapid moves toward actual alignment. After all, Sadat was the man who initiated the 1973 war, helped in establishing the Arab oil embargo against the United States, and still refused to recognize America's major regional ally, Israel. But some of these psychological obstacles had been partially removed by Sadat's expulsion of the Soviets and his cooperation with the United States in the negotiations. What remained of these barriers was removed, almost magically, when Sadat surprised the world and embarked on his historic visit to Jerusalem. Overnight, Sadat became the most popular man in America.

The potential for American-Egyptian relations was viewed by Egypt as an important leverage in the negotiations with Israel. The Egyptian assessment was that Israeli strategy in the region could be successful only with unlimited support from the United States. This was possible only if Israel could maintain its position as the United States' primary military and political ally in the Middle East.[44] If Egypt could compete with Israel for alliance with the United States, the Israelis would have to compromise in the short term, and their regional hegemony would be prevented in the long term. But in order to compete effectively, Egypt would have to align her interests and positions more closely with those of the United States. It was thus that Sadat developed close ties with the Carter administration, often making the extra gesture, always responding positively to Carter's requests. By the time the negotiations at Camp David took place, the American position was considerably closer to that of Egypt than it was to Israel; so much so that, at one point before Camp David, Carter and Sadat had secretly agreed on a joint strategy that would manipulate Israel into accepting a settlement that they considered acceptable.[45] Throughout the negotiations at Camp David Sadat sought to assure an identity of views with the United States, dealing with President Carter as a "partner" when it should have been apparent that Carter was only capable of playing the role of a mediator. When President Sadat threatened to leave the negotiations and return to Egypt during the final days at Camp David, he changed his mind only after Carter threatened to blame the failure of the talks on Sadat.

That Egypt viewed this new relationship with the United States as bargaining leverage with Israel can be seen from the private statements of several Egyptian officials. Butrus Ghali, Egypt's Minister of State for Foreign Affairs, saw the Egyptian competition for alliance with the

United States as the "most important leverage" that Egypt held in the negotiations, and the "secret weapon that Israel feared most."[46] According to Ghali, this was the way President Sadat saw things as well.[47] Ibrahim Kamel, former Egyptian Foreign Minister also confirmed this view.[48] Israel, too, perceived the situation along similar lines, and sought to frustrate Egyptian objectives.

Egypt's strategy continued beyond Camp David. In addition to the advantage held by Egypt in its agreement with the views of the Carter administration, Egypt also attempted to stress its strategic utility for the United States. Egypt argued that, because Egypt is an Arab state it is in a much better position than Israel to intervene on behalf of American interest in the Arab world. Similarly, Egypt offered the use of its territory to the American Rapid Deployment Force, arguing that launching the force from Egypt would be "more acceptable" than from a non-Arab state. When the Shah was deposed Sadat resolved a potential problem for the Carter administration by hosting the Shah in Egypt, at some risk to the regime. During the American attempt to free the hostages held in Iran, American forces used Egyptian territory. When the new Reagan administration emphasized a Soviet threat, Sadat announced that he now viewed the Soviet Union as the most serious threat to the Middle East, and called for American and regional cooperation to counter it. It is rather doubtful that Sadat actually took the Soviet threat very seriously, since even when thousands of Soviet troops and their bases were present in Egyptian he was able to expel them with a simple order.

Despite Egypt's efforts, this strategy had little chance of success. Aside from America's fundamental commitment to the state of Israel, emanating from domestic variables, Egypt gave up any military, economic or political influence in the Arab world after Camp David. Israel, on the other hand, retained both the military power and the political capacity for an initiative to alter the nature of regional affairs, and to creating a *fait accompli* which would force America to favor Israel. The invasion of Lebanon is a good case in point.

Conclusion

I have argued that Soviet influence over Egypt in the 1950s and early 1960s was limited as a result of global strategic disparity, and that the Egyptians perceived themselves as being nonaligned. But by the late sixties, increasing parity between the superpowers forced Egypt toward alignment, especially given Egypt's regional objectives. Sadat's early strategy of consolidating relations with the Soviet Union should discredit the thesis that his personal preferences resulted in his later moves toward the United States.

In addition, I have also argued that the eventual shift toward alignment with the United States was due partly to Soviet priorities (which were largely an outcome of *economic disparity* between the Soviet Union and the United States), and partly a result of shifts in Egypt's regional objectives, resulting from change in the distribution of power in the Middle East.[49] Of these Egyptian objectives, I have outlined only the one pertaining to the state of Israel, and simply alluded to others. A full articulation of these objectives and how they affected Egyptian choices is now in order.

APPENDIX 3A

"MODERATE" AND "RADICAL" STATES IN THE MIDDLE EAST: PATTERNS OF INTERNATIONAL TRADE

ONE COMPONENT of American interests in the Middle East is an economic one. Aside from securing the flow of Middle Eastern oil to the West at reasonable prices, the West seeks to secure a good share of the trade in the region. This appendix is intended to determine whether the division of the Middle East into "radical" and "moderate states" is a useful indicator of the trade patterns of Middle Eastern states. In particular, do radical states conduct more trade with the Soviet bloc countries than do moderate states? Do moderate states conduct more trade with the West than do radical states?

The tables below show that the answer is largely negative. First, of the oil-exporting states of the Middle East, the moderate states do not appear to behave differently from the radical states; indeed, the oil-exporting state that conducted the greatest percentage of its trade with the Soviet bloc is the Shah's Iran, not Libya, Algeria, or Iraq. Second, a change in regime from moderate to radical in one state does not appear to alter the pattern of that state's foreign trade. Libya, for example, was governed up until 1969 by a conservative pro-Western monarchy; since 1969 Libya has been governed by the radical government of Muammar al-Qaddafi. Yet its trade pattern has remained almost constant. The percentage of trade conducted with the Soviet bloc nations has been as follows:[50]

1960	1965	1970	1975	1980
1.9%	1.9%	1.8%	1.3%	1.0%

Of the states that are not major exporters of oil, Egypt has conducted more trade with the Soviet bloc nations than have other Middle Eastern states, especially during the 1960–1975 period. But the case of Egypt is somewhat unusual in the sense that most Egyptian trade with the Soviet Union had been an economic debit rather than a credit for the Soviet Union, just as later increased Egyptian trade with the United States was mostly an economic burden for the United States. Moreover, even during the years when Egypt conducted a high share of its trade with the Soviet Union, it still conducted a higher percentage with the Western world.

The years 1970–71 witnessed the highest share of Middle Eastern trade with Soviet bloc countries. This increase seems to hold regardless of the radical-moderate distinction. Furthermore, a noticeable increase in Soviet political and military influence in the region seemed to accompany the trade increase. An explanation for this surge in Soviet influence which does not rely on the radical-moderate dichotomy is offered in Appendix 3B.

APPENDIX 3B

THE BALANCING TENDENCY OF STATES IN THE MIDDLE EAST:
CAUSES OF SOVIET MILITARY INFLUENCE

*I*NCREASED SOVIET influence in the Middle East follows a clear pattern: a weakened state facing increased regional polarization and stepped-up commitment to its opponents by the United States accepts increased Soviet influence in order to remedy the perceived imbalance.

TABLE 3.1. Trade Patterns of Middle East States

	INDUSTRIAL WEST			SOVIET BLOCK			NON-OIL DEVLP.		
	E	I	T	E	I	T	E	I	T
S. Arabia									
1960	70.1	65.5	69.2	–	0.2	–	29.9	34.1	30.7
1965	74.5	84.6	77.1	–	–	–	6.0	12.9	7.8
1970	68.3	63.7	67.7	0.1	0.7	0.1	24.0	26.4	24.3
1975									
1980	75.3	79.6	73.5	–	1.6	0.4	20.8	14.7	18.7
Syria									
1960	29.7	70.1	57.6	20.6	9.0	12.6	25.8	17.1	19.8
1965	24.4	54.7	41.3	33.7	16.7	24.3	28.0	11.4	18.7
1970	39.7	47.8	44.7	27.1	26.3	26.3	23.3	22.2	22.4
1975	48.7	59.2	55.5	11.4	9.2	10.0	20.9	23.8	22.8
1980	67.0	52.1	57.1	7.0	6.4	6.6	18.1	17.6	17.7
Kuwait									
1960	88.5	88.4	88.5	–	0.1	–	10.8	9.4	10.6
1965	91.5	81.9	89.5	–	–	–	3.5	9.9	4.8
1970	78.9	66.9	75.9	–	8.9	2.9	15.3	17.7	15.9
1975	62.4	77.1	65.6	–	2.3	0.5	24.9	17.4	23.2
1980	50.3	74.1	56.1	0.7	1.2	0.8	29.1	19.9	26.9
Iran									
1960	59.1	79.6	63.9	2.9	8.7	4.2	37.7	8.4	30.8
1965	62.2	80.3	69.4	3.0	4.5	3.6	22.9	7.4	16.7
1970	77.4	82.9	79.7	–	6.7	2.8	16.3	6.3	12.0
1975	86.3	83.0	85.1	0.5	3.4	1.5	12.3	12.4	12.4
1980	61.3	67.0	63.9	0.5	8.8	4.3	36.3	18.5	28.2
Israel									
1960	71.0	80.2	77.4	1.8	0.9	1.1	23.6	10.7	14.6
1965	70.6	80.1	77.4	4.0	2.0	2.7	12.2	5.1	7.5
1970	69.8	82.3	77.9	2.6	2.3	2.4	15.9	11.1	12.8
1975	69.6	53.1	57.1	0.4	0.1	0.1	19.2	4.7	8.3
1980	69.0	54.6	59.8	0.1	–	0.1	16.5	4.7	9.0
Egypt									
1960	26.0	57.5	42.8	44.4	25.1	34.1	26.8	14.0	19.9
1965	25.3	52.2	41.6	52.8	22.9	34.6	11.4	11.5	11.4
1970	26.5	57.0	41.5	48.8	15.2	32.3	15.4	14.3	14.9
1975	14.5	65.8	52.3	67.2	12.8	26.0	16.0	15.1	15.3
1980	59.8	72.5	66.8	7.6	5.4	6.2	29.5	16.3	21.0

	INDUSTRIAL WEST			SOVIET BLOCK			NON-OIL DEVLP.		
	E	I	T	E	I	T	E	I	T
Algeria									
1960	92.4	91.3	91.6	0.5	7.7	0.8	6.5	7.7	7.4
1965	80.3	79.8	80.0	8.9	6.6	7.6	8.0	10.3	9.3
1970	88.3	89.3	88.9	3.8	3.4	3.6	7.9	7.1	7.4
1975	90.3	83.6	87.2	1.8	3.4	2.5	5.4	12.8	8.8
1980	–	–	–	–	–	–	–	–	–
Jordan									
1960	1.0	57.4	53.1	11.2	3.5	4.1	60.2	24.8	27.4
1965	6.5	57.4	51.4	3.7	11.7	10.7	45.3	18.5	21.7
1970	0.3	54.1	45.6	3.5	12.2	10.8	52.8	25.9	30.1
1975	8.0	52.4	44.8	5.2	2.5	3.0	34.0	20.4	22.7
1980	6.5	56.4	46.0	1.4	2.7	2.4	22.5	12.8	14.8
Iraq									
1960	85.1	66.7	78.2	0.6	9.7	4.1	13.4	22.7	16.9
1965	75.3	85.4	77.9	–	–	–	21.9	9.4	12.0
1970	61.4	49.2	57.6	1.9	26.4	9.6	13.7	17.6	14.9
1975	60.1	74.5	65.3	0.2	6.5	2.5	39.4	18.2	31.8
1980	59.4	76.8	65.1	0.2	3.5	1.2	44.1	15.4	32.1
Libya									
1960	67.6	88.7	87.4	6.7	1.5	1.8	25.7	9.5	10.4
1965	94.0	82.8	90.8	–	8.7	1.9	2.4	7.2	3.6
1970	91.5	72.7	87.9	–	9.8	1.9	1.6	12.9	3.7
1975	84.6	74.1	80.7	0.5	2.8	1.3	14.9	20.6	17.0
1980	89.8	84.2	88.0	0.3	2.4	1.0	9.5	12.8	10.6
Morocco									
1960	73.3	77.3	75.4	4.4	5.5	5.0	21.9	16.8	19.2
1965	72.5	69.4	70.9	11.4	16.0	13.7	6.6	10.2	8.4
1970	72.5	74.2	73.5	10.4	12.3	11.5	5.9	5.6	5.8
1975	66.3	69.9	68.5	13.6	8.6	10.5	16.2	14.1	14.9
1980	62.9	61.1	61.8	18.7	6.2	7.2	15.4	7.7	10.5

E = Percentage of Exports to Group of States Indicated
I = Percentage of Imports to Group of States Indicated
T = Percentage of Total Trade to Group of States Indicated
SOURCE: *Direction of Trade: Annual*, 1960–1964; 1964–1968; 1970–1976 (Washington DC: International Monetary Fund); and *Direction of Trade Yearbook*, 1981 (Washington, DC: International Monetary Fund). Percentages are calculated from figures presented in these sources.

When states have consented to Soviet presence and influence they do so only reluctantly, for all states wish to remain independent to the greatest extent possible. Weakening Soviet clients, it turns out, does not weaken Soviet influence as some American administrations have tended to expect, but exactly the opposite. Moreover, increasing regional polarizations are demonstrably conducive to increased Soviet influence.

There are three indicators of concrete Soviet military and political influence that concern the United States: the actual presence of Soviet troops (especially in their own bases), the access of the Soviet navy to Middle Eastern ports, and the number of political and military treaties between the Soviet Union and Middle Eastern states. Three major cases of increasing Soviet influence, as measured by these indicators, demonstrate the pattern described above.

The first case is that of Egypt, which signed a "treaty of friendship and cooperation" with the Soviet Union in 1971, and offered naval and air bases to the Soviets. Soviet military influence peaked with the presence of some 15,000 Soviet troops in Egypt. The events leading to this are clear: even after its devastating defeat in 1967, Egypt refrained from succumbing to Soviet pressure insofar as was possible. But when the United States failed to achieve a political settlement with the Roger's Plan, and in fact increased the U.S. military commitment to Israel by supplying new attack aircraft with the capacity to strike Cairo, the Egyptians moved closer to the Soviets.

The second case is that of Iraq, which signed a treaty with the Soviet Union in 1972. The Iraqis were facing increasing conflict with Iran, as they both were competing to fill the vacuum in the Persian Gulf created by the withdrawal of Britain. The United States committed itself fully to Iran as part of the Nixon-Kissinger strategy for the Middle East. Iraq's consolidation of relations with the Soviet Union was a reluctant one, and Iraq indeed came under attack from its own friends in the Arab world for signing the treaty; Libyan leader Qaddafi recalled his ambassador from Baghdad in protest.

The third case is that of Syria, which concluded a treaty with the Soviet Union in 1980. Perhaps more than other Arab states, Syria had resisted concluding a treaty with the Soviets, refusing to follow suit with its Egyptian allies in 1971. Not until after the Camp David accords and the signing of the Israeli-Egyptian peace treaty (which was fully supported by the United States) did the Syrians conclude their treaty with the Soviets. Moreover, Soviet military presence in Syria peaked only after the Syrians' 1982 defeat by Israel as they invaded

Lebanon; the number of Soviet troops in Syria reached over 7000, with many manning military equipment.

The pattern continues beyond these three cases. Libya, for example, has rejected Soviet requests for a naval base on its territory; but one day after the United States attack on Libya in 1986, Libyan vice-president Abdul Salam Jalloud declared that Libya was now seriously considering granting the Soviets a naval base. Later, asked if he was serious in saying he would join the Soviet bloc, Libyan leader Qaddafi replied: "We will do this if we have to."

APPENDIX 3C

INDICATORS OF US-SOVIET MILITARY AND POLITICAL POWER IN THE MIDDLE EAST

A CRITICAL argument in this study is the shift in relative U.S. and Soviet power on both the systemic and regional levels. While the measurement of "power" is problematic, it is still possible to examine several of the more important indicators of military and political influence.

Examining indicators of Soviet systemic power shows that Soviet military and political power was clearly more substantial in the early 1970s than it was in the late 1950s and early 1960s. Regional indicators, such as the number of Soviet troops and bases in the Middle East, the number of formal treaties between the Soviet Union and states in the region, naval presence in the Mediterranean, the peaceful use of force in and arms transfers to the Middle East, reflect this change in more local terms by 1972. Similar indicators point to an increased American role in Middle East politics by the early 1970s.

General indicators of relative military power will be loosely categorized as being on the systemic or regional levels, since systemic parity plays a central role in my arguments. These measures can also be seen as static or dynamic. A static indicator of power is one that operates without being overtly invoked by its source, such as military forces-in-being; such indicators would tend to measure a state's potential power as seen by friends or adversaries whether the source intends to exercise the power or not. A dynamic measure is one that is deliberately invoked by the source, such as naval maneuvers in a region; these indicators would address the source's general intent to display or exercise power.

These indicators will be examined for the 1960s and 1970s. Three general types of indicator will be considered: military, economic, and political. There is, of course, an extremely broad range of variables which could be considered indicators of power; those chosen are merely representative examples drawn from readily available sources. These indicators are neither comprehensive nor definitive, but should strengthen the arguments presented in the narrative.

MILITARY INDICATORS

Systemic. Indicators of the relative military power of the United States and Soviet Union on this level have been widely examined and discussed, and many interpretations offered. It is not my purpose to unravel or take sides in the debate(s) on the US-Soviet military balance. With this in mind, the number of nuclear warheads possessed by each side should serve as a simple static measure of overall military power. This information is presented in table 3.2.

Dynamic measures present their own set of difficulties. Still, the data collected in two Brookings studies of the peaceful use of military power should be very useful. These data are presented in table 3.3. While the individual cases are divergent in terms of location, instru-

TABLE 3.2. Deliverable Nuclear Warheads, 1955–1975

	UNITED STATES		SOVIET UNION	
	Regional	*Long Range*	*Regional*	*Long Range*
1955	698	2310	324	0
1960	772	4362	1034	294
1965	862	4002	2085	381
1970	748	3689	2281	1403
1975	1294	7725	2467	1875

SOURCE: Robert P. Berman and John C. Baker, *Soviet Strategic Forces: Requirements and Responses* (Washington DC: The Brookings Institution, 1982), pp. 42–43. U.S. regional figures include European allies and China, but these figures are quite small for the period indicated.

ment used, and purpose, they can serve as an indicator of the exercise of military power in a political context.

Regional. Indicators similar to those presented above are useful in looking at regional power. These indicators apply to the Middle East only. Data on superpower troop deployments and/or basing in the region is sketchy and difficult to find, particularly for the 1960s, often appearing only in widely scattered sources. One can note, however, the dramatic change in Soviet military presence in Egypt: from little or no presence in the fifties and sixties, by 1971 the Soviets had 15,000–20,000 troops in Egypt. These figures include instructors, advisers, six fighter squadrons, and air defense units. The Soviet Union also operated six airbases in Egypt, and had facilities at two ports; at Mersa Matrouh both air and naval facilities were under construction at that time.[51]

Two simple dynamic indicators offer more possibility for comparison with the United States: the peaceful use of force in the region, as presented in table 3.3 for the systemic level, and the maneuvering of naval forces, as presented in table 3.4. Although these forces need not be used in their primary military roles, their responsiveness and potential for quick use would qualify them as a dynamic measure.

"Peaceful" use of force in the region can be examined as it was in a system-wide context above. These data are presented in table 3.5. Data are available only to the middle of the 1970s, indicating the generally increasing Soviet tendency to use force in this way.

TABLE 3.3. *Use of Force as a Political Instrument, 1955–1975*

	NUMBER OF INCIDENTS OF THE PEACEFUL USE OF FORCE	
	United States	Soviet Union
1955–1960	46	33
1961–1965	75	12
1966–1970	21	35
1971–1975	25	27

SOURCE: [U.S. data] Barry M. Blechman and Stephen S. Kaplan, *Force Without War: U.S. Armed Forces as a Political Instrument* (Washington DC: The Brookings Institution, 1978), pp. 547–553; [Soviet data] Stephen S. Kaplan, *Diplomacy of Power: Soviet Armed Forces as a Political Instrument* (Washington DC: The Brookings Institution, 1981), pp. 689–693.

Economic Indicators

Systemic. As with military indicators, a wide variety of economic indicators could be chosen. Trade with the two superpowers, presented in terms of exports to and imports from them, has been chosen as a good general indicator of both economic interaction and strength. The precise dollar figures in these tables are less important than the relation-

TABLE 3.4. *U.S.–Soviet Naval Presence in the Mediterranean, 1965–1976*

	SHIP-DAYS "OUT-OF-AREA"	
	Soviet Navy	U.S. Navy
1965	4,200	8,000
1969	15,800	19,000
1972	18,100	15,000
1974	20,200	15,400
1976	18,600	15,200

SOURCE: *Understanding Soviet Naval Developments*, 4th ed., NAVSOP P-3560, Rev. 1/81 (Washington DC: US Government Printing Office, 1981), p. 16. A 'ship-day out-of-area' is defined as one where a ship "is deployed beyond the normal operating and training areas of home waters." Soviet naval presence in the Mediterranean before this period was generally negligible.

TABLE 3.5. *Use of Force as a Political Instrument in the Middle East, 1955–1975*

	NUMBER OF INCIDENTS OF THE PEACEFUL USE OF FORCE	
	United States	Soviet Union
1955–1960	11	4
1961–1965	5	1
1966–1970	7	6
1971–1975	2	6

SOURCE: [U.S. data] Barry M. Blechman and Stephen S. Kaplan, *Force Without War: U.S. Armed Forces as a Political Instrument* (Washington DC: The Brookings Institution, 1978), pp. 547–553; [Soviet data] Stephen S. Kaplan, *Diplomacy of Power: Soviet Armed Forces as a Political Instrument* (Washington DC: The Brookings Institution, 1981), pp. 689–693.

ship between them; for this reason the ratio of each year's U.S. and Soviet figures is given. Not surprisingly, the U.S. is consistently ahead of the Soviets; though the U.S. relative "lead" does increase for the period of most interest, the Soviets seem to gain somewhat later in the period.

Regional. The figures in table 3.7 are presented in a similar fashion to those in table 3.6. Note, however, that the ratios show a significantly different relationship for the 1960–1975 period; exports to the Soviet Union actually slightly overtake those to the United States for 1975.

Arms trade figures can be seen as economic, political, or military

TABLE 3.6. World Trade with the Superpowers, 1960–1980

	EXPORTS		EXPORT RATIO	IMPORTS		IMPORT RATIO
	US	USSR	US:USSR	US	USSR	US:USSR
1960	20,587	5,368	3.8	16,209	6,192	2.6
1965	27,393	2,291	11.9	22,869	2,467	9.2
1970	43,231	3,913	11.0	42,452	4,523	9.4
1975	107,586	11,363	9.5	103,418	17,000	6.0
1980	220,703	29,498	7.5	252,995	31,121	8.1

TABLE 3.7. Middle East Trade with the Superpowers, 1960–1980

	EXPORTS		EXPORT RATIO	IMPORTS		IMPORT RATIO
	US	USSR	US:USSR	US	USSR	US:USSR
1960	313.0	124.0	2.5	634.1	106.9	5.9
1965	258.1	184.8	1.4	738.4	169.0	4.3
1970	339.4	379.4	0.9	1242.8	349.3	3.6
1975	5612.8	997.0	5.6	7314.7	836.0	8.7
1980	30624.8	519.6	58.9	13198.4	669.6	19.7

SOURCE: *Direction of Trade: Annual,* 1960–1964; 1964–1968; 1970–1976 (Washington DC: International Monetary Fund); and *Direction of Trade Yearbook,* 1981 (Washington DC: International Monetary Fund). Figures are in $US million, as reported by the countries themselves. For this table, the Middle East consists of those countries in Table 3.1 in Appendix 3B.

indicators; though they are relevant to all three areas, they will be considered as economic indicators for the purposes of presentation. Table 3.8 gives constant dollar values for arms flows into the Middle East for our period. Though Soviet transfers are consistently greater than those for the U.S., they represent an approximately constant percentage of total transfers to the region, while U.S. figures grow steadily throughout the period.

Political Indicators

Regional. Potential indicators of systemic political power are probably too general to be of much real value; regional-level indicators can, however, be more focused.

One important political indicator is major treaties of friendship or alliance with regional actors. There are, of course, a broad range of formal agreements between the superpowers and Middle Eastern states for specific economic, military, or other purposes, but these would tend to be reflected in the data presented above. For present purposes, less-specific treaties of friendship or alliance will be considered.

While having no formal treaties with Middle Eastern states in the 1950s and 1960s, the Soviets came to have two important "friendship" treaties by 1972 with Egypt and Iraq; the United States had no such treaties with Middle Eastern states.[52]

Like arms transfers, naval forces serve many functions. Apart from the more military-related deployments of naval forces out of area, as mentioned above, navies engage in port calls as political gestures, to "show the flag" and indicate (among other things) support for friends

TABLE 3.8. Arms Transfers to the Middle East, 1956–1975

	US	USSR	Total
1956–1960	386 (14%)	1,325 (48%)	2,760
1961–1965	1,434 (29%)	2,423 (49%)	4,946
1966–1970	5,737 (35%)	8,032 (49%)	16,392
1971–1975	14,438 (41%)	15,847 (45%)	35,217

Figures are in billions of constant 1985 dollars. "Total" refers to arms transfers to the Middle East from all sources, figures in parentheses are percentages of this total. Calculated from Michael Brzoska and Thomas Ohlson, *Arms Transfers to the Third World, 1971–1985* (New York: Oxford University Press, 1987), pp. 338, 344.

and the interest or commitment of their countries in particular areas. The brief port-call data in table 3.9 indicate shifts in the use of this instrument.

Conclusion

The above indicators of relative Soviet and American power, though not strictly comparable or comprehensive, do suggest a pattern. Overall, the indicators seem to favor the United States early in the period, and show a significant growth of Soviet "power" in the late sixties and early seventies. Though for some indicators (systemic economic and nuclear, for instance) the United States retains an absolute lead throughout the period, Soviet increases are clear. In general, this increase in power wanes in the later seventies and into the eighties. Although the significance of any one of these indicators is open to question and debate, and the precise measurement of power is still beyond us, the fact of a *shift* in *relative* power for the period in question seems beyond dispute.

TABLE 3.9. U.S. and Soviet Port Visits to Arab States in the Mediterranean, 1964 and 1974

1964		1974	
US	USSR	US	USSR
Lebanon	–	Egypt	Algeria
Libya		Morocco	Egypt
Morocco		Tunisia	Morocco
Tunisia			Syria
			Tunisia

SOURCE: Jesse W. Lewis, Jr., *The Strategic Balance in the Mediterranean* (Washington D.C.: American Enterprise Institute for Public Policy Research, 1976), pp. 45, 69.

4

Regional Politics and the Preferences of Egypt

IN THIS chapter I will make some basic assumptions about Egypt's enduring regional preferences and, in the framework of these preferences, show how Egyptian objectives changed as a result of changes in the distribution of power in the Arab world that had taken place by the mid-seventies. These changes help explain Egyptian policies leading to the Camp David accords.

My basic assumption about Egypt's regional objective is that Egypt has consistently sought to lead the Arab world and that, since the creation of the state of Israel, Egypt has also sought to prevent Israeli regional hegemony, partly as a means of furthering this same objective. Given this objective, the policy changes leading to the Camp David accords are an outcome of shifts in the regional distribution of military and economic power.

The acceptability of these propositions is determined by two criteria. One is the extent to which they explain Egyptian regional policy in comparison with competing propositions; a demonstration of the degree to which they do this across time will take up much of this chapter. The second criterion pertains to the reasonableness of the assumption of Egypt's drive for regional leadership. This criterion is particularly relevant here, since it is not necessarily obvious that it is consistent with the core propositions of the research program that guides this work (which, one will recall, assumes only that states minimally seek self preservation). A discussion of state preferences in general is therefore appropriate here, in order make a preliminary statement about the conditions under which this assumption is reasonable.

The External Objectives of States

All states seek security and independence to the fullest extent possible, but do all states seek to "maximize" their power? Hans Morgenthau argued that, in the context of the anarchic nature of the international environment, states do tend to seek power. Kenneth Waltz, on the other hand, makes the more basic assumption that states seek primarily to preserve themselves, and that while some also seek to maximize power, others may not. Yet Waltz and Morgenthau may not be that far apart: the objective of security and independence in the context of international anarchy may require the maximization of power. Even if this relationship between self-preservation and power maximization is not logically necessary, it may be likely in practice: the objectives of security and independence can easily be exploited by small interest groups within the state who may be interested in power maximization. Nevertheless, there is little doubt that there are substantial differences among states in terms of the degree to which they commit themselves to the pursuit of power. Some states seek to dominate, others do not; some states are expansionist, others are not. What variables explain this variance? This question deserves a systematic study, and although such a study is beyond the scope of this work, a brief general discussion is in order.

First, it should be pointed out that the distinction generally made in the international relations literature between "status quo" and "non-status-quo" states is not the same as the distinction between states that seek to dominate and those that do not; a state could be a status quo state precisely because it already dominates, while another state may be non-status-quo because it seeks to free itself from domination. The question, therefore, is which states tend to seek domination of others?

A related debate, concerning the causes of "imperialism," already exists in the literature of international relations. Several explanatory variables have been emphasized in this debate, most prominent among these the link between capitalism and imperialism, initially advanced by John Hobson and further developed along Marxist lines by V. I. Lenin, and a number of others. While these explanations differ as to the logic of the link between capitalism and imperialism, most argue that the capitalist mode of production inclines capitalist states toward domination. Aside from the many theoretical and empirical objections that have been raised against these arguments, it should be at once apparent that they do not apply to the case of Egypt, since Egypt has rarely known a system of government resembling capitalism. A limited version of the neo-Marxist theories was applied to Egyptian behavior under the rule of Anwar Sadat, when Egypt pursued the "open door" economic policy of *infitah*.[1]

A second prominent linkage between state characteristics and the will to dominate is the prevalent ideology of the state. If a state's ideology is conducive to the pursuit of dominance, then the state in question is likely to pursue it. Aside from the potential conflict between this assumption and other more widely accepted theoretical assumptions about state behavior, and much empirical evidence to the contrary, there is the question of the prominence of any such link in terms of the given state's priorities. Perhaps more significantly, it is apparent that states advocate different ideologies at different times, so that one still needs to explain the reason for the emergence of a particular ideology. In the case of Egypt, it will be shown clearly that the Egyptian tendency to seek regional domination is independent of ideological changes within Egypt.

A third variable linking states and the pursuit of dominance is atavism, or the extent to which the state reverts to historically prominent internal variables. The arguments advocating this as an explanatory variable can be divided into two groups: "structural" and "cultural" atavism. By structural atavism, I mean arguments that are based on the assumption that a state may have a class that fulfilled a specific function in the past, but that has created a new expansionist role for itself, in order to guarantee the continuation of its existence after that function has ceased to operate. Joseph Schumpeter's explanation of imperialism and Dimitri Simes' explanation of Soviet foreign policy fit into this category.[2] By "cultural atavism," I mean the proposition that there are enduring cultural tendencies, whatever their origins may have been, that incline some states toward domination. Adam Ulam and Richard Pipes advocate explanations of Soviet foreign policy that are along these lines.[3] Both types of atavistic explanations are limited in scope in that they do not pretend to have the ability to predict a priori *which* states will have atavistic inclinations that move them to seek domination; rather, these are explanations about the behavior of particular states based on the observation of historical patterns.

While the latter is less than a scientist hopes for, it may be that more general patterns about state objectives, beyond the basic requirement of security, do not exist. It may be that we simply need to propose hypotheses about the behavior of each state, so long as these hypotheses do not conflict with our general propositions and are confirmed by historical patterns of behavior for that particular state. As I argue later in this chapter, in the case of Egypt such a pattern exists dating back to the beginnings of modern Egypt in the early nineteenth century. Moreover, the assumption of Egypt's will to "lead" states in the region is so minimal that it approaches the basic assumption of the pursuit of independence and does not entail the expansionism expected in theories of imperialism. In fact, it raises the following important question: are there generalizable circumstances under which a state's pursuit of independence and security by themselves incline that state to seek domination?

This last question sidesteps the more general question of whether or not the pursuit of independence automatically involves a tendency to maximize power. It may be that while such a derivation is not automatic, it is justifiable under some particular, specifiable circumstances. A systematic exploration of this question is therefore worthwhile, although it is substantially beyond the scope of this work. Instead, I shall mention several conditions where such linkage is likely, with the understanding that further, more systematic exploration is required.

States are generally affected by their immediate environment; consequently, whatever their objectives may be, states desire at a minimum a stable and predictable environment, and at a maximum they seek to have the ability to shape the order of the environment. It follows from this that the more unstable the immediate environment is, the more a particular state would be inclined to attempt to shape it; and whenever major changes in the environment appear likely, the tendency to play a leading role manifests itself more clearly. Of states that exist in an unstable environment, the ones that possess the capability to play a leading role (i.e., states that possess a relative advantage in size and resources) are more likely to be inclined to dominate the shape of the environment.

Among variables that contribute to enduring instability, geography is especially significant. Its relevance is twofold: the more a given region is strategically and economically important to the rest of the world, the more the competition for the region and thus the greater the instability; the less conducive geography is to the security of states in a given region, the more the instability. This latter point can be perceived as an extension of Robert Jervis' hypothesis about instability resulting from situations where offense has an advantage; geography may incline states to pre-emption, even when unnecessary.[4] And if the environment of a given state is enduringly unstable, that state is likely to attempt to maintain the capacity for dominance through pre-emption, especially if the failure to deter potential opponents can have disastrous consequences. The state of Israel is a good example of this latter point. Aside from the fact that Israel's environment is inherently unstable (given the circumstances of its creation), Israel is also militarily vulnerable in terms of both geography and population; Israel cannot afford to lose even once. As a result, Israel's drive for security requires the capacity for initiative, prevention, pre-emption, and control of the environment, all of which dictate a tendency toward regional military hegemony whether Israel has expansionist ambitions in the Middle East or not.[5]

As for Egypt, it can be argued that given the instability of its environment (which derives partly from geography), and given its superior size and resources, it has historically attempted to play a dominant role in regional affairs. This has been true especially when major regional changes appeared likely, and this Egyptian tendency may also derive simply from the objective of security and independence.

The Pursuit of Independence

While states seek to maximize independence, absolute independence is of course unattainable; the mere existence of other states entails a degree of interdependence. In the end, there is no alternative to effective deterrence for maximizing state security, even though deterrence involves interdependence. But there are of course degrees of dependence, and these are of significance to most states. It is pertinent,

FIGURE 4.1. Regional and Systemic Dependence

RELATION TO REGIONAL ACTORS

	Independence	Dependence
Independence (Relation to Superpowers)	P1	P3
Dependence	P2	P4

therefore, to ask: Can one establish a minimal generalizable set of state preferences about the types and degrees of dependence? The answer to this question will be significant for my explanation of Egyptian motives and behavior.

One can conceive of two types of dependence: on other regional actors and on superpowers. Figure 4.1 illustrates four possibilities for each state.

In this figure P1 through P4 indicate the preferences of each state in descending order. That P1 should occupy the upper left cell of the matrix should be obvious; in this situation a given state has a reasonable degree of military and economic independence from both regional actors and superpowers. France and China are examples of this situation. The least preferable outcome, P4, corresponds to a situation where the given state is highly dependent, militarily and economically, on both regional actors and the superpowers. Jordan is an example of such a state. That P2 and P3 should fall between P1 and P4 is clear enough; but that P2 is preferable to P3 is not at once obvious. The following illustration may be helpful. Following the Israeli invasion of Lebanon, when the government of Lebanon found itself potentially dependent on superpowers and regional powers, it attempted to protect itself from both Israel and Syria by attracting an apparent American commitment; dependence on America was preferable to dependence on either Syria or Israel. But when a full American commitment could not be secured, Lebanon was forced to accept dependence on Syria (P3). Israel, on the other hand, is an example of a state that is highly independent regionally yet extensively dependent on the United States (P2).

There are several reasons for states to prefer high dependence on a superpower to high dependence on a regional power. First, every small state is partly dependent on superpowers regardless of its regional circumstances. Second, because of the obvious superiority in power and resources, a commitment from a superpower is generally more stable and rewarding than one from a regional power. Third, a relationship with a superpower, regardless of how dependent, rarely becomes a situation of true hegemony because of the inevitable existence of at least another alternative superpower. Fourth, the extent of regional independence partly determines the extent of independence in the relations with the superpowers; the more regionally independent a state is (or, at a maximum, the more dominant a state is regionally), the more attractive it becomes to the superpowers and the more influence it can wield with them. Empirically, this hypothesis seems to hold: faced with threats from regional powers, small states seem to throw their lot with a willing superpower. Reflecting on Egypt's choices in the 1970s, Former Egyptian Foreign Minister Ismail Fahmy remarked that, "for a country like Egypt it is in many ways easier and safer to deal with a superpower than with a small or medium-sized country. A superpower will not bother to go to war over the abrogation of a treaty, but simply write off the loss as a bad investment. Examples of this abound."[6]

Independence, Domination, and the Preferences of Egypt

I am now in a position to state my arguments about the changes in the regional distribution of power that resulted in transforming Egypt's position from nearly P1 in the late fifties to P2 in the sixties, and to nearly P4 (constituting, at a minimum, significant regional interdependence) in the early seventies.[7] Egypt's "peace initiative" in the late seventies was an attempt to get to at least P2, and to P1 if possible. In either case, Egypt hoped to eventually regain its position of prominence in the region, by altering the structure of its relations with regional and global powers, even if such moves would not pay off immediately.

In specific terms, the argument can be summarized as follows: in the 1950s Egypt was regionally independent and in a position to dominate Arab politics at a time when the European empire in the region was disintegrating; the advocacy of Pan-Arabism, centering around the issue of Palestine, served Egypt's interests well. At the international level, as has been discussed, the gradual emergence of a new international system with a disparity in power between the new superpowers allowed Egypt superpower support while maintaining a degree of policy independence. By the 1970s, major changes in the distribution of military and economic power in the Middle East region, as well as increasing parity between the superpowers, made Egypt dependent on both regional actors and superpower support. Militarily, Egypt's power was paralyzed by Israel's strength; partly because of military commitments, Egypt became increasingly dependent on the oil-rich Arab states whose influence in shaping Arab politics was enhanced at the expense of Egypt's. Simultaneously, increasing superpower parity inclined Egypt toward international alignment. Egypt's move toward the United States and the Egyptian peace initiative were designed to alter this situation; by replacing Arab economic aid with American aid Egypt hoped to gain regional independence; and by competing with Israel for alliance with the United States, Egypt hoped to eventually block Israeli hegemony and gain enhanced regional status that would once again enable it to take the lead in inter-Arab politics.

THE EMPIRICAL ACCEPTABILITY OF THE ASSUMPTIONS

Having argued that the assumptions about Egypt's foreign policy objectives are theoretically reasonable, I will now turn to the issue of empirical acceptability. Are the assumptions consistent with the historical pattern of Egyptian foreign policy? Since a serious examination of the historical pattern of Egypt's foreign policy is beyond the scope of this work, I will limit myself to two specific tasks. The first is to note the prevalent interpretations of significant periods in the modern history of Egypt, dating back to the nineteenth century, that are consistent with Egypt's drive for regional leadership.[8] The second and more central task is to reconcile this assumption with the apparently conflictive Egyptian foreign policy during the three decades preceding Camp David, when Egypt advocated Pan-Arabism; and with the decision to abandon this advocacy signified by the Camp David Accords. I shall now turn to this second task.

PAN-ARABISM AND EGYPT'S DRIVE FOR REGIONAL LEADERSHIP

Two strikingly different interpretations of Egypt's advocacy of Pan-Arabism stand out in the literature. The first is that Egypt during the Nasser era *deliberately* used Pan-Arabism in order to enhance Egypt's national interest. P. J. Vatikiotis has argued, for example, that "a good case can be made for the deliberate choice by Egypt, under Nasser or any other ruler, of an Arab nationalist policy on the basis of her economic and strategic needs, without the necessary conversion of its rulers or people to a political ideology of Arab nationalism," and that "on purely economic grounds Nasser's policy made eminent sense."[9] The second interpretation is that Nasser's advocacy of Arab nationalism was genuine, received high priority, and was advocated at some cost to Egypt's national interest. For example, R. Hrair Dekmejian maintained that "though it is difficult to assess the depth to which Nasser internalized Arabism, the intensity of his identification with the doctrine, as well as the high priority he eventually gave to its achievement, even to the point of hurting his own Egypt, makes it difficult to doubt his sincerity."[10]

My own propositions about Egypt's advocacy of Arabism are different from both of these explications. To be sure, I argue that Egypt's active advocacy of Pan-Arabism was pursued and sustained only as long as it was generally conducive with Egypt's objective of Arab leadership (and in that sense, Egypt's advocacy of Arabism was a function of Egypt's national interest); but, unlike Vatikiotis, I do not see this as necessarily indicating a conscious and deliberate use of Arabism by its leaders and elites. Indeed, such a leap from state behavior to individual intentions is methodologically erroneous.[11] Moreover, it is often the case that states and individuals alike pursue several, sometimes conflictive objectives; in that sense, one need not doubt the sincerity of the Egyptian leaders. But, whatever the preferences of Egypt and its leaders have been, a good case can be made that Egyptian national interest, most notably the historical tendency to lead the Arab world, dominated Egyptian behavior: whenever serious conflict emerged between the Pan-Arabist objectives and Egypt's drive for leadership, the latter won at the expense of the former.[12] On the other hand, selective sacrifices of state interests in favor of Pan-Arab objectives do not necessarily entail a superior ranking of Pan-Arabism in the preferences of Egypt and its leaders, as Dekmejian would have it: If the overall benefits of a long-term policy are conducive to Egyptian national interest, occasional costs, which are almost inevitable, are tolerated. In fact, Egypt's ultimate abandonment of the Pan-Arabist policy came when the overall benefits of this policy were overwhelmed by its costs; instead of enhancing Egypt's leadership position, the policy came to undermine this position, following the major shifts in the distribution of economic and military power that had occurred in the Middle East by the 1970s.

A better understanding of Egypt's active advocacy of Pan-Arabism can be attained by thinking of Pan-Arabism as an international "regime," since a rich body of literature on this subject already exists.[13] A dominant school of thought within this literature, which is also consistent with realist theory, argues that regimes come into being when there is a strong state, a hegemon, who generally benefits from its existence. But the regime must be able and willing to use both threats and incentives, which may be costly in the short time, in order to maintain the stability of the regime.[14] Such costs are tolerated because they are outweighed by the overall benefits of the regimes. For example, the hegemonic role that the United States played in the inception of the General Agreement on Tariffs and Trade following the second world war entailed that the United States had to make trade concessions to other members. Such concessions were not indications of weakness but of strength; not of values that are more important than the national interest but the opposite, since the stability of Europe was helped by this regime and thus Soviet threat was reduced. A good case can be made for a similar role for Egypt in the Pan-Arabist movement in the late 1950s.

But a regime declines when power becomes diffused among its members, as the old hegemons can no longer issue threats and incentives to maintain the old rules; the costs of maintaining the regime, when power becomes diffused, could outweigh the general benefits. The old hegemon's commitment to the regime thus disappears, and while regimes can develop a "life of their own,"[15] they become vulnerable to "shocks" in the absence of hegemonic protection.[16]

Accordingly, it can be argued that the decline of both Egypt and Arabism are functions of the diffusion of military and economic power in the Middle East by the late 1960s. In this regard, several points can be made. First, Egypt's active advocacy of Pan-Arabism emerged in the mid-1950s, as its utility in generating public Arab support for Egypt became obvious following the Baghdad Pact and the Suez war.[17] Before that period, Pan-Arabism as an ideological movement had little support in Egypt, and the early Nasser years indicated a tendency toward Egyptian nationalism.[18] Second, the change in the political order in the Middle East following the second world war, and the decline in the influence of Britain after the Suez crisis, created a vacuum for a new regime to fill. Third, among Arab states, Egypt's relative power and resources (as specified in the next section) made it the primary candidate to fill the gap by creating a new regime. Fourth, while Egypt's hegemonic role in the Pan-Arab regime entailed some sacrifices, such as extending aid to other Arab states and the deployment of troops in Yemen, these could be sustained only so long as the overall benefits from the Pan-Arab movement enhanced Egypt's drive for leadership. This drive preceded Nasser's government and dominated all other objectives even when Pan-Arabism was advocated:[19] whenever conflict emerged between the drive for leadership and Pan-Arab objectives, the former won out.[20] Fifth, by the late 1960s major shifts in the distribution of military and economic power in the Middle East had two important outcomes: they weakened Egypt's ability to issue the threats and incentives necessary to maintain the regime and to build a consensus; and they transformed the utility of regime norms and rules, when the central symbol of the Pan-Arab movement, the commitment to a collective decision on the issues of Israel and Palestine, became counterproductive for Egypt's leadership drive. Specifying these important regional shifts in the distribution of power and their impact on the behavior of Egypt is thus central for the task at hand.

Change in the Distribution of Power in the Arab World

By the time Anwar Sadat came to power, major shifts in the distribution of power in the Middle East had already taken place. In order to see these shifts clearly, it is useful to compare Egypt's position in the Arab world in the fifties with its position in the seventies.

In the fifties Egypt had one of the most stable state infrastructures in the region, with a remarkably homogeneous population and a well-developed sense of nationalism. Many newly created Arab states, on the other hand, were less stable and therefore more vulnerable. On the whole, Egypt maintained the largest and strongest Arab army, and had the largest population from which to draw reinforcements. Economically, Egypt had the largest GNP in the Middle East, with the apparent ability to use economic aid for influence. Egypt also held a decisive advantage in terms of other means of influence in the Arab world: it had the most effective information network, served as an intellectual guide to many Arabs, and possessed expertise in engineering, agriculture, arts, and education which could fill the needs of many Arab states. Finally, in institutional terms Egypt was in control of the Arab League, contributing more than other Arab states both economically and in human resources. In short, Egypt was in a position to play a dominant role in Arab politics, and Pan-Arabism seemed an effective vehicle.

In contrast, Egypt of the 1970s had become, in relative terms, a much weaker state with few means of influence. After more than two decades of independence, most Arab states had developed reasonably stable institutions, and many Arab regimes demonstrated a remarkable capacity to survive against great odds. State nationalism had become a reality as a new generation emerged which knew only the prevailing boundaries.

Egypt also no longer maintained the potential for military hegemony in the region. Several factors account for this. In general, it had become apparent that relative military superiority at the regional level could not be measured in isolation; superpowers had the capacity to negate the translation of military superiority into political influence, and a regional "subsystem" could be understood only within the context of the overall system.[21] Egypt discovered, for example, that it could not directly coerce Libya, Jordan, or Saudia Arabia militarily because of American commitments to these states. It also discovered that when it used its military forces in the civil war in Yemen, aid provided to its opponents by outside powers was sufficient to neutralize its effectiveness.

Within the Arab world several states had succeeded in building relatively impressive armies on their own; as table 4.1 indicates, several other Arab states surpassed Egypt in military expenditures in the 1970s. And the regional but non-Arab state of Israel occupied much of the Egyptian army's attention, even before the destructive confrontation of 1967. And, while Egypt professed to be the only Arab country capable of countering Israel, which provided Egypt with *political* power in its inter-Arab campaign, the devastating defeat of 1967 removed whatever leverage Egypt could derive from its military power.

In the seventies Egyptian superiority no longer prevailed in the fields of information, education, the arts, and technical skills. Arab regimes, anxious to develop a sense of statehood in their constituencies, had managed to build impressive information networks including television, radio and print media; many even employed skilled Egyptian journalists and writers who seemed eager to work for other Arab governments at higher salaries. Similarly, most Arab states had dramatically improved their educational institutions.

Perhaps most significantly, Egypt no longer dominated the economic scene in the Middle East, particularly as a result of the rise of the oil states. As table 4.2 and figure 4.2 indicate, by the mid-1970s Egypt had been superseded in total GNP by *five* Arab states. Egypt's percentage of combined Arab GNP declined dramatically from 23.4% in 1965 to 7.9% in 1977 (table 4.3 and figure 4.2). By 1977 Egypt's per-capita GNP became the second lowest in the Arab world (table 4.4). Significantly for the politics of economic aid, Egypt ran huge deficits while several Arab states accumulated healthy surpluses. This remarkable change in the distribution of regional economic power is especially relevant since the military dimension had, of necessity, been neutralized.[22] Economic power became the primary means of influence in Arab politics.

Finally, on the institutional level Egyptian dominance of the Arab League had substantially diminished. Although at the inception of the Arab League Egypt had been the largest contributor and had come to host the majority of its projects, by the late 1970s the picture had changed noticeably; 55 percent of the capital used in all inter-Arab economic ventures came from five oil-producing countries, with most

TABLE 4.1. Military Expenditure and GNP of Selected Arab States

		1970	1971	1972	1973	1974	1975	1976	1977	1978	1979
Egypt	GNP	6.7	7.1	7.6	8.9	9.5a	11.7	12.9	13.3	16.9	16.5
	MILEX	1.3	1.5	1.5	2.8	4.1	6.1	4.9	4.4	2.8	2.2
	%	18.9	21.1	19.9	31.0	42.8	52.4	37.0	32.8	16.5	13.1
Syria	GNP	1.5	1.5	2.1	2.5	2.9	0.7	6.1	7.1	7.8	9.2
	MILEX	0.2	0.2	0.3	0.4	0.5	0.7	0.7	1.0	1.1	2.0
	%	11.9	11.8	12.1	16.0	15.7	15.1	16.3	15.0	14.2	22.1
Iraq	GNP	3.8	3.7	6.6	9.2	10.2	13.4	13.4	14.2	16.3	15.5
	MILEX	0.3	0.2	0.5	0.8	1.6	1.6	1.6	1.7	2.0	2.7
	%	7.7	6.5	7.2	9.8	15.7	11.8	9.6	10.2	13.0	12.5
Saudi Arabia	GNP	4.0	4.3	5.2	8.3	24.8	37.2	51.1	55.8	87.8	94.6
	MILEX	0.4	0.4	0.9	1.5	1.8	6.8	9.0	7.5	13.2	14.2
	%	9.8	8.9	18.1	18.3	7.3	18.0	17.7	13.5	15.0	15.0

SOURCE: *The Military Balance*, IISS, various years; and World Bank Atlas. Figures are in US$ billion, % is military expenditure as percent of GNP.

FIGURE 4.2. Relative GNP of Selected Arab States

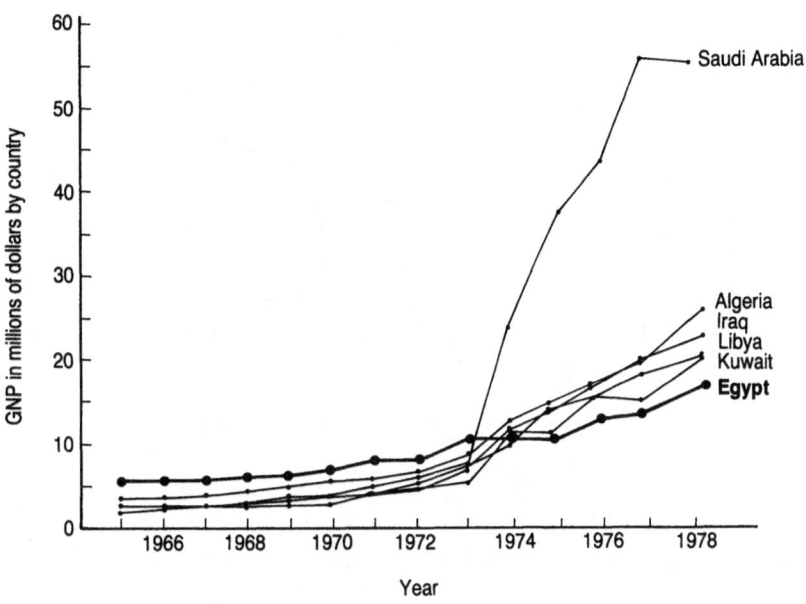

TABLE 4.2. Annual GNP of Middle East States

	1960	1965	1970	1975	1978
Algeria	2,932	3,240	5,065	14,421	25,730
Egypt	4,155	5,350	6,928	9,294	16,890
Iraq	1,418	2,197	3,127	13,245	22,540
Jordan	–	–	–	1,145	2,370
Kuwait	–	1,655	2,546	12,038	19,410
Libya	355	1,339	3,390	11,311	19,820
Morocco	2,057	2,966	3,825	9,410	12,890
Oman	44	63	196	1,679	2,340
S. Arabia	–	1,854	3,090	36,955	54,200
Sudan	1,534	1,963	2,659	4,285	5,900
Syria	810	1,218	1,709	5,349	7,820
Tunisia	–	976	1,405	4,327	6,010
Y.A.R.			294	1,180	2,301

SOURCE: World Bank Atlas. Figures in US$ million.

FIGURE 4.3. GNP as Percentage of Total GNP for Six Arab States

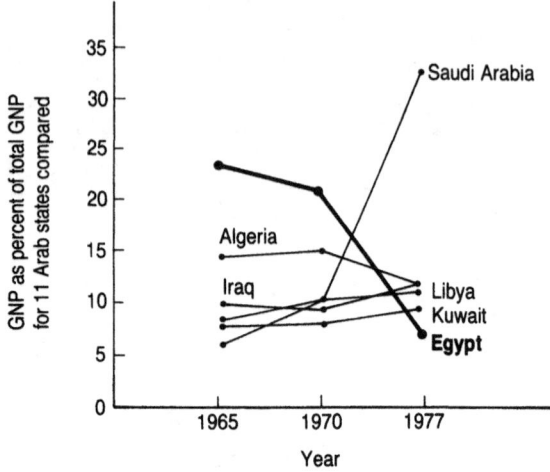

TABLE 4.3. Percentage Share of Middle East GNP

	1965	1970	1977
Algeria	14.2	14.9	11.3
Egypt	23.4	20.4	7.9
Iraq	9.6	9.2	11.3
Kuwait	7.3	7.5	8.4
Libya	5.9	10.0	10.4
Morocco	13.0	11.3	6.3
Oman	0.3	0.6	1.2
Saudi Arabia	8.1	9.1	32.8
Sudan	8.6	7.8	3.5
Syria	5.3	5.0	4.0
Tunisia	4.3	4.1	2.9
TOTAL GNP (US$)	22,821	33,940	170,004

SOURCE: World Bank Atlas. Columns are percentages, rounded to 0.1. Total GNP is expressed in millions of current US$.

FIGURE 4.4. Egypt's Military Expenditure as Percent of GNP

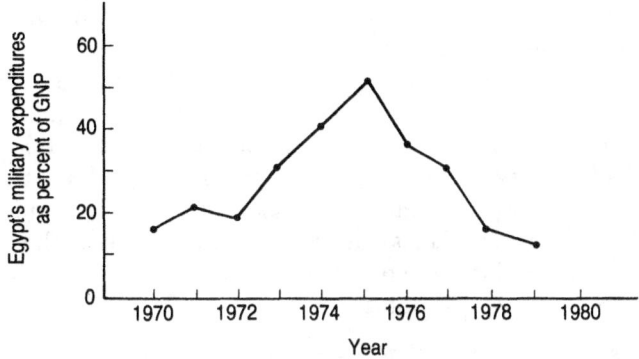

of the ventures headquartered in these countries.[23] Egypt had lost a major institutional means of influence.

THE IMPACT OF CHANGE IN THE DISTRIBUTION OF POWER ON EGYPT

Pan-Arabism meant two things for Egypt in its attempt to lead the Arab world. First, Egypt could influence Arab politics, bypassing Arab governments. Second, because Israel and the Palestinian issue were the common denominator for the Arabs and the central issues for the Pan-Arab movement, Egypt could earn its right to lead by projecting its ability to counter Israeli military hegemony and its commitment to the Palestinian cause. But by the end of the 1960s, as a result of the military and economic changes in the Middle East, Egypt suddenly found that its commitment to the Palestinian cause and its confrontation with Israel could no longer serve to legitimate its position in the Arab world. Indeed, the very commitment to the cause brought about increasing Egyptian dependence on the Arab states that Egypt sought to dominate in the first place, and diminished Egypt's capacity to influence regional events instead of enhancing it. Not only did the 1967 war demonstrate Egypt's inability to stop Israel, but it also entailed massive economic losses. The loss of income from the Sinai oil fields, the closure of the Suez Canal, the abandonment of cities along the canal and the subsequent influx of refugees into already overcrowded Cairo, the need to rebuild the army, the added preoccupation with Israel now that Egyptian territories were under occupation all added up to an incalculable Egyptian loss. Egypt alone could not accomplish the task it had set for itself.

The first visible sign of emerging Egyptian dependence came after the 1967 war, during the Arab summit conference in Khartoum, when Nasser found himself having to appease the very leaders he had attempted to undermine. The result was that while Egypt, Syria, and Jordan would rebuild their armies and focus their efforts on the state of Israel, the oil-rich Arab states would provide financial support. The Arab Cold War was over; Egyptian influence had dramatically declined. The psychological impact of the new Egyptian dependence was noticeable even before Sadat came to power. Referring to the decisions of the Arab summit conference following the 1967 war, Egyptian historian Salah al-Aqqad put it this way:

> It was the first time that Egypt had received aid from Arab states. Nasser apparently felt a deep wound to his leadership, for he had been accustomed to dispensing Egyptian aid to Arab liberation movements and to the many political refugees. How

TABLE 4.4. Population and Per Capita GNP of Middle East States

	1960		1965	
	Pop. x 000	GNP $ p/c	Pop. x 000	GNP $ p/c
Algeria	10,319	284	11,394	284
Egypt	25,929	160	29,389	182
Iraq	6,647	207	7,975	275
Jordan	1,695	–	1,962	–
Kuwait	278	–	471	3,514
Libya	1,349	248	1,624	825
Morocco	11,640	177	13,139	226
Oman	505	87	571	110
S. Arabia	4,787	–	5,405	343
Sudan	11,256	136	12,533	157
Syria	4,561	178	5,325	229
Tunisia	4,221	–	4,630	211
Y.A.R.				

SOURCE: World Bank Atlas. Population figures in thousands; per capita GNP given in current US$.

could Nasser now extend his hand to aid from (reactionary) Arabs? Perhaps in order to relieve some of the pain, Nasser recommended that the aid allocated to Egypt be reduced by twenty million in favor of Syria.[24]

While the 1973 war succeeded in regaining some Egyptian prestige in the Arab world, the outcome hardly improved Egypt's ability to influence other Arab states. Indeed, since the war was largely responsible for the dramatic increases in oil prices, it also contributed to the very changes in the distribution of economic power that found Egypt more dependent on other Arab states. The fact remained that Egypt was unable to regain its occupied territories through the war and was unable to secure an overall settlement through the diplomatic efforts that followed.

While Arab aid to Egypt reached a maximum of $1,264 million in 1974, it declined to $625 million in 1976, despite the quadrupling of Arab oil revenues. In the meantime, Egypt continued to suffer from the loss of its Sinai oil fields, with an estimated annual income of $1,000 million, and still needed to maintain a large army whose expenditures reached a remarkable high of 52.4% of Egypt's total GNP in 1975. This can be compared with a defense expenditure of 13.1% of

1970		1975		1977	
Pop. x 000	*GNP* $ p/c	*Pop.* x 000	*GNP* $ p/c	*Pop.* x 000	*GNP* $ p/c
13,758	368	16,105	895	17,152	1,120
32,563	213	36,079	258	37,796	354
9,355	334	11,020	1,202	11,803	1,628
2,299	–	2,702	424	2,888	673
744	3,422	1,002	12,014	1,137	12,585
		2,430	4,655	2,636	6,707
15,126	253	17,160	548	18,310	586
654	300	766	2,192	814	2,569
6,198	499	7,180	5,147	7,633	7,309
14,100	189	16,015	268	16,919	348
6,258	273	7,345	727	7,835	857
5,127	274	5,608	772	5,899	837
4,356	67	4,758	248	4,982	508

the GNP in 1979, following the Camp David accords (table 4.1 and figure 4.3).

To be sure, oil-rich Arab states were willing to dispense economic aid when they felt it necessary, but the political conditions they generally attached to economic aid were generally embarrassing to Egypt; these visibly demonstrated that Egypt had become weaker and unable to fulfill its perceived destiny. The irony remained: while Egypt's commitment to Pan-Arabism (and thus to the Palestinian cause and confrontation with Israel) was intended to enhance Egyptian influence, it achieved exactly the opposite. Egypt's political efforts at the Rabat summit conference of 1974 were telling on this score. As Egypt spearheaded the effort to declare the Palestine Liberation Organization to be the sole legitimate representative of the Palestinian people, its effort was seen as another step in its never-ending commitment to the cause. Ironically, the Rabat declaration signaled the end of Pan-Arabism, for the Palestinian issue which for decades remained the collective responsibility of all Arabs suddenly became the responsibility of the Palestinian people—and of them alone.

That Egypt's main concern became its increasing political dependence on other Arab states and its declining regional position can be seen from several facts. In the end it was apparently this political issue and not purely economic need that inclined Egypt to embark on a separate course from other Arab states. While Arab states were often reluctant to meet Egypt's demands for substantial economic aid, they seemed willing, when it was politically necessary, to make unilateral offers of aid. Often, however, this aid was linked to political conditions that entailed diminished Egyptian influence. What Egypt resented most was this increased influence on the part of other Arab states. One example is Qaddafi's proposal in July 1973 to grant Egypt a total of $1 billion over five years, to help Egypt resolve its economic problems. Sadat had asked for half that amount.[25] In exchange, however, Qaddafi demanded the prohibition of all advertisements from Saudi Arabia, Kuwait, and Abu Dhabi in Egyptian newspapers. This demand, however, was unacceptable in principle to the Egyptians, and the deal fell through.

Saudi Arabia, which has been most successful among Arab states at translating economic aid into political influence, had made the largest contributions to Egypt's economy, but political strings were almost always attached. In 1975, for example, when Egypt's military expenditures reached a high of 52.4% of GNP, Saudi Arabia offered to pay for all of Egypt's military needs for a period of five years, deposited approximately $1 billion in the Central Bank of Egypt, and contributed to the establishment of the Gulf Organization for the Development of Egypt.[26] In return, however, the Saudis expected reduced Soviet influence in Egypt and desocialization of the economy;[27] perhaps more importantly, the Saudis were constantly threatening to hold off aid to Egypt when unhappy with articles in Egyptian newspapers and statements by Egyptian officials.

When Egypt embarked on its unilateral course toward Israel, Arab states that were anxious to prevent a bilateral Egyptian-Israeli agreement offered to replace American aid that had been promised to Egypt. Moreover, Egyptian leaders were apparently convinced that the issue was not strictly economic. Asked whether or not the biggest incentive for concluding an agreement with Israel was economic aid from the United States, former Egyptian Foreign Minister Ibrahim Kamel replied:

> What economic incentive? In effect, we are receiving approximately $1 billion a year in actual economic assistance from the United States. This aid could have been easily replaced by other Arab states.[28]

Although Kamel, having supported Sadat's initiative and accompanied the Egyptian delegation to Camp David, resigned before the conclusion of the accords, his resignation was primarily over the details of the accords; he did not seem to object to the idea that Egypt would pursue its interests even if other Arab states objected. Kamel put it thus:

> [Sadat] said, suppose, I mean, we reach a very good agreement with the Israelis and other Arabs refuse it. Shall we tie ourselves to them? And I told him at the time, no, if we reach an agreement on principle—mainly concerning withdrawal from all Arab territories and realizing the fundamental rights of the Palestinians —if we reach that, we can register this at the United Nations and have a guarantee for the implementation of this agreement. And if other Arabs wouldn't go along we would start implementing this agreement on what concerns us, on Sinai, and then continue and help the other Arabs in realizing the other parts. So, I was rather flexible.[29]

Minister of State for Foreign Affairs Butrus Ghali echoed the view that Egyptian concerns went beyond economics. The following interview is revealing:

> Q: Everyone recognizes that Egypt's economic problems are serious, and that there is a need for outside assistance. But it is not clear why you have opted for American aid, when in fact you could have received even more from Arab states.
> A: It is not that simple. Arab states have often made some impressive offers of aid, but when it came down to it, they set unacceptable conditions. I mean, you will have the Saudi government calling and threatening to cut off aid to us, because one of our magazines wrote an unfavorable story about a given prince. They want to dictate our domestic and foreign policies. That is unacceptable. American aid is stable and predictable.[30]

Sadat, perhaps more than most of his aides, was simultaneously resentful of Egypt's diminished influence in the region, and confident that a change in policy, even if costly in the short term, would inevitably regain Egypt's position of leadership. In his speeches and statements Sadat persistently argued that Egypt was, is, and will always remain the leader of the Arab world. His view, which was shared by other Egyptian leaders, saw Egypt's leadership role as its "fate" and "destiny" which was dictated by Egypt's geographical location and history:

> Egypt was and remains the central and major factor in our Arab Nation. Egypt can never escape her role, and any outside attempt to isolate her can only end in failure and shame. We did not claim that role, nor do we invoke it as a way of boasting. It has simply been thrust upon us by history and circumstances; we maintain it only as a way of bearing our responsibility, and this sometimes entails our being subject to rancor.... The entire world knows that Egypt is not merely an insignificant dot on the world map, but that Egyptian history is very long and it has contributed much to human history and civilization.... neither peace nor war can be pursued without Egypt.[31]

According to this view, other Arab states derived their temporary strength from Egypt's and will decline without Egypt; the rise in the oil prices was a result of Egypt's military power and effort, and Arab states must be reminded of this fact. All those Arab states that opposed Egypt's peace initiative, as Sadat saw it, will have no alternative but to follow in Egypt's footsteps, for it is Egypt that sets the shape of politics in the region. Those who oppose Egypt's role will come back, for without Egypt they cannot obtain their objectives.[32] When Israeli

Defense Minister Ezer Weizman inquired about the likely reaction of other Arab states to Egypt's moves toward Israel, Sadat replied confidently: "The Jordanians will follow our footsteps. So will the Syrians. Things in the Arab world happen the way Egypt decides."[33]

While Sadat may have resented Egypt's dependence on other Arab states more than other Egyptians, prompting him to prefer dependence on a superpower instead, Nasser had been similarly inclined even before Sadat. Salah al-Aqqad put it thus:

> At the Rabat Conference in December 1969, a debate raged between Qaddafi and Feisal about the level of aid [to Egypt]. . . . This debate led Nasser to withdraw from the Rabat conference determined to increase his dependence on the Soviet Union. . . . For Nasser found it easier to accept aid from the Soviets, even if in the form of loans, just as Sadat later came to prefer grants and loans from the United States.[34]

The upshot of the above is that Egypt's behavior in the 1970s seemed motivated by the inclination to rid itself of its increasing economic (and thus political) dependence on other Arab states, and to pursue a policy that would first attain a degree of regional independence eventually leading Egypt to regain its position of leadership in the region. The Camp David process promised to achieve Egypt's objectives in several ways. First, aside from regaining its occupied territories and thus reducing its economic burdens, Egypt could free itself from economic dependence on other Arab states through aid from the United States; Egypt could thus regain the political initiative in the Arab world. Second, by forging close ties with the United States, Egypt hoped to compete with Israel for a central role in American regional strategy, and thus to prevent Israeli hegemony by reducing the American commitment to Israel. Third, by playing a leading political and military role in American strategy Egypt could enhance its relative military and political power in the Arab world.

These objectives thus rested on Egypt's ability to compete with Israel for strategic alliance with the United States, which would simultaneously undermine Israel's regional hegemony and eventually increase Egypt's regional influence. Some Israelis became concerned about the potential for such strategic competition as soon as Sadat expelled Soviet troops from Egyptian soil.[35] Prime Minister Menachem Begin told President Carter at Camp David that his primary concern was to protect Israeli-American relations.[36]

Egyptian leaders were clearly aware of the centrality of this strategic interest at Camp David.[37] Sadat himself was apparently willing to live with a failure to reach an agreement with Israel at Camp David as long as the result would be closer American-Egyptian relations at the expense of Israel's relations with the United States.[38] If he could be assured of this in case of failure, Sadat may have been willing to forgo more compromises with Israel in order to preserve his relations with at least some Arab states like Saudi Arabia. In the end, however, the Egyptians were forced to make a choice: it turned out that a failure at Camp David could result in weakening Egyptian-American relations. Perhaps the single most important event forcing the Egyptian choice was Carter's confrontation with Sadat on the eleventh day of Camp David, as the Egyptian leader threatened to abandon the negotiations. Carter warned Sadat that if he left, "it will mean first of all an end to the relationship between the United States and Egypt."[39] Forced to choose between his relations with the United States and his relations with other Arab states, Sadat, for the very reasons that I have articulated here, decided to choose the former.

Conclusion

I have argued in the last two chapters that Egypt's inclination toward a bilateral agreement with Israel at the expense of Pan-Arabism emanated from both international and regional changes in the distribution of military and economic power. Moreover, the assumptions about inter-state relations from which the conclusion was derived originated in widely accepted theoretical propositions that seem to hold in other cases.

Nonetheless, while changes in the international and regional distributions of power explain the tendency of Egypt to conclude a bilateral agreement with Israel at the expense of Egypt's relations with other Arab states, given Egypt's enduring objectives, the specific terms of the agreement could not be specified by these variables. The bargaining framework in chapter 7 promises to explain these specific terms.

5

International Politics and the Preferences of Israel

*H*ow DID international and regional politics affect the preferences of Israel? What were Israel's international preferences at Camp David? These questions will be treated in this chapter through analogical reference to a game-theory model called the "chain-store paradox," which is based on assumptions that are consistent with the research program being used in this study.[1] Once again the primary variable is the distribution of power, both regionally and internationally. It turns out that one does not need to decide whether or not Israel has expansionist designs in the Middle East in order to explain Israeli foreign policy. More minimal assumptions go a long way on their own.

These assumptions are reasonable in that they are consistent with the core assumptions of the research program. The hypotheses derived from them about Israeli preferences will be shown to hold by examining the extent to which they explain Israeli foreign policy across time.

My general argument is that Israel, because of its limited resources and hostile environment, tends to pursue a dual international strategy. On the regional level, Israel seeks to prevent *collective* Arab action. The most important aspect of this regional strategy is the decoupling of Egypt, the most powerful Arab state, from the rest of the Arab world. On the international level, Israel needs strong and durable ties with the United States. Even under the best of conditions Israel strives to project itself to the Arab world as an extension of the United States, and therefore as having unlimited resources. Israel cannot simply rely on America's traditional commitment and on domestic lobbies in pursuing this objective, but also seeks an indispensable role in America's international strategy. As a result, any Middle Eastern competitor with Israel for alliance with the United States is perceived as a threat. Consequently, Israel seeks to prevent closer ties between the United States and Arab states. Yet in the case of Egypt, the attainment of Israel's regional objective of de-coupling Egypt from other Arab states resulted in a potential challenge to the international objective when Egypt then sought alliance with the United States. This competition was apparently perceived by both the Egyptians and the Israelis, resulting in a visible set of constraints at Camp David.

Reference to the formal model, the chain-store paradox, is made not for the purpose of deriving some unconventional and counterintuitive hypotheses, but rather, simply to show that the two general hypotheses about Israeli foreign policy are consistent with the proposed research program; they are deducible from the minimal assumptions about Israeli drive for security given limited resources in a hostile environment which is constituted by several potential opponents. Since this situation is structurally similar to the chain-store game in some respects, the deductive solution to this game is relevant.[2]

Once the reasonableness of the two hypotheses about Israeli foreign policy is established, the task is to demonstrate empirically that these hypotheses can explain major decisions in Israeli foreign policy across time. The empirical interpretations, while general and brief, will not be entirely unconventional. Their relevance in this work pertains to the specific connections between historical patterns in Israeli foreign policy and Israel's preferences during the Camp David process.

The Chain-Store Paradox and Israel's International Strategy

Before articulating several features of the formal model that make it useful in explaining Israeli strategy, it is worth noting that a key feature of the model is the projection of power through action; that is, by establishing a historical record of behavior that is conducive to effective deterrence. But Israel's human and economic resources are so transparently limited in comparison with those of its adversaries that actions alone could not be expected to achieve the required deterrence. Israel's solution to this problem has been straightforward from the early days of statehood: the consolidation of close relations with the United States to the point that Israel becomes virtually an extension of the United States and its resources; this prevents close Arab-American relations that could compete with Israel's coveted role. Indeed, this enduring aspect of Israeli foreign policy will be shown to be central in shaping Israeli preferences at Camp David.

There are several aspects of the chain-store paradox that resemble Israel's situation in the Middle East. First, the chain store faces several potential rivals on a single important issue, and if all these rivals choose to challenge it collectively and continuously they are likely to "win" in the long term. Second, the key to the successful strategy for the jeopardized store is to *deter* its potential rivals from competing. It achieves this deterrence by projecting the perception that whenever challenged, it will meet the challenge and prevail. Perceptions are formed by the adversaries' assessments of the chain-store's previous behavior. Third, the store keeps potential competitors guessing about its *real* capabilities, always attempting to appear stronger than it may actually be. Fourth, to project this strength requires that when a competitor decides to challenge, the store must fight all out and drive the competitor to bankruptcy even though a compromise might be better in the short term. Fifth, while the chain store must fight when challenged, it is evident that it prefers neither to be challenged nor have to fight; fighting diminishes the store's capabilities, and it could eventually undermine the very deterrence it seeks.

The following features of Israel's international environment have recommended specific strategies that Israel has tended to pursue. First, Israel has sought to prevent collective Arab action and has therefore often preferred division in the Arab world. Israel's short-term policies, as Wilfred Knapp put it, "naturally seek to divide the Arab states, which in any case are only too able to present divisions amongst themselves ready to be exploited."[3] An important component of this Israeli strategy has been to separate Egypt, the most important rival, from the rest of the Arab world.

Second, because deterrence is a function of projected perception of capabilities, and because these perceptions are a function of previous behavior, Israel can succeed even with limited resources, provided that it projects the proper image efficiently. But, given that the perception of Israel held by many Arab states has often been that of a temporary entity that lacks staying power, Israel's task has been all the more difficult. One way for Israel to transcend this difficulty has been the continuous attempt to project itself as an extension of the United States; this end was sought by solidifying strategic ties with the U.S. and by the constant attempt to prevent Arab states from forming similar ties. Israel's opposition to proposed arms sales to the Arab world, while often explained by concern for the more obvious military threat, sometimes appears motivated by this broader Israeli strategy.[4] Israeli author Amos Kenan described it thus: "Israel pursued a policy of 'making the West always choose between us and them [the Arabs], and if it is not us, we'll create enough trouble to make sure that it must be us.'"[5] More recently, the *New York Times*, reporting on Israel's decision to join the Strategic Defense Initiative, wrote that "senior [Israeli] officials welcome what one called 'another manifestation of intimacy' as an important additional deterrent to Israel's enemies," as well as further evidence that "efforts to draw Israel and the United States apart to bring about an imposed solution in the Middle East is futile."[6]

Third, lest the real limitations of its power be exposed, Israel sought to act quickly and massively to prevent long and protracted wars that would reveal the lack of depth in Israeli human and economic resources;[7] some Arab states have been aware of this Israeli strategy, which has led them on several occasions to attempt to counter it.[8]

Fourth, in building a history of reaction to Arab threats that would promote effective deterrence, Israel sought, when challenged, not only to meet the challenge but also to inflict a great deal of pain on the challenger, often more than would be considered commensurate with the level of the challenge, and sometimes at an avoidable short-term cost to Israel. When Egypt and Syria attacked Israeli forces in 1973, indicating a failure of Israeli deterrence, an editor of the Israeli newspaper *Maariv* wrote:

> Our counterattack must be so fierce, so crushing, so pitiless and cruel that it causes a veritable national trauma in the collective consciousness of the Arabs; their Yom Kippur adventure must cost the Arabs so dear that the mere thought of new adventures makes them tremble with fear. . . . We must strike a blow that

exceeds all reason, so that the Arab people's instinct of self-preservation makes them accept Israel.[9]

Fifth, because the extensive use of force diminishes resources and could therefore undermine the very deterrence that a state is attempting to build, the reckless use of force is highly undesirable; a state projecting deterrence must respond forcefully when challenged but it must not invite challenges. The problem is that decision makers, once they succeed in projecting a perception of superior power, tend to confuse perceptions and reality, often at some high cost to themselves. In invading Lebanon, for example, some Israeli leaders had apparently come to accept what they were attempting to project: that Israel is a 'mini-superpower' in the Middle East.[10] The outcome, however, was such that Israeli weaknesses were unnecessarily exposed, so that Syria, although defeated, perceived that Israel was move vulnerable than it had previously supposed, and so became more willing to confront Israel.

Israel, the United States, and Egypt: The Historical Pattern

It has been theoretically argued above that Israel's international environment recommends the consolidation of relations with the United States while preventing Arab competition for such relations, the prevention of collective Arab action through the specified tactics, and the specific task of decoupling Egypt from the rest of the Arab world. My remaining task is to show how these propositions explain many of Israel's strategic policies, including those that appear puzzling. It will also be argued that Israel's regional and international preferences posed a serious dilemma for Israel at Camp David, a fact of which the Egyptians were fully aware.

Before proceeding, it should be noted that the historical interpretations here are by definition brief and incomplete; that other variables are, as always, relevant; that the concern here is to show how the variables introduced help explain *patterns* across time; and that, given the focus at one level of analysis here, other interpretations, focussing on other levels are not necessarily incompatible with this analysis.[11]

Israel, a small country with limited resources surrounded by hostile Middle Eastern states, could not expect to survive long without continued massive support from a major power, even with its superior organization and technology. Whether or not Israel has had expansionist designs in the Middle East, the minimalist assumption of survival instinct dictates a major commitment by a superpower, given Israel's hostile environment. This conclusion was recognized by the British as the Jewish state was being established in Palestine. In assessing the 'viability' of the new state, the issue for some British diplomats boiled down to the question of whether or not a major power would be prepared "to maintain Israel as a more or less permanent pensioner,"[12] for it seemed clear that, "the poorness of her soil, her lack of raw materials and high wages obtaining there make it uncertain whether Israel can ever hold its own as an industrial or agricultural country on purely economic ground."[13]

The British initially feared that Israel might become a Soviet base in the Middle East, because of its close relations with the Soviet Union during the first two years of its existence, the military supplies Israel was receiving from Czechoslovakia, and the socialist ideology advocated by most political parties in Israel. But by 1949 most British diplomats in the Middle East had concluded that the viability of Israel was intimately linked to unlimited support by one superpower only: the United States.[14] Sir John Troutbeck, the head of the British Middle East office in Cairo, wrote that:

> all one can predict is that the Israelis will be quickly aware of the anxiety of the United States Government to keep them within the Western fold and will not miss the opportunity for blackmail which will afford them both in the financial and territorial spheres.[15]

Even though many British diplomats concluded that the survival of Israel seemed to depend on the willingness of the United States to support it, they did not take American commitment for granted:

> It may be that Israel will be able to carry on as a subsidized State. How long Jewry will go on paying the subsidies as an act of charity cannot be foreseen and whether it will be worth while for the United States Government to continue to do so. . . . is also doubtful.[16]

Soon after, however, the British grew more optimistic about American support for Israel; the United States had decided to grant Israel economic aid amounting to $100 million. The British found this amount staggering in 1949, for it was no less than the total of British economic assistance throughout the entire world.[17]

As for Israeli perceptions of its own international options in the early years, they too moved quickly toward the necessity of strong ties with the United States. To be sure, the Israelis pursued a policy of 'nonidentification' during the first two years and received political and material support from the Soviet bloc countries. Moreover, Israeli leaders saw a need for a policy of nonidentification to the greatest extent possible because of the distribution of world Jewry. As David Ben-Gurion put it, "About two-thirds of our people in the Diaspora are scattered among the Western nations, and one-third in the East. This decisive fact, which will not speedily be altered, is enough in itself to compel us in the Land of Israel to follow a foreign policy of peace and goodwill towards all nations in the world."[18]

Although it was not until 1949 that Israel clearly linked itself to the United States, the necessity of this course was realized much earlier. As early as 1939 Ben-Gurion pointed out that: "outside Israel, there is only one Jewish community that has substantial capabilities for the task of removing the heavy weight of saving the people and the homeland: the American Jewish community."[19] And in 1943, even though Britain was the primary actor in Palestine, Ben-Gurion saw the centrality of the United States in influencing Britain:

> As long as America is a democratic state, where the opinion of every citizen is expressed on election day, Britain has no interest in adding to its many haters in America—the Irish, Germans, Italians, and the remaining Catholics—another active element that is centered in cities in key states, and that is influential in the media, numbering five million people. Britain will need America for a long time to come . . . It is clear that Jewish opinion, which, by itself, does not yet determine the position of the American government, nonetheless has much weight on Jewish issues—sometimes a decisive weight in shaping American public opinion. And there is no doubt that the opinion of the American government—whatever becomes of American foreign policy after the war—will weigh more heavily in the eyes of the British government than the opinion of any other government in the world, especially the opinions of Arab leaders.[20]

There were two primary reasons for this shift in Israeli policy in 1949–50: (1) Among the major international powers during that period, only the United States had both the will and the ability to provide the massive economic aid that Israel required. (2) The nature of the American system of government allows for considerable influence on the process of foreign policy formulation by domestic interests, such as the American Jewish community; the Soviet system does not.

On the first point there was wide consensus in Israel after the United States announced its substantial aid package to Israel. The Israeli newspaper *Haboker* wrote that "Even if the assumptions of those who declare that the American loan was granted on the eve of the elections in order to pre-judge them prove true, we now have concrete evidence that America is at least interested in achieving some influence over us and in gaining our friendship."[21] Ben-Gurion made his views on both these points very clear in a broadcast on January 31, 1949. Referring to Israel's early experience in purchasing arms, he declared that both Eastern and Western countries "wanted dollars from us— and dollars are only to be had in one country. . . . Neither the United States nor the Soviet governments gave us arms. But when the Soviet says 'No,' that goes for everybody in Russia. It is not so in America."[22]

President Truman apparently agreed with Ben-Gurion on one point. As early as 1946 he told a group of diplomats: "I am sorry, gentlemen, but I have to answer to hundreds of thousands who are anxious for the success of Zionism. I do not have hundreds of thousands of Arabs among my constituents."[23]

Nonetheless, during the first two years of Israel's existence Ben-Gurion continued to insist that "as long as there are millions of our people on both sides, we must guard our independence."[24] Such a posture, however, could be maintained for only a few months, for the outbreak of the Korean war in 1950 and the subsequent globalization of American containment policy forced the Israelis to take sides. Israeli condemnation of North Korea signaled the end of a short honeymoon with Moscow, and Israeli-American relations went from good to better.

It is useful to keep in mind that American involvement in the Middle East during this period was still minimal, and that Western interests were in practice guarded by the European allies. It is remarkable, therefore, to note the extent of American aid to Israel at that point, and to note that both the British and the Israelis saw the United States as the ultimate guarantor of Israel's survival. This is particularly noteworthy in the case of the British, who at that time had no intention of relinquishing their dominant influence in the Middle East.

Following the massive American loan to Israel, the British grew more optimistic about the survivability of the state of Israel and about its pro-Western orientation, and moved to improve relations with the new state. Nonetheless, some British diplomats worried that the Arab-Israeli polarization could be detrimental to Western interests in the Middle East. Specifically, they were concerned that Israel might drive a wedge between Egypt, which was of major importance in British strategy, and the West. Sir John Troutbeck, for example, thought that the British "were in a position to control the Arab governments but not Israel." He foresaw that the Israelis might drag the Arab States into a neutral bloc, "and might even attempt to turn us out of Egypt."[25]

Accepting the same premise, that the Arab-Israeli conflict could affect Western-Arab relations in important ways, other British diplomats thought that a pro-Soviet Israel might actually better serve Western interests in the Middle East, given that the Arab states in themselves were more important than Israel. Argued Bernard Burrows: "Even if the Jewish state was strongly subject to communist influence this would have its good side since the Arabs would automatically dislike communism because it is associated with the Jews."[26]

Nonetheless, the worsening relations between Britain and Egypt that followed the overthrow of the Egyptian monarchy in 1952 made Egypt the primary competitor with Britain for dominance in the Arab world. This development fundamentally changed Israeli-British relations and eventually led to the joint military attack against Egypt in 1956.

In the meantime the United States had recognized the importance of Egypt in the Arab world and sought to cultivate a close relation with it, distancing itself to the extent possible from British policy in the region. This American approach led to the promise of substantial American economic aid to Egypt in 1954. These American gestures caused the Israelis considerable worry and they became concerned that closer Egyptian-American relations would ultimately undermine the American commitment to Israel. This major Israeli concern manifested itself in covert actions against Western installations in Egypt in order to portray Egypt as an unstable, anti-Western state that could not become a reliable ally. These operations were later revealed in 1960, during a governmental crisis in Israel over what came to be known as the "Lavon Affair," described below.

Following improved Egyptian-American relations in 1954 an Israeli espionage ring operating in Egypt placed bombs in American installations in Egypt, including the USIA libraries in Alexandria and Cairo. The purpose of these attacks, according to the instructions given by the head of Israeli military intelligence, was "to break the West's confidence in the existing (Egyptian) regime" and "to prevent economic and military aid from the West to Egypt."[27] Even though the perpetrators were caught by the Egyptians and confessed to the crimes, few in the U.S. believed the Egyptian story, and some accused Nasser of anti-Semitism in arresting Jews for the purpose of rallying the Egyptian population against Israel. Not until the governmental crisis in Israel in 1960, when admission of Israeli involvement in the attacks leaked out, did Western media take Nasser's charges into account. But by then Egypt had embarked on an independent road.

It should be pointed out, however, that while it is now clear that some Israeli officials gave orders to carry out these attacks in Egypt, it is not clear at what level the orders were approved. Moreover, there is little doubt that many high level officials were kept in the dark, and that some, like Israeli Prime Minister Moshe Sharrett, would not have been inclined to approve such attacks. Nevertheless, although there was no Israeli unanimity on the *means* of undermining Egyptian-American relations, the incident does illustrate the extent of Israeli concern over the improving relations between Washington and Cairo. This concern, which declined in the sixties as a result of worsening relations between Egypt and the U.S., reintensified in the 1970s as Egypt once again became a candidate for alliance with the U.S.; Israeli policies in the seventies were heavily influenced by this concern.

While Israel saw the fundamental importance of its relations with the United States as early as 1949, this was largely for economic, political and long-term military considerations. In the short term it was Britain, and to a lesser extent France, that had an actual military presence in the Middle East and the apparent willingness to use force to achieve Western objectives. Thus, as early as 1951, Ben-Gurion actually considered a military alliance with Britain in order to guarantee Israel's survival, even though he still ultimately preferred ties with the United States. With the new government in Egypt in 1952, short-term Israeli and British objectives seemed to coincide. Their eventual collaboration against Nasser in 1956 reveals several facts about Israeli strategy.

One Israeli objective in collaborating with France and Britain was to demonstrate Israel's utility and reliability for Western interests in the Middle East. Assessing the outcome of the Sinai attack, former Israeli Defense Minister Moshe Dayan wrote that Israel's "military victory in the Sinai brought Israel not only direct gain . . . but more important, a heightened prestige among friends and enemies alike."[28] While Israel's Western friends in this case were France and Britain, the Israelis had little indication that the United States would actively oppose the operation, especially during an election year. And indeed, American reaction was stronger toward the European allies than it was toward Israel.

Once it became clear that both the United States and the Soviet Union would actively oppose Israeli occupation of Egyptian territory the Israelis made serious attempts to derive some political benefit from the adventure by striking an agreement with Egypt that would lead to the decoupling of Egypt from the rest of the Arab world. Indeed, one apparent cause of the Israeli decision to attack Egypt was Nasser's emerging ability to lead and unite the other Arab states. Just before the start of the Suez War Egypt had succeeded in concluding a tripartite agreement with Jordan and Syria, setting up a unified command for the three armies under Egyptian direction. Moreover, had Nasser been left unpunished after challenging the European powers and nationalizing the Suez Canal Company, his regional influence and capacity to rally Arab states behind him would have been dramatically enhanced. Such a prospect was particularly threatening to Israel.

While Israeli objectives were not achieved in the short term, events unfolding soon after the Suez War seemed to turn the tide in Israel's favor once again. The sudden upheavals in the Arab world against the West and the dramatic rise in Nasser's popularity forced the United States into a role it did not wish to play.[29] Egyptian-American relations worsened, and Egypt became preoccupied not with Israel but with what came to be known as the "Arab Cold War." For the next decade Egypt expended most of its political and military energy competing with its rivals in the Arab world, culminating in a highly draining military involvement in Yemen that ended only after the 1967 Arab-Israeli war.

Between the 1956 and 1967 Arab-Israeli wars both Israeli strategic objectives were, therefore, easily achievable. This put Israel in a strong position to prepare itself for the confrontations of the sixties. During this period Israel succeeded in building an impressive army while Egypt was draining its own in a losing battle. When Israel felt it necessary to act as a result of major regional and international changes it was in a position to exploit those changes.

By 1966, Egypt was losing its edge in the inter-Arab rivalry. Many of the gains made in the late 1950s had been reversed as Egypt found itself unable to bring a successful end to the military involvement in Yemen. But Nasser, ever the resourceful leader, saw an opportunity in the troubled front between Egypt's ally Syria and Israel. It was his chance to prove to the Arab world that Egypt was the only Arab state that could defend Arab interests against Israel. And Nasser's rivals in the Arab world were all too willing to bait him into an all-out conflict with Israel.

By now, it is clear to most analysts that Egypt's aggressive acts and escalating rhetorical war against Israel in 1967 were not preparation for an attack against Israel, nor was Egypt in a position to mount such an attack. The question remains as to why Israel had decided to launch an attack against Egypt and Syria.[30] One possible explanation is that Israel saw a good opportunity to make substantial territorial gains, though this explanation does not seem likely for several reasons.[31] A second and more plausible explanation is that even if Egypt did not intend to attack, Israel could not be sure of this. Given that the military strategic situation was such that the offense had the advantage, the temptation to preempt was irresistible.[32] What makes this explanation less likely is the evidence indicating the Israelis were told by the United States that Egypt did not plan to attack, and that they would easily win even if Egypt were to attack first.[33]

A more likely explanation for the Israeli attack fits the pattern that I have been outlining.[34] There were four Israeli considerations that can be derived from the model proposed in this study. First, in the context of the Israeli strategy of establishing a reputation which would deter challenges from the Arab states, Israel could not allow Nasser to get away with his provocations, lest other Arab states be emboldened to follow suit. Second, the strategy of preventing collective Arab action dictated that Israel defeat Egypt. Had Nasser been allowed to score the political victory he sought by his provocative actions and claiming to have prevented an Israeli attack on Syria, he would have almost overnight reversed his fortunes in the Arab world and would have been able to rally the insecure Arab states behind him.[35] Indeed, just before the Israeli attack his strategy seemed to be working; one of his rivals in the Arab world, King Hussein of Jordan, anxiously flew to Cairo in order to sign a new pact.[36] The parallel between this situation just prior to the 1967 war and the conditions prevailing immediately before the attack on Egypt in 1956 should be evident.[37] Third, because of Israel's evident limitations in human and economic resources, it must overshadow Arab perceptions of these limitations in order to successfully project deterrence. Arab leaders have often argued that even if Israel wins several limited rounds with the Arab states, it is bound to lose at some point. The massive Israeli victory over three Arab states served to anchor in Arab minds the reality and the durability of the state of Israel. Fourth, long-term projection of Israeli power hinged on solid, unchallenged relations with the United States. This was especially true in 1967 as the European powers were planning their final withdrawal from the Middle East and leaving the United States with major new tasks in the region. By demonstrating its impressive military dominance in the Middle East, Israel would make itself an attractive ally for the United States. Ironically, although the United States advised Israel against initiating the war, heeding American advice was not, as is often the case, the best way for Israel to insure closer ties with the United States. What mattered was that the outcome of Israeli action be such that closer American-Israeli relations were the best option available for the United States.[38]

The situation facing the United States after the 1967 war favored consolidation of relations with Israel; Soviet influence and presence in the Middle East had reached a peak as a result of the destruction of the Arab armies and the consequent increasing Arab dependence on the Soviet Union.[39] Furthermore, the United States was moving to fill the gap created by the withdrawal of the European powers from the Middle East at the very same time as the difficulties in Vietnam were preventing direct American involvement elsewhere. Even before the Nixon-Kissinger administration came to power, President Johnson had decided to sell Israel the sophisticated weapons it requested.

For Israel, the period between the wars of 1967 and 1973 was a relatively easy one for its relations with the United States. While the Arabs posed no real military threat and Israel held a decided political and strategic advantage in occupying Arab territories, American support for Israel did not seem to threaten other American interests in the region. Iran, America's other Middle East ally, seemed capable of maintaining control and order in the Gulf, and oil-producing Arab states appeared either unwilling or unable to use oil as a political weapon. Even increasing Soviet influence did not seem too threatening in the emerging atmosphere of détente. The inherent conflict among American objectives in the Middle East did not surface.

The expulsion of Soviet troops from Egypt in 1972 signaled the beginning of potential tension in American-Israeli relations. Egypt was making itself available as a possible U.S. ally, at some risk to Israel. Former Israeli Defense Minister Ezer Weizman wrote: "In driving out the Russians from Egypt he [Sadat] brought the West closer to him, necessarily diluting its loyalty to us. His campaign was successful, costing us our position as the cosseted godchild of the Western world. Our political situation went from bad to worse."[40]

While Egypt was making itself available, its apparent military and strategic inferiority did not, however, make it an appealing candidate. Not until its impressive showing in the 1973 war, after it had also demonstrated its capacity to rally other Arab states for an oil embargo against the United States, was Egypt taken seriously. Egypt followed with additional gestures toward the United States, accepting unilateral American mediation with Israel. American-Egyptian relations were rapidly improving.

Despite the Arab oil embargo and its detrimental effect on Western economies, the United States did not reduce its commitment to Israel, but there emerged a new awareness in the United States of the inherent conflict among American objectives in the Middle East which was potentially threatening to American-Israeli relations. By the time Jimmy Carter became president few people in Washington considered Israel a strategic asset and some, including a high ranking military officer, considered it a strategic burden.[41] Instead, most officials emphasized America's moral and traditional commitment to Israel. But as some American Jewish leaders recognized, moral and traditional commitment alone cannot sustain close ties, even if there are strong domestic interests to support them. The former director of the American-Israeli Public Affairs Committee put it this way: "unless you can always translate this in terms of what's in America's interest, you're lost."[42]

The general foreign policy outlook of the Carter administration also favored closer relations with Egypt at the expense of Israel. The United States seemed less obsessed with overall strategic issues in the Middle East vis-à-vis the Soviet Union, and more concerned with economic interests, particularly in the Persian Gulf. In this context Egypt, as the most important Arab state, was in a better position to play a constructive role. Despite Israel's military predominance in the region, as a Pentagon official later put it, although "everyone appreciates what the Israelis can do militarily," their "proximity to the gulf is not enough to be of real use as a base for fighting there, except on paper."[43] The prevailing atmosphere under the Carter administration was such that presidential candidate Ronald Reagan later accused the administration of being the only one to have "deluded itself that Israel was not of permanent strategic importance to America."[44]

Given the vital nature of continuous American support to Israel, many Israeli leaders and strategists became seriously concerned. For the next few years Israel worked to solidify the foundation of American-Israeli relations. Political scientist Shai Feldman reflected the Israeli concern in arguing that, even though Israel "tried to justify continued American support by emphasizing its strategic importance to Western defense. . . . American commitment is based on cultural, ideological and moral affinity—not on strategic interests."[45]

Feldman went on to recommend that for Israeli security to be guaranteed, this unreliable moral foundation of American-Israeli relations must be replaced with formal treaties of alliance, defining a clear role for Israel in Western defense. His views were echoed by some Israeli leaders both before and after the Camp David accords. The pursuit of this important Israeli objective became more intense after Sadat's initiative and the Camp David accords, and was later aided by a new president, Ronald Reagan, who declared that "Israel is a strategic asset to the U.S." and that "we must have policies which give concrete expression to that position."[46] The effort later culminated in the signing of the "memorandum of strategic understanding" between Israel and the United States, highly sought after by Israel but reluctantly agreed to by the U.S. As Shlomo Avineri put it, the American purpose of the agreement was "merely to placate the Israelis in the wake of the AWACS sale to Saudi Arabia."[47]

As welcome as Sadat's initiative was to the Israelis, it posed a real dilemma to Israel's relations with United States. On the one hand, one long-term regional Israeli objective was within reach: a bilateral agreement between Egypt and Israel would simultaneously neutralize Egypt as a military threat and divide the Arab world. On the other hand, the agreements would result in closer American-Egyptian ties that might lead to the weakening of American commitment to Israel. This could be true particularly if Egypt seemed more cooperative and useful in aiding American interests in the Middle East than did Israel, and if Egypt seemed capable of repairing its relations with the Arab states without jeopardizing its relations with the United States.

While Egypt could be instrumental for the United States because of its historic role in the Arab world, the Israelis were concerned because Egyptian objectives in an Arab-Israeli settlement seemed to coincide substantially with those of the United States. As Israeli Defense Minister Weizman put it:

> My objections to excessive American involvement in the negotiations with Egypt stemmed from a simple consideration: I foresaw that U.S. interests lay closer to Egypt's than to ours, so that

it would not be long before Israeli negotiators would have to cope with the dual confrontation as they faced a Washington/Cairo axis.[48]

This meant that not only could American participation in the negotiations be advantageous to the Egyptians, but also that Israeli failure in the negotiations would likely lead to strained Israeli-American relations and to closer Egyptian-American ties, especially given the nature of Egyptian objectives and Sadat's personal determination.[49]

The above considerations led to a strategic debate about the role of the United States in the negotiations. Egypt called for triangular negotiations in which the United States would be a "full partner," while Israel called for bilateral Egyptian-Israeli negotiations in which the United States would be limited to the role of a "mediator." In the end, while the United States preferred to be a full participant, it was forced by other American priorities to play the role of a mediator.[50] Throughout the Camp David process Israeli concerns over relations with the United States affected Israeli behavior noticeably.

The Pattern Continues After Camp David

On his first visit to the United States after the Camp David accords, Prime Minister Begin asked for more arms, and suggested that Israel and the United States conclude a mutual defense treaty.[51] Referring to Begin, President Carter remarked that "his purpose seemed to be to convince us that Israel should be the dominant military power in the area, and that it was our only reliable ally in the Middle East."[52]

While the Camp David accords were acceptable to all sides, Egypt and the United States perceived them as only one step in a process to be aggressively continued, while Israel was not anxious to proceed further on the West Bank and Gaza. This meant that the possibility of closer American-Egyptian relations at the expense of Israel remained high, especially since Egypt had made several gestures for strategic cooperation with the United States, including offering bases for the Rapid Deployment Force. Egypt could become an even more attractive ally if it were to improve relations with other Arab states, thus enhancing its effectiveness and utility. Thus both long-standing Israeli objectives remained in jeopardy: closer American-Egyptian relations could undermine America's commitment to Israel encouraging reconciliation between Egypt and the Arab world. There was a new qualification to the Israeli strategy, however: while close Egyptian-American strategic cooperation should be prevented, a minimal economic relation should be encouraged in order to give Egypt the incentive for maintaining its treaty with Israel.

Several steps taken by Israel after the signing of the Israeli-Egyptian peace treaty indicate that Israel continued to pursue its major objectives. The Israeli attack against the Iraqi nuclear reactor, for example, took place only hours after a meeting between Begin and Sadat, causing Egypt a great deal of embarrassment in the Arab world. This also delayed the possibility of Egypt's rapprochement with other Arab states and forced it to downplay its relations with the United States. The timing of the Israeli invasion of Lebanon was also conducive to cooler American-Egyptian relations.[53]

Israeli strategy proved successful.[54] As the eighties came to an end, Israel had achieved close strategic cooperation with the United States, culminating in the inclusion of Israel in the research for the Strategic Defense Initiative; American-Egyptian relations cooled off dramatically; the state of the Egyptian army, the separation of forces in the Sinai, and the peace treaty between Egypt and Israel effectively neutralized the Egyptian military threat; and Egypt remained dependent on the United States for economic support.

Conclusion

I have argued that, because of its inherent vulnerability and hostile environment, Israel has sought two primary objectives from the first years of its existence: the prevention of collective Arab action (which in practice meant separating Egypt from the rest of the Arab world), and unchallenged relations with the United States (which meant the prevention of strong Arab-American relations).

The Egyptian peace initiative brought mixed blessings to Israel: it made possible the attainment of Israel's regional objective, while it threatened to undermine Israels relationship with the United States. At Camp David these Israeli concerns were translated into two specific problems, one for the short term and the other for the long term. The immediate problem was how to prevent this tension from forcing Israel to grant more concessions to Egypt. The long term problem was that if Egypt succeeded in gaining enough at Camp David to accelerate its return to the Arab fold and to consolidate Sadat's power at home, then Egypt could become a more serious and attractive competitor with Israel for alliance with the United States, thus undermining Israel's long-term strategy. But the final terms of the Camp David accords can be explained only by additional variables, in the context of the bargaining framework to which I will now turn.

III

Specifying the Parameters of Bargaining: Domestic and International Preferences at Camp David

6

Preferences, Perceptions, and the Structure of Bargaining

*A*s a prelude to the central chapter on bargaining, this chapter will undertake the specification of the international and domestic preferences of the actors at Camp David; "preferences" being the agenda of ends, the set of priorities, that are axiomatically ascribed to the actor, and that are shown to explain the actor's behavior across time.

I have already argued in the previous chapters that changes in the distribution of power, both at the international and regional levels, had caused a change in the international preferences of Egypt and Israel which made a bilateral agreement between them preferable to the status quo. In this chapter I will undertake two additional tasks. The first will be to attempt to articulate, using both domestic and international level variables, the additional objectives each side hoped to maximize.

The second task is to consider a potential objection to the method employed in identifying preferences: my analysis relies on indicators that are independent of the perceptions and apparent expectations of policy makers. One might ask if this does not pose a threat to the method, at least in the case of Camp David. I shall begin by considering this question.

Expectations, Perceptions, and Actors' Behavior

Does avoiding the issue of possible misperception as a cause of Egyptian and Israeli behavior threaten the propositions advanced so far? This is a particularly relevant question, since one can explain Egyptian behavior as having been caused by Sadat's misperception of the strategic possibilities in the triangular Israeli-Egyptian-American relationship. Indeed, was Egypt's failure to attain the very end that was said to motivate its behavior, the enhancement of its regional role, due to misperception? I would like to first consider issues of perception and expectation in general terms, and argue that (a) the issue of perception/misperception does not threaten the propositions of the research program that rely on other indicators and that (b) the expectations of policy makers are rarely good predictors of their actual preferences or behavior.

EXPECTATIONS, PERCEPTIONS, AND PREFERENCES

How does one separate perceptions from other objective indicators? Can one deduce preferences from specific indicators without reference to the perceptions of policy makers?

It is useful to separate the question into three related issues. The first has to do with the usefulness of policy makers' perceived expectations in predicting their behavior. The second deals with the extent to which explanations which pretend to derive from objective indicators actually derive from the perceptions (or misperceptions) of policy makers. The third asks whether a systematic method can be devised that will establish the kinds of situations in which perceptions or misperceptions are likely to affect behavior significantly. This last question will be treated in the next chapter, drawing on existing literature, most notably the work of Robert Jervis.[1]

ACTORS' EXPECTATIONS AS PREDICTORS OF BEHAVIOR

The first issue seems particularly relevant to the case of Camp David. On several occasions there appeared to be serious discrepancies between policy makers' expectations about their own behavior and the expectations of their behavior that can be derived from other indicators. In such cases, which one is a better predictor of behavior? I shall briefly argue that policy makers' own expectations, even when they can be accurately identified, are not good predictors of their behavior.

It is generally recognized that individual actors cannot predict their own behavior well in hypothetical situations. The problem is that actors are rarely conscious of their real priorities *unless* and *until* they are forced to choose among them. And although some people are better than others at realistically evaluating their future behavior, the case at hand reveals that the behavior of all three leaders at Camp David did not match their expectations. Several striking illustrations can be given.

One example is Sadat's expectations upon arrival at Camp David. Sadat had told his aides that he could not leave Camp David without an agreement committing the Israelis to withdraw from the West Bank and Gaza; he would simply not accept a bilateral agreement with Israel that only returned the Sinai to Egypt.[2] Moreover, before departing to Camp David Sadat summoned several prominent Egyptian ambassadors and other diplomats to Cairo to brief them on a future international mission that would immediately follow the conclusion of the Camp David negotiations. Given the necessity of an agreement on the West Bank and Gaza, and given Israeli refusal to make concessions on that issue, Sadat told his audience he expected the negotiations to fail. Consequently these Egyptian diplomats were asked to board the presidential airplane on the way to Camp David and disembark in Europe, for the purpose of launching a major public relations campaign to blame the failure of the talks on Israeli intransigence. At least some of his diplomats voiced skepticism about Sadat's expectations; they argued that, when offered all of the Sinai back and an American commitment to Egypt, the President would find it difficult to turn down such an agreement, no matter what his expectations and perceptions were.[3] The President remained sure of himself. He told Carter on the second day of the Camp David negotiations that "I will not sign a Sinai agreement before an agreement is also reached on the West Bank."[4] Yet the outcome of the Camp David negotiations proved Sadat wrong, in spite of his attempt to rationalize the outcome to hide the inevitable dissonance. In the end, Sadat's expected behavior was not well predicted by his perceptions.

A second example also relates to Sadat. Several months before the formal negotiations began, Sadat adamantly told Carter that although he was willing to sign an agreement with Israel and to put an end to the state of war, normal diplomatic relations could not be expected for a generation;[5] time would be required for the psychological adjustment necessitated by such a dramatic step. President Carter took this point for granted as he entered the talks. In his notes he wrote that although he wanted normal relations between Israel and Egypt, "Sadat was not at all ready for full diplomatic recognition of Israel."[6] Yet, within a matter of days Sadat had reconciled himself to the idea of full diplomatic relations.

A third example pertains to the perceptions and expectations of President Carter. At the start of the negotiations, Carter set himself the goal of a comprehensive settlement which would include the West Bank and Gaza, and was determined to "use every influence we have at Camp David to make it successful."[7] Members of the National Security Council advised him to limit his expectations; given the domestic and international constraints on the U.S., it was likely to accept much less as an alternative to failure.[8] Carter remained optimistic, but when critical decisions had to be made a few days later, he reconciled himself to much less.

A final example relates to Israeli perceptions and expectations. When the Carter administration suggested closed, intensive negotiations involving the three states, several Israeli policy makers became concerned. They feared that the United States and Egypt, who shared close views about the nature of a desirable agreement, would be in a position to corner Israel. Moreover, without media participation the Carter administration would be in a better position to use its potential leverage with Israel. Prime Minister Begin, on the other hand, seemed less worried, since he apparently saw that international and domestic constraints could make the bargaining situation work in favor of Israel. In the end the negotiations proved Begin correct and many of his aides mistaken; objective indicators gave Israel the advantage in the isolated setting at Camp David.[9]

The point of these examples is to demonstrate the difficulty in employing actors' expectations as predictors of their behavior. There is always, of course, the additional problem of discriminating real expectations from tactical posturing, which complicates the situation even further. In the examples above there was little doubt that the policy makers perceived the situation as stated, but one can never be certain. The point, however, is that even when policy makers are honest about their expectations their eventual choices are generally dependent on factors outside of their control. What this entails, of course, is a great deal of psychological dissonance, both individual and collective, which has to be confronted. An example of this inevitable dissonance was confronted by President Nasser immediately before his death in 1970. Nasser had been the hero of Pan-Arabism and of its central issue, the Palestinian cause. Although I have argued before that Egypt's advocacy of these causes was largely an instrument for furthering Egyptian national interest, I have little doubt that Nasser may have felt a strong personal commitment to them so long as there was no conflict with Egypt's national interest. As long as no choices between these objectives had to be made, the potential dissonance could be ignored. But in 1970, following the failure of the "war of attrition," when Nasser confronted serious choices in relation to the Rogers Plan and in relation to Jordan's attack against the bases of the Palestine Liberation Organization, his choice was clearly in favor of Egypt's national interest. But, while this may have been a predictable choice, the emerging dissonance must have been difficult to confront; Malcolm Kerr ventured to speculate that in the end, Nasser's fatal heart attack was a result of the heavy burden of the moment.[10]

MISPERCEPTIONS AS A CAUSE OF BEHAVIOR

Misperceptions can, of course, often explain behavior. But to the extent that the degree of misperception and its relative importance vary according to situations and personalities, two general questions become important. The first, alluded to earlier, asks what situations and personalities are likely to lead to the kind of misperception that will affect behavior. This is the central question of Robert Jervis' *Perceptions and Misperceptions in World Politics,* and which I will examine in the context of Camp David in the next chapter. The second question asks about the relative importance of misperceptions as an explanation of state behavior, in comparison to other variables. This latter question is particularly relevant to the Camp David case: although it has been argued that Egypt pursued its own interests, as defined by the necessities of regional and international changes, in attempting reconciliation with Israel and consolidation of relations with the United States there are reasons to raise some serious doubts about this explanation. The outcome of the negotiations raise an interesting point: although Egypt succeeded in regaining the occupied Sinai, it failed to achieve the central objectives which were said to motivate its behavior. Egypt's influence in Arab affairs declined markedly, American-Israeli relations reached new heights at the expense of Egyptian-American relations, Israel's regional military hegemony peaked while Egypt lacked the capacity to contain it, and the domestic economic problems remained. Does this not suggest that President Sadat and other Egyptian leaders misperceived the situation?

Several general observations are in order before answering this specific question. Implicit in the research program proposed in the theoretical chapters is the assumption that objective indicators, such as the rough distribution of military and economic power, tend to dominate general patterns of behavior in international politics. Put differently, perceptions tend to conform to reality in most cases, especially over time. In the end, the ultimate test of this assumption is an alternative research program which relies on perceptions as a causal variable, and which does away with objective indicators of military and economic power. But also implicit in the theoretical assumptions is the possibility that, in any one case, misperceptions could prevail as a dominant causal variable. The key, therefore, is that the research program should provide a consistent framework for testing the relative importance of misperception as an explanatory variable. In answering the empirical question posed above, I will attempt to devise some useful general propositions about the relevance of misperception.

The most widely accepted interpretation of the role of misperception at Camp David is that President Sadat, who seemed to dominate Egyptian decisions, misperceived his ability to influence the United States at the expense of Israel. This misperception led to the specific outcome of Camp David. While there is little doubt that Sadat often misperceived the situation confronting Egypt, and that both the Egyptian system of government and Sadat's personality were particularly vulnerable to misperception (as will be argued in the next chapter), such a causal link between misperceptions and Egyptian behavior is unlikely.

First, Sadat's perception of the need to move unilaterally away from other Arab states was shared by most of his aides, including some of those who abandoned him during the negotiations. Later, after Sadat's death and the return of the Sinai to Egyptian control, many other Egyptian officials found it easy to blame it all on Sadat's incompetence. Prominent intellectual critics like Muhammad Haykal and Sayyid Yasin voiced disagreements with Sadat's tactics and bargaining strategy, though not with the necessity of negotiating with Israel or the need to act even without the support of other Arab states. Former Egyptian Foreign Minister Ismail Fahmy, who resigned over Sadat's decision to visit Jerusalem and deliver a speech to the Israeli Knesset, disagreed primarily with Sadat's bargaining strategy. "I then reminded Sadat that we had only two cards to play—recognizing Israel and ending belligerency."[11] By proclaiming "no more war" in Jerusalem, Fahmy reasoned, Sadat was in effect giving up both cards before the negotiations began. The man who succeeded Fahmy as foreign minister, Ibrahim Kamel, resigned during the negotiations over major provisions of the final agreement,[12] although he had no objection in principle to concluding a treaty with Israel, even if all the other Arab states rejected it. He later stated, "if we reach an agreement on principle. . . . and if other Arabs wouldn't go along we would start implementing this agreement on what concerns us, on Sinai, and then continue to help the other Arabs in realizing the other parts."[13]

Presidential assistant Usama al-Baz, whom some Israelis considered to be a hardliner, often disagreed with Sadat's tactics but found the accords better than no agreement, and remained in the government. In fact, he was promoted by Sadat's successor, Husni Mubarak.[14] Secretary of State for Foreign Affairs Butrus Ghali expressed frustration with Sadat's bargaining behavior and considered the President to be an "amateur," but still saw no alternative to the accords and did not believe that better strategy on Egypt's part could have achieved much more.[15]

It should be apparent from the above that Sadat's inclination toward a bilateral agreement with Israel was shared by many prominent officials and intellectuals. This may, however, imply one of two other possibilities: the first is that while Sadat's *personal* misperceptions were not directly responsible for Egypt's behavior, the *collective* misperception of Egyptian elites is responsible. The second possibility is that while no misperceptions account for Egypt's inclination toward a treaty with Israel and closer ties with the United States, tactical mistakes in the bargaining process which were due to misperceptions account for Egypt's failure to attain its major strategic objectives.

Although this second possibility bears on the first, I shall treat it independently in the next chapter. Here I shall limit myself to some general propositions about the first possibility: the extent to which the failure to attain objectives through a chosen course of action indicates misperception.

As asked earlier, if Egypt failed to achieve the regional and international objectives that motivated it toward Camp David in the first place, does this failure indicate misperceptions on the part of Egypt? It would be a mistake, I will argue, to make this assumption too hastily.

The problem is that whatever indicators a theorist can devise, they are not likely in themselves to predict a particular outcome. While the appropriateness of these indicators is determined by their comparative utility in explaining a given phenomenon in general, over time, their employment in any single case will result in underdetermination. From a decision maker's point of view, even if all indicators are taken into consideration there remains at least some risk (and often complete uncertainty) as to the likelihood of a specific outcome; the utility of the indicators for a given decision maker is in helping to maximize the chances of some particular outcome or range of outcomes. Therefore situations occur where a perfectly rational actor, behaving in a manner consistent with objective constraints, will choose a course of action that fails. An elaboration of this point is in order, although part of the discussion relates more to the section on "abstractive" theorizing in chapter 2.

Decisions and Risk

Formal decision theory is divided into three branches, based on the type of decision. These involve: (a) decisions under *certainty*, (b) decisions under *risk*, and (c) decisions under *uncertainty*.[16] Decisions under certainty are those in which the actor can be certain that a given choice will lead to a specific outcome. Decisions under risk are those in which the actor has an objective method of evaluating the probability of a given outcome for a particular course; buying a lottery ticket is an example. Decisions under uncertainty are those in which the actor is at least partly unable to ascertain the probability of a given outcome for a particular course of action; betting in a horse race is an example. It should be evident that most political decisions are at least of the second type, and can often be of the third. This entails the following simplified structure of choices.

Assuming a situation of risk with two possible choices (A and B) and four possible outcomes (O1 to O4), the probabilities of each outcome are indicated by p1, p2, 1−p1, and 1−p2. If O1 is the most preferable outcome, then the choice between A and B will depend on

FIGURE 6.1. Choices Under Risk

A	(p1) O1	(1-p1) O2
B	(p2) O3	(1-p2) O4

the relative values of the four possible outcomes and the estimated values of p1 and p2. If O1 is much larger than the others and p1 much larger than p2, choice A may be preferable to B. But to say that p1 is much larger than p2 does not mean that p2 is very large in absolute terms. It could be, for example, that p1 is much smaller than .5, indicating that the most likely outcome of choice A is O2, not the desired O1. O2 may in fact have a smaller value than O3 and O4.

Yet choice A may still be "rational." The third independent factor on which the choice depends is the conception of rationality being employed. Regardless of the objective values of choices, probabilities and outcomes, an actor's behavior depends on what conception of rationality one ascribes to; it should be apparent that one can define rationality as either "conservative" or "liberal," in that an actor may choose to behave in a way that tends to minimize losses (conservatively), or in a way that tends to maximize gains (liberally).[17] Neither choice seems to be inherently preferable, and the fact that an actor may prefer one over the other cannot be said to determine that actor's rationality, nor does it necessarily mean that the values of the outcomes or their probabilities were misperceived. In terms of developing positive theory, however, one can determine which actors are likely to subscribe to what concept, and on the basis of that and other indicators, the likely choices of a particular actor could be predicted.

In the real-world case of Egyptian behavior at Camp David, objective indicators may be sufficient to determine the value of the possible outcomes to Egypt and perhaps their rough probability; but actual behavior still depends on other, independent Egyptian inclinations that must be determined separately; this is partly the task of chapter 7. Moreover, it should be apparent that even if Egypt's chosen course of action did not lead to the desired outcome, this does not necessarily mean that the desired outcome was not the motivator of Egyptian behavior, or that the chosen course of action was "irrational," in the pursuit of the desired objective. Although it may of course be possible that Egyptian decision makers misperceived the probability of their ability to reduce American commitment to Israel, it is also possible that they viewed the rewards of this possibility to be so high, and the losses to be so minimal, in comparison to the continuation of the status quo, that they saw the risk worth taking, even if failure was more probable. The point is that failure to attain desired objectives does not automatically indicate misperceptions.

In conclusion, although perceptions and actors' expectations need to be considered in the context of strategies and tactics of bargaining, the issue does not pose a serious threat to the determination of the actors' preferences from the higher-level indicators that have been discussed in the previous chapters. Consequently, I will proceed to analyze the preferences of the three states at Camp David from international and domestic indicators. This will be accomplished through the hierarchical procedure discussed in chapter 2.

American Preferences at Camp David

THE INTERNATIONAL COMPONENT

American policy in the Middle East has been consistent, since the late 1940s, in three broad objectives: limiting Soviet influence in the region, securing Western economic interests in the region (especially the flow of oil at reasonable prices), and the survival, security, and well-being of the state of Israel. The means of attaining these objectives and their relative weight have varied over time. Moreover, as argued in chapter 4, these objectives are potentially in conflict with one another. Although this conflict did not always surface and rarely forced the United States to make definite choices between these objectives, the tension between them has been often evident, preventing the United States from implementing effective policies.[18]

By the mid-1970s, however, the United States found itself facing tough choices. As Western dependence on Middle Eastern oil grew, Arab states, frustrated with American support of Israel, appeared willing and able to use the oil weapon, forcing new choices. While the United States could endure Arab pressure, and was unlikely to yield to it by reducing the commitment to Israel, some undesirable tension emerged. Kissinger's diplomacy temporarily defused the immediate economic and military crisis following the Arab-Israeli war of 1973 (and the subsequent Arab oil embargo), but there emerged a new view in the United States about the centrality of the Arab-Israeli conflict to

America's Middle East interests. Arab states, especially Egypt, became more willing to weaken their ties to the Soviet Union and move closer to the United States, as illustrated during Kissinger's "shuttle diplomacy" and by Egypt's abrogation of its treaty with the Soviets. In this environment active American involvement in settling the Arab-Israeli conflict promised a dual reward.

When the Carter administration came to office there were some in the United States who viewed Israel as a strategic burden, both militarily and economically.[19] But many other American officials continued to see Israel as being potentially useful, and there was little doubt that America's commitment to Israel would endure as a fundamental aspect of U.S. policy in the Middle East. The task for American foreign policy, therefore, was not to choose between Israel and other American objectives, but to attempt to resolve the tension among American objectives by arriving at an acceptable and comprehensive settlement to the Arab-Israeli conflict. Such a settlement would not only reduce the threat to Western economic interests, but Soviet influence in the Middle East as well.[20]

America's instrumental objective in the 1970s became, therefore, the achievement of a comprehensive settlement to the Arab-Israeli conflict. The Carter administration, upon coming to office, played an active role in moving Arab-Israeli negotiations forward through the Geneva process, and moved to better define the American position in relation to the Palestinian issue. American national interest in the region dictated the pursuit of a settlement to the Arab Israeli conflict as a primary objective.

While the Geneva talks moved slowly and encountered many obstacles, the Carter administration remained optimistic as it sought to retain the political initiative. When President Sadat surprised the world with his visit to Jerusalem, however, American reaction was not one of immediate enthusiastic support. Sadat's dramatic move had stolen the political initiative in a manner that could have undermined American strategy for a comprehensive settlement. But, given the momentum created by Sadat's initiative, it was best to seize upon it as an opportunity to push forward the settlement process.

The internationally derived objective of an overall settlement remained America's preference until the very last moment of the Camp David negotiations.[21] And even when the United States had reconciled itself to achieving much less, there remained the hope (or perhaps the rationalization) that the Camp David accords would be a constructive step toward an eventual comprehensive settlement. But while America's international preferences recommended a comprehensive settlement, its domestic preferences pulled in a different direction; given the nature of American politics, domestic preferences can often dominate.

THE DOMESTIC COMPONENT

As mentioned previously, an assumption of this study's research program is that when international issues of security and vital economic interests are involved, they tend to dominate state behavior regardless of the domestic system of government. It is important, therefore, to begin the research procedure by beginning at the international level. But this does not mean that these international considerations always dominate a state's preferences or behavior; the hierarchical "nesting" procedure may reveal other variables that dominate in specific situations. In the case of American Middle East policy, a brief examination of the American system of government reveals a set of domestic priorities in American preferences that often undermines its international objectives.

The United States commands such relative wealth and power that few regional international issues, whether military or economic, are vital to it. Given the decentralized system of government in the United States, America's regional preferences are often set according to domestic influences, and American policy tends to be more concerned with short-term tactics than with long-term strategy.

A highly decentralized system of government tends to lead to policy priorities that do not best respond to international objectives, and this issue has been considered by several analysts.[22] In chapter 7, I deal with this issue in more general theoretical terms. Here I will simply consider the major implications of this proposition for American policy in the Middle East, of which there are two.

First, when a foreign policy issue is not of vital interest, domestic interest groups can determine a government's position over that issue even if their views conflict with those of the majority of Americans. If issues matter at all in the voting behavior of Americans, there are usually only one or two that dominate; among these are, typically, the economy, issues of war and peace, and relations with the Soviet Union. If another issue of marginal concern to the majority of Americans is a top priority for a well-organized special-interest group, that group can determine policy unless there is a significant counterweight. This is true even if a majority of Americans does not agree with the views of the interest group (and especially when the President is weak), since most Americans will vote on the basis of other issues and a strong interest group can tip the balance in favor of one candidate or the other. The pro-Israel lobby in the United States is by any measure such a group, and it plays a critical role in American Middle East policy. This brings to mind a statement David Ben-Gurion made when contemplating the choice between the Soviet Union and the United States during Israel's early days: "when the Soviets say 'No,' that goes for everybody in Russia. It is not so in America."[23] America's decentralized political system permits much leeway for the influence of interest groups.

Second, American policy in the Middle East tends to be primarily reactive, concerned with short-term interests; only during crisis situations are Middle East issues elevated to the top of the priority list, and when that occurs it is politically safer simply to diffuse the crisis than to launch a major long-term policy. As a consequence, American diplomacy in the Middle East has been characterized by the motive of achieving diplomatic success for its own sake, with little effective regard to the consequences. Several diplomatic "achievements," originally hailed as successes and popular domestically, have turned out to have undesirable consequences.[24] Taking advantage of America's political limitations, effective regional actors can often take the initiative in such a way that when crises emerge, the new facts of the situation and the domestic constraints in the United States will substantially limit American choices; the Israeli invasion of Lebanon and the Egyptian-Syrian attack on Israel in 1973 are good examples. But there can be little doubt that Israel, combining its military hegemony (which gives it the capacity for the initiative) in the Middle East with its sizable influence in American domestic politics, benefits most from this situation.

MEDIATION OR PARTICIPATION

The Carter administration was clearly aware that a durable settlement of the Arab-Israeli conflict was a prerequisite for the attainment of American objectives in the Middle East. This became more apparent to policy makers after the 1973 war and the oil embargo. But, while the administration sought a long-term American policy designed to achieve a comprehensive settlement, it clearly underestimated both the domestic political constraints and the ability of powerful regional actors to preempt American policy. Domestic variables are bound to alter American priorities; an American politician is not likely to risk losing power over a noncritical issue. As a consequence the Carter administration's desire to be a participant in the negotiations was bound to give way to Israel's desire of limiting the American role to that of mediation.

If one ignores the domestic constraints on American Middle East policy, one may be led to believe that America is in a position to maintain the initiative, especially in relation to Israel. After all, Israel is economically and militarily dependent on the United States, and without U.S. support Israel's very survival could be threatened. An administration acting on this basis might be led to overestimate its leverage. On the eve of Camp David President Carter, intent on achieving a comprehensive settlement which would require some difficult Israeli concessions, seemed confident about his leverage with Israel and committed to employing it. In his diary, Carter wrote a few weeks before the negotiations: "We will use every influence we have at Camp David to make it successful, and will not put a time limit on how long we stay there."[25] But by the third day of the negotiations Carter seemed more concerned with success for its own sake than with the provisions of the agreement, and preventing the breakdown of the negotiations became his top priority: "Our efforts at Camp David were now prominent in the eyes of the world, and we did not want to fail."[26] When it appeared that the negotiations were headed toward failure Carter's earlier threat to blame Israel for the failure in front of the American people seemed more of a threat to Carter himself than to Begin. A weakened American president who had just failed in his most important foreign policy endeavor would not have been likely to find receptive ears. And Carter would have been in a bad position given the inevitable campaign of Israel's supporters in Congress. The "wise men" of the Democratic Party, as Carter called them, would have been all too happy to remind Carter of their earlier advice to "stay as aloof as possible from direct involvement in the Middle East negotiations; this is a losing proposition."[27] Indeed, although Carter felt that the apparent failure of the negotiations was due largely to Israeli intransigence, he found it politically safer to warn Sadat that he would blame the failure on Egypt, when Sadat was ready to walk out of the talks.[28]

AMERICAN PREFERENCES: CONCLUSION

While America's international objectives recommended that the United States seek an overall settlement to the Arab-Israeli conflict and play the role of an independent participant in the negotiations, domestic objectives pulled toward a less comprehensive settlement and toward an American role of mediation. Given the decentralized American system of government, the relative power of the pro-Israel lobby and the absence of an effective counterweight, and given American policy priorities, domestic policy considerations were likely to shape American preferences more than international objectives. At Camp David, perceptions aside, the primary American objective was bound to be success for its own sake.

In short, America's minimally acceptable outcome at Camp David was any agreement acceptable to Egypt and Israel. Beyond that, the preference function of the United States involved maximizing the chances for a comprehensive settlement to the Arab-Israeli conflict and securing maximum concessions from Israel in order to obtain the most acceptable outcome possible to other Arab states.

Egyptian Preferences at Camp David

THE INTERNATIONAL COMPONENT

I have already argued (in chapter 5) that Egypt's international objectives recommended both closer ties with the United States and a bilateral agreement with Israel, even at the expense of Pan-Arabism. These objectives would have led to greater regional power for Egypt, since it would have had an independent source of support and a role as "proxy" for a major power in the region. It seems ironic that this effort to regain its leadership role in the Arab world recommended the termination of its commitment to Pan-Arabism.

Beyond this basic objective, Egypt sought to maximize three more specific objectives. First, Egypt sought to achieve the closest possible relations with the United States and maximal separation between the United States and Israel. Second, in order to enhance its future influence with other Arab states, Egypt sought to maximize Israeli concessions on the issue of Palestine and the other occupied Arab territories. Third, for the purpose of enhancing its future leverage with Israel, Egypt sought to minimize the number of immediate concessions made to Israel over the issue of "normalization of relations" between the two states.

THE DOMESTIC COMPONENT

Having derived the international preferences of Egypt at Camp David there remains the question of whether or not there were overriding domestic preferences, and if so how they affected Egyptian international preferences. I shall argue here that domestic preferences had minimal affect on Egypt's international preferences, although they may have constrained Egypt's tactical performance. A further exploration of the relation between the Egyptian system of government and optimal bargaining behavior is pursued in the next chapter.

Given Egypt's centralized system of government, characterized by Leonard Binder as "a modern autocracy dominated by a bureaucratically oriented elite,"[29] there were three potentially serious threats to the government of Anwar Sadat: the military establishment, the bureaucratic elite, and massive popular discontent. None of them posed a serious threat to Egypt's international objectives.

The military establishment, which had been humiliated as a result of the 1967 war, owed a great deal to Sadat for restoring its stature in the 1973 war. Moreover, those elements within the officer corps that posed a potential threat to him were successfully replaced with loyal men.[30] In addition, there was a prevailing resentment of the Soviet Union for failing to supply the Egyptian army with the most modern weapons, and for the patronizing attitude that Soviet officers displayed toward their Egyptian counterparts. The lure of sophisticated American military hardware also had some effect on many Egyptian officers.[31] As for the cessation of hostilities with Israel, the prospect could only be met with relief since most of the military establishment was not prepared for another war with the superior Israeli army. In short, the military establishment did not appear to pose a serious challenge to Egypt's political objectives at Camp David.

Second, Egyptian elites may have appeared to pose the most serious threat to the objective of a separate agreement with Israel at the expense of Pan-Arabism. For three decades these elites had advocated Pan-Arabism, and any major shift was bound to create substantial dissonance which, added to other dissatisfactions, would be bound to show itself in some form or another. Aside from this, however, the abandonment of Pan-Arabism was not likely to affect Egypt's bureaucratic elites to any great degree for two primary reasons. The first, with which I have dealt earlier, is that the roots of Pan-Arabism in Egypt were not very deep, and the role of this movement during the

Nasser Era was secondary to Egyptian national interests. The second is that as a result of the massive changes in the distribution of economic strength in the Arab world, also described earlier, Egypt became a dependent nation in the context of Arab politics. As a result Egyptian elites suffered dissonance from the decline of their role in inter-Arab organizations and projects in favor of the apparently less capable elites from oil producing states.

The resentment of the Egyptian elites symbolically reflected itself in their new economic status in Cairo during the two years preceding Sadat's visit to Jerusalem. As a result of the Lebanese civil war, already-overcrowded Cairo became the new haven for the Gulf state rich, who were prepared to spend in one week what most members of the Egyptian elite could earn in one year. Taxi drivers, scarce to begin with, became less anxious to cater to the low-paying Egyptians, and were glad to attach themselves to the oil state rich for a full day. Apartments, which were becoming even more scarce in Cairo, were now being rented for short periods of time to the Gulf state visitors at rates that no Egyptian bureaucrat could afford. In other words, the more fundamental resentment that Egyptian elites held toward their oil-rich Arab brethren was reinforced in matters of day-to-day life. Whatever dissonance would emerge from the abandonment of Pan-Arabism could probably be easily rationalized.

The third potential challenge to the government of Egypt, massive popular uprisings, was not likely to materialize over foreign policy issues. For one thing the centralized Egyptian government controlled the opinion-shaping media, so much so that at Camp David Begin infuriated Sadat by remarking that "the people of Egypt could be easily manipulated by Sadat, and their beliefs and attitudes could be shaped by their leader."[32] Furthermore, the roots of Pan-Arabism among the masses were even more shallow than among the elite. As for their apparent hostility toward Israel, the author was surprised to discover its lack of relevance during a research trip to Egypt one year before Sadat's initiative.[33] Most of those interviewed appeared more interested in their deteriorating economic condition than in war and peace with Israel. Sensing this sentiment, Sadat subsequently sold the Camp David accords to the Egyptian people as the road to economic rebirth. While such a strategy would backfire in the event of economic difficulties, it is not obvious that a different strategy would have been better on this score. In conclusion, domestic political concerns within Egypt did not appear to alter the preferences of Egypt as derived from the international circumstances.

Israeli Preferences at Camp David

THE INTERNATIONAL COMPONENT

As argued in chapter 5, Israel had two major international objectives. The first, and perhaps most important, involved maintaining a close and unchallengeable relationship with the United States. As President Carter wrote, Begin pointed out that there had to be two agreements at Camp David, "the most important [of which] was between the United States and Israel. . . ."[34] Israel's second objective was a bilateral agreement with Egypt that would simultaneously neutralize militarily and separate Egypt from the rest of the Arab world. In other words, Israel sought to ensure its survival by substituting the resources of the United States for its own, which were insufficient, and by decreasing the effective hostility of its environment by dividing its enemies.

Aside from that, Israel sought an agreement that would put an end to formal hostilities between the two countries. In this regard, Israel's international objectives recommended the normalization of relations with Egypt and the limitation of concessions by Israel on other issues. The limitation of concessions was necessary in order to maintain effective leverage with other Arab states in future dealings, and to deprive Egypt of a big political victory that might encourage collective Arab political action.

A remaining international-level issue involves Israel's military situation relative to Egypt. Israel's desire to reach a bilateral agreement with Egypt was motivated by two primary considerations, one of which was the previously discussed objective of preventing collective Arab action. The second is that Egypt has traditionally been Israel's most serious military opponent, and the cessation of hostilities between the two nations would improve Israel's military situation substantially. But no agreement, no matter how firmly founded, can be taken for granted forever. Consequently, the question arises as to what compromises Israel could make and still retain a military advantage. Specifically, did the return of the Sinai, a natural military barrier, alter the situation in a way that would put Israel at a serious disadvantage in the event of some future war with Egypt? A brief examination of this question reveals that it does not. Indeed, Israel's military situation, the peace treaty aside, would improve with the return of the Sinai, subject to some conditions.

First, Israel does retain a buffer between its heartland and the Egyptian border in the vast and largely uninhabited Negev desert. Second, during the 1973 war it became apparent that the vastness of the Sinai desert and its treacherous conditions posed a serious problem for the Israeli army. Since a fully mobilized Israeli army is made up largely of reserves, Israel is faced with the task of mobilizing and transporting most of the soldiers from its populated areas to the front in the event of war. In 1973 this proved quite difficult, and major delays allowed the Egyptians to attack Israeli convoys before reaching the front. The return of the Sinai resolves this problem. Third, the return of the Sinai to Egypt could decrease the chances of a large Egyptian surprise attack. Specifically, a partially demilitarized Sinai (as agreed to at Camp David) would not allow Egypt to maintain a military force in the Sinai sufficient to launch an attack against Israel, and any substantial troop movement across the Suez Canal would be easily detected. In short, military considerations alone did not conflict with Israel's objectives as described above.

THE DOMESTIC COMPONENT

In the next chapter I will consider the extent to which the Israeli system of government is conducive to the attainment of Israeli objectives and the way that specific Israeli preferences related to the bargaining process. Here, I will limit myself to considering the way that Israel's domestic politics affected Israeli objectives at Camp David. I will argue that domestic politics did not appear to have dramatically altered Israel's international objectives except in perhaps allowing more compromise than the political leadership seemed willing to accept.

Israel's multi-party parliamentary system allows a greater role for popular opinion than does Egypt's. Moreover, by the time the Camp David negotiations were held Israeli politics had become so polarized that no single party held a decisive advantage in the Knesset. While Begin's Likud party won the largest plurality, its lead over the competing Labor party was slim. In forming a government, Likud had to rely on the support of a number of smaller parties. Under these circumstances, Israeli public opinion mattered even more than usual, since the smallest political issue would be seized upon by opposition groups anxious to defeat the government. In determining the minimal boundaries of Israeli preferences one must therefore attempt to derive the minimal preferences of Israeli popular opinion as well as the minimal preferences of the leading political parties.

The central issue related to domestic preferences involves the degree of compromise that would be tolerated domestically in exchange for the achievement of Israel's international objective. Here one must ask what the minimal preferences of the major political parties and of the Israeli population at large were, and what constraints these preferences put on Israel's representatives at the negotiations. Specifically, what degree of compromise would be domestically acceptable on the issues of the West Bank and Gaza, Jewish settlements, and the Palestinian question in exchange for an agreement that secured peace, maintained the special relationship with the United States, and split the Arab world?

An examination of the long-held positions of the major political parties in Israel not only shows some serious differences between them but also reveals some surprising similarities in terms of the issues in question here. Israeli public opinion at the time of Camp David may have been more willing to compromise than both parties had been historically inclined to do.

The Likud party, and its main predecessor the Hirut party, have been traditionally committed to the inclusion of the West Bank ("Judea and Samaria") in the state of Israel. This commitment seemed so central to Menachem Begin that he resigned from the Labor-led national unity government in 1967 when it accepted United Nations Resolution 242, which was understood to imply withdrawal from parts of the West Bank. On the face of it, therefore, the basic principles of the then-governing Likud party seemed to prevent any compromises on the West Bank and the Palestinian issue that entailed Israeli withdrawal. Yet it is not easy to determine the importance of this issue in relation to other important issues such as Israeli security, long-standing Israeli strategic objectives, and the continuation of Likud rule. Although Begin's personal commitment to the West Bank seemed unshakable, I will argue in chapter 7 that this is the type of uncertainty that only optimal bargaining behavior by one's opponents (Egypt in this case) could resolve.

Although Labor's public position on the West Bank and Gaza differed markedly from Likud's, there are some fundamental similarities between the two that seem to have endured since the creation of Israel. The platform of the Labor party envisioned a settlement of the West Bank issue based largely on the Allon Plan,[35] which involved the return of the population of the West Bank and part of the territory (approximately 60%) to Jordan, while Israel would retain all of Jerusalem, many of the other historical sections of the West Bank, and a good percentage of the arable land. The basic Labor argument has been that the territories that Israel would retain are needed for security; little mention is made of any part that, with the exception of Jerusalem, would be retained on the basis of the historical claim to Eretz Yisrael. But there has been some convincing evidence that while the Labor party may have ranked historical claims somewhat lower than Likud, it has based its foreign policy at least partly on these claims.

One surprising example can be seen from recently revealed material about the deliberations of Israeli leaders over relations with Arab states in 1949. Israeli leaders were apparently preparing a long-term foreign policy toward the Arab world that would eventually fulfill the historical claims on the West Bank. Former Israeli Prime Minister Moshe Sharrett has been considered one of the most moderate leaders of the Labor party's predecessor, and his stance toward the Arab world, the Palestinians, human rights, war and peace, has been more compromising than perhaps any Labor leader of his stature. For him security seemed the dominant issue for Israel, while ideology did not appear to be a primary motivator. It is surprising, therefore, to note his recommendations on agreements with Arab states in 1949:

> In general, total and absolute peace is desirable for us. But, there is no certainty that we are about to conclude a peace treaty with any (Arab) state. Even if this does not come about, however, we will lose nothing if we enter negotiations without giving up any of our cards. This consideration applies to Jordan as well, but there is a difference between Jordan and others. With Egypt, it is certainly desirable that we conclude a peace treaty that will stabilize our relations, will permit mutual trade, and will allow the return of the previous status of Egyptian Jews. This also applies to Lebanon, and perhaps to Syria with some reservations about the new government there. This does not apply to Jordan however. We are not interested in officially recognizing the annexation of any part of [Eretz Yisrael] or any part of Jerusalem by Jordan. At this stage, it is desirable to the extent possible, to limit ourselves to resolving the urgent problems by widening the cease-fire agreement, or by concluding a series of special practical agreements.[36]

There seemed to be unanimity within the Israeli leadership over this issue as no one raised any objection to this general reasoning. In other words, the ideological ambition in relation to the West Bank has been a component of Labor policy since the creation of Israel, and it seemed to rank sufficiently high in Israeli priorities to determine the nature of desired agreements with the Arab states since a peace treaty with Jordan, though it would lead to greater security and stability, was ruled out over this issue. Nonetheless, the degree to which the Labor party would compromise on this issue in order to obtain the other, strategic objectives is probably uncertain even to policy makers themselves; only when critical either/or choices have to be made can such an issue be settled, though ideology does tend to give place to issues of security. The exact boundary cannot be established a priori, however, and bargaining usually settles the issue.

Even if the Labor party had not been more inclined than the Likud to compromise over the West Bank, a failure of the negotiations between Israel and Egypt and the possible deterioration in relations with the United States would have been seized upon by Labor for its domestic struggle with Likud. Consequently, given the nature of the Israeli system, the Likud government had a greater incentive toward achieving an agreement and avoiding failure than the Egyptians seem to have estimated.[37] This was even more true given the state of Israeli public opinion at the time of the negotiations.

While political parties may have been motivated at least partly by ideological commitments, Israeli public opinion has generally been concerned with security. The evolution of Israeli public opinion in relation to the West Bank reveals that the ideological motivation is a luxury that Israelis sought only as their ability to afford it increased. Whatever the political leadership may have felt about peace treaties with Arab states, for the Israeli public the idea was sensationally attractive. Sadat's trip to Jerusalem succeeded in breaking a major psychological barrier, and the prospect of peace with Egypt captured the Israeli imagination. A failure of the negotiations with Egypt over the failure of the Israeli team to compromise would have seriously threatened the Likud government. This point was apparently foreseen by Sadat as he devised his strategy for Camp David. As Carter put it, Sadat's "first preference was obviously a settlement; his second, an agreement with me which would be so good for Israel that Begin would be condemned if he rejected it."[38] Israeli public opinion, therefore, may have increased the pressure on the Israeli government to succeed in the negotiations.

In conclusion, Israel's system of government and the role of public opinion in that system seemed to enhance Israel's chances of achieving their objectives of a bilateral agreement with Egypt and closer ties with the United States. However, other domestic Israeli objectives in relation to West Bank, which appear to have been widely shared, bring to question the extent of compromise that would have been acceptable in order to attain these objectives. An exact determination of the boundary could be determined only through optimal bargaining by the Egypt, which would force the choice.

This typical uncertainty about the specific boundaries of compromise is the primary explanation for the prevalence of bargaining. If the boundaries for all actors are fully certain, no bargaining need take place. In the next chapter, I will examine the extent to which Israel, Egypt, and the United States followed their optimal strategies, thus forcing the others to determine their minimal boundaries.

Tactical Preferences at Camp David

Aside from the general international and domestic preferences of the negotiating parties, each party had some tactical preferences about the structure of the bargaining situation. Two central issues are considered below: the role of the United States in the negotiations and whether this would be one of a full partner or a detached mediator, and the isolated, open-ended form of the Camp David negotiations, to include the influence of the element of time.

THE ROLE OF THE UNITED STATES

I have argued earlier in the present chapter that America's international objectives would move the United States to seek to play the role of a full participant in the negotiations, but that domestic considerations would push the United States toward the role of a mediator. It is also apparent that American officials were clearly aware of their preferred role. Carter wrote that he "saw no possibility of progress if the United States should withdraw and simply leave the negotiations to the Egyptians and the Israelis," and on Begin's arrival at Camp David Carter told him that "we wanted final decisions at Camp David and that we were going to put forward our positions forcefully."[39]

For several reasons, the Egyptian objectives also favored a full partnership role for America. First, the general American objectives seemed to coincide more with Egypt's objectives than with Israel's; an American participation could therefore help Egypt's hand. Second, while Egypt held some leverage with Israel, the United States held much more; an American involvement would therefore be more conducive to Israeli compromise. Third, to the extent that a major Egyptian objective was to weaken the relationship between the United States and Israel, the more-detached role of mediator did not threaten as much loss of face in the event that the negotiations failed. These considerations were obvious to the Egyptians, who consistently called for the United States to become a "full partner" in the negotiations and to advance independent American positions. "Sadat has urged me," wrote President Carter, "to play an active role, to be a full partner."[40]

The Israeli preference for the American role was directly opposed to the American and Egyptian preferences; Israel actively sought to limit the role of the United States to that of mediation. The reasons for this should be apparent, since Israel based this preference on similar objective conditions but an opposed set of objectives. Limiting the U.S. to a mediator's role removed the potential leverage in favor of Egypt, so that the negotiations would be determined by the relative positions of Israel and Egypt. Israel held a decisive short-term advantage over Egypt in that it occupied Egyptian territories and maintained a far superior military force. Limiting the role of the United States to mediation would also limit the Egyptians' potential to reduce the American commitment to Israel. Consequently, the Israelis argued both publicly and privately that the United States should not advance its own proposals, but should simply try to bridge the gap between Egypt and Israel. And when the United States advanced its own positions the Israelis were quick to accuse American officials of taking sides and straying from the role of mediator. On the fourth day of the negotiations, for example, Begin "complained that the United States negotiators were all agreeing with the Egyptian demand that the Sinai settlements be removed, and that this was no way for a mediating team to act."[41]

In conclusion, America and Egypt preferred, for tactical reasons, that the United States be a full participant in the negotiations, while Israel preferred that the U.S. confine itself to a role of mediation. The reasons for this were clearly recognized by all parties. In the end, as argued earlier in this chapter, the American role was dictated by America's domestic priorities, which recommended an agreement for its own sake.

THE BARGAINING SITUATION

The isolated, open ended form of the Camp David negotiations was chosen by the United States, and supported by Egypt, on tactical grounds. It was thought that to conduct the negotiations in a more public setting would make compromise and departure from previous positions less likely, while making it easier for Israel's supporters in the United States to influence the negotiations.[42] Moreover, Israel was expected to be more forthcoming when confronted in an isolated environment by both the United States and Egypt. These considerations aside, an analysis of the objective characteristics of the form of the negotiations seems to show that, for several reasons, Israel retained the tactical edge.

First, both the isolated setting of the negotiations and the full involvement of the highest levels of government in them raised public expectations both internationally and in the United States. This put the Carter administration under greater pressure to avoid failure, which made it more inclined toward success for its own sake, but this diminished its leverage against Israel. The same could be said of Sadat, who in effect made his initiative (and its benefits) hostage to the success of the negotiations; his options, however, were extremely limited by Carter's own dilemma. Having increasingly moved toward an agreement for its own sake, Carter found himself having to threaten Sadat, not Begin, against abandoning the negotiations.[43]

In contrast with the United States and Egypt, Israel had less to fear from the format of the negotiations, despite its own dilemma. Israel wanted to prevent a long-term deterioration of its relations with America at almost any cost, which inhibited conflict even with a weak American president. Carter, however, would probably have been the primary victim of a failure, and Israel's supporters in Congress could probably have ensured that any deterioration in American-Israeli relations would have been of limited extent and duration. Israel held a decisive military superiority over combined Arab forces, so that short-term tension with the United States would not have affected its security. This is not to say that Israel was unconcerned; there is every indication to the contrary. What it does imply is that Israel held some real leverage which allowed it to test Carter's position to the limit; given its more limited options, the Carter administration would likely buckle under first.

A second effect of the intensive and isolated form of the negotiations was the implicit atmosphere of crisis. The issue at hand became the center of life for all actors. As Carter put it: "although we had been at Camp David only three days, the affairs of the rest of the world seemed to fade rapidly from our minds. My world became the negotiating rooms, the study where I poured over my notes and maps of the Middle East."[44]

In this atmosphere, the element of accelerated "diplomatic time" is relevant. As Pierre Allan describes it, "diplomatic time runs faster than normal time when more things occur than usual."[45] In crisis situations policy makers, focusing on specific issues and under pressure to make decisions, experience "diplomatic time" in that they must resolve internal dissonance to accommodate a necessary decision more quickly than usual. Thus, thirteen days at Camp David may have been sufficient time for the Egyptians to resolve the dissonance entailed in their acceptance of a bilateral treaty with Israel. Indeed, while Sadat began with the idea, apparently sincere, that full diplomatic relations with Israel were unthinkable, he quickly accommodated himself to the necessary change. Had it not been for the crisis atmosphere, the tendency might have been to avoid confronting the dissonance for as long as possible.

The open-ended nature of the negotiations also had a tactical impact on the talks. The Carter administration apparently saw a tactical advantage in open-ended talks, pledging that "we will . . . not put a time limit on how long we stay there."[46] The basic idea was that under such circumstances Egypt and Israel could not escape making decisions. The objective facts, however, indicate that this format was disadvantageous to the United States. For Israel and Egypt the talks concerned their most vital interests, over which few issues can take precedence. They could therefore afford to remain preoccupied with the talks for a long time. This is not the case for the United States, a superpower with major international responsibilities and with domestic issues that usually took precedence over the Middle East. Extended talks were bound to put more pressure on the United States than on Israel and Egypt. By day eleven Carter wrote:

> The pressures from Washington were building up. Attorney General Griffin Bell and FBI Director William Webster had come to Camp David the previous day with urgent business, and Harold Brown needed to see me today about matters relating to our

nation's armed forces. These kinds of visits were becoming more frequent and time-consuming.[47]

Aware of these pressures, the Egyptians and the Israelis could stall if need be, realizing that time diminished the value of American leverage. This may have contributed to some hasty decisions by the American negotiating team toward the end of the negotiations.

In conclusion, while the United States and Egypt believed that the intensive, isolated, open-ended form of the negotiations would increase their leverage against Israel, a closer examination indicates the contrary.

IV

*Bargaining Performance:
An Evaluation*

7

Bargaining Performance: A Case in Comparative Foreign Policy

*M*Y OBJECTIVE in this chapter is to evaluate the bargaining behavior of Egypt, Israel, and the United States, and the degree to which the outcome of the negotiations conformed to the specified preferences of each actor. In the process, I will introduce some general hypotheses about comparative foreign policy which relate states' systems of government and leaders' personalities to optimal bargaining behavior.

I have argued so far that, given the enduring objectives of Israel and Egypt, their inclination toward a bilateral agreement by the mid-1970s can be best explained by one primary variable: the change in the distribution of regional and international power. But such an explanation cannot by itself explain the particulars of the agreement; there are many possible variations. A central question therefore remains: what explains the specific terms of the Camp David accords? This is a particularly relevant question since some components of the agreements that are somewhat independent from bilateral relations have significant consequences for both Egypt and Israel.[1] This question, I argue, is best answered by examining the actors' bargaining behavior and positing it as a function of several domestic variables.

Specifically, two general arguments are made. The first is that contrary to intuitive expectations, decentralized systems of government are more conducive to optimal bargaining behavior than centralized ones. In this regard the centralized system of government of Egypt impaired Egypt's bargaining ability with Israel, and affected the outcome of the negotiations on some specific issues in a detrimental way for Egypt. The second is that, when personality traits are taken into account, Sadat's personality proved less conducive to optimal bargaining than Begin's or Carter's. Nonetheless, the outcome fell within the range expected by the (structurally) specified preferences of the three actors at Camp David.

Section A: Criteria for the Evaluation of Bargaining Performance

Four different methods stand out as candidates for evaluating bargaining performance:

(1) Comparing each actor's opening bargaining position with the final outcome;

(2) Comparing each actor's objectively derived preferences with the final outcome;

(3) Comparing the bargaining behavior of each actor with the recommended strategies of prescriptive bargaining theory;

(4) Comparing the actual outcome to the solution predicted by abstractive bargaining theory.

I will argue that the first is least useful, and that the other three are necessary but insufficient individually, though employed together in a complementary fashion, they can yield powerful explanations. Most of this chapter will focus on the third method, but the fourth will also be considered at the end of the chapter.

OPENING BARGAINING POSITIONS OF ACTORS

One typical and intuitive criterion of evaluation is the degree to which the outcome of negotiation deviates from the opening positions of the participants. By this standard the success or failure of the states at Camp David would involve a comparison of the provisions of the final accords with the opening positions of each actor.

By this criterion Camp David was a stunning victory for Israel's bargaining team and an embarrassing defeat for the Egyptian and American teams. As the Documentary Appendix shows, a comparison between the opening positions of the three actors with the Camp David accords reveals that the accords correspond most closely to the Israeli opening position on most central issues. Indeed, this opening position was advanced by the Israelis long before Camp David, as the first response to Sadat's speech at the Knesset. And when Begin proposed, at Ismailiyya,[2] that the inhabitants of the West Bank and Gaza be granted "autonomy," the Egyptians saw it as a step backward and an attempt by Israel to control the territory without having to incorporate the undesirable population. Israeli Defense Minister Ezer Weizman agreed with this assessment: Begin's "unshakable adherence to the perpetuation of Israeli rule over the West Bank and Gaza Strip led him into the autonomy plan. . . . Rather than viewing autonomy as the beginning of Arab self-rule, Begin saw it as the way to prevent Israeli withdrawal. . . . 'A plan of genius!' was the verdict of Deputy Prime Minister Yigael Yadin."[3] Sadat became "completely disillusioned with Begin's 'ridiculous' position,"[4] and "when Begin spelled out his self-rule proposal. . . . it was obvious that Egypt could not accept it."[5] Yet the final accords were not significantly different from the original Begin proposal.

Nevertheless, this criterion is not a good indicator of success or failure; assuming that the opening positions are sincerely held, it may indicate at best the extent to which perceptions change in order to conform to positions that are necessitated by other factors.[6] The fact is that opening positions can be deliberately exaggerated, unrealistic, or based on misperceptions. Judging the outcome on this basis is often misleading, and better criteria for evaluating bargaining behavior are necessary.

ACTORS' OBJECTIVELY DERIVED PREFERENCES

One alternative to the opening position criterion is the objectively derived preferences of the actors and their relative leverage in relation to each other, as articulated in the previous chapter. On the basis of this criterion one can assess the extent to which the final agreement corresponds to the actors' objectives in the negotiations. But while this is an essential component in the evaluation process, there are two problems that make this approach insufficient in itself.

First, assuming that the boundaries of the preferences can be fully drawn, the outcome remains largely *underdetermined*. That is, preferences may indicate the actor's minimum and maximum goals in the specific bargaining situation, but this may still leave a wide range of possibilities for the exact nature of the final agreement. The specifics of the final agreement cannot be predicted on the basis of preferences alone. One way out of this dilemma involves the introduction of speculative abstractive theory through the imposition of additional theoretical assumptions that are capable of explaining specific outcomes. This will be discussed briefly later in this chapter. Second, as seen in the previous chapter's discussion of Israeli preferences, boundaries can rarely be specified exactly. Indeed, a major reason why bargaining takes place is the uncertainty about the exact limits of the opponent's (and often one's own) position; actual bargaining forces the actors to specify these limits. The objectively derived preferences are therefore necessary to an evaluation but are also insufficient in themselves. Supplementary criteria are needed.

OPTIMAL AND ACTUAL BARGAINING BEHAVIOR

A third criterion of evaluation is not the outcome of bargaining but bargaining behavior itself. While it may be impossible to predict the precise outcome of different bargaining behaviors, it may be possible to establish the behavior most likely to maximize the chance of achieving the desired outcome. Given that, it becomes possible to assess the extent to which actual behavior deviates from this optimal behavior. Hypotheses may then be derived to explain the deviation from optimal bargaining. The articulation of such a method and its application in the Camp David accords is now in order.

Section B: Prescriptive Theory and Camp David Bargaining

DERIVING OPTIMAL STRATEGIES: PRESCRIPTIVE BARGAINING THEORY

Students of bargaining have long recognized several general strategies that are likely to maximize the bargainer's chances of attaining the desired outcome; these strategies seem to hold regardless of the actual situation or specific preferences of the actors. While there is a rich literature recommending numerous bargaining strategies and tactics,[7] most strategies derive from a single (but central) feature of bargaining situations.

The starting point is that bargaining takes place because of the actors' *uncertainty* about the minimally acceptable position of the opponent (the preference function), and about the opponent's "rationality" (the abstractive assumption). Bargaining occurs because, although both parties may be better off with an agreement than without, there is a space within the range of possible agreements where one actor's gain becomes another's loss—i.e., the game becomes zero-sum. If each actor seeks to maximize his own gains, and knows that the opponent is better off with an agreement than without, it can make sense to project a tougher stance than the actor actually holds. This strategy could backfire, of course, preventing an agreement when both parties would be better off with one, but unless the situation is one of immediate crisis, failure usually leads only to another session, and another chance.

When time becomes an important variable, however, its impact on bargaining may be asymmetrical in that one actor may need an agreement sooner than the other, giving the less-pressured actor a decided advantage in its ability to exaggerate its minimally acceptable position. For example, the structure of the bargaining situation discussed in the previous chapter gave a decided advantage to Israel, in that Israel seemed better able to project the ability to afford short-term failure. Aside from this general constraint of the bargaining situation, however, the strategy of exaggerating minimally acceptable positions seems optimal; one's real position should be hidden for as long as possible.

This central bargaining strategy has organizational implications: a hierarchical organization of the bargaining team, with most of the work relegated to subordinates, is optimal. This prescription serves to ensure that an error by one individual, especially in relation to projecting an exaggerated minimum, can be corrected by others. Since a mistake by a top leader could not be easily corrected, the leaders' involvement should come only at the end of the process. This is particularly true in situations of closed, intense bargaining, since the bargaining situation becomes one of both professional and social interaction, where errors resulting from the confusion of roles become likely. Anyone who has purchased an automobile from a dealership should be able to recognize this tension, and recognize the success of the dealer's hierarchal team in avoiding its negative impact.

Projecting uncertainty also entails that bargainers must avoid being overly predictable. This conclusion can be shown mathematically in games where a static equilibrium solution cannot be found.[8] The point of this strategy is to avoid giving the opponent any certainty, not only about your actual position, but even about your "rationality," although some consistency must be maintained to prevent a breakdown in bargaining.

On the basis of these general recommendations, deriving from the central bargaining feature of projecting uncertainty, I will evaluate the extent to which the actual bargaining behavior of the actors at Camp David corresponded to optimal strategies. Before I turn to this issue, however, it is useful to define the specific bargaining issues at Camp David, taking into account the specified preferences of the actors.

ISSUES OF BARGAINING

I have already argued that shifts in the distribution of power at the international and regional levels made a bilateral agreement between Israel and Egypt better than the status quo for both, other factors aside; and that Camp David accomplished at least the minimal goals of both. The questions that remain are: how much more than the minimum did each side accomplish? What accounts for this? What would the outcome have looked like if all actors had pursued optimal strategies? In order to consider these questions, one needs to define the issues that were open for bargaining.

We can rule out some issues. A comprehensive settlement of the Arab-Israeli conflict could not have been accomplished. The negotiations were by definition between Israel, Egypt, and the United States; for a comprehensive settlement Syria, the Palestinians, and the Jordanians would have had to have been included. Moreover, Israel needed some leverage for any future negotiations with these parties. Similarly, it is unrealistic to have expected that the Egyptians could have accepted anything but a full Israeli withdrawal from the Sinai. Given the peace treaty with Israel and the establishment of full diplomatic relations, Egypt would have had nothing to bargain with in the future, and would probably have been unable to sell the accords domestically.

There remained four basic zero-sum issues between Israel and Egypt. First, Israel needed, in the context of long term regional strategy, at least a peace treaty with Egypt and sought to normalize relations to the maximum; Egypt sought to minimize normalization so as to retain a degree of leverage over other issues. Second, Israel sought maximal demilitarization of the Sinai so as to make the Egyptian military option more remote; Egypt sought minimal demilitarization, so as to retain the military option. Third, Egypt sought maximal linkage between normalization and the resolution of the problem of the West Bank and Gaza; Israel sought the opposite. Fourth, Egypt sought some a priori general agreement on principles; i.e., the right of the Palestinians to self-determination and the Israeli intention to withdraw from occupied Arab territories.[9] For all of these issues there was both ambiguity about the bottom line and a zero-sum situation; in other words, these were truly bargaining issues. The task now turns to evaluating the actual performance of each actor at Camp David.

BARGAINING BEHAVIOR AT CAMP DAVID AND OPTIMAL STRATEGIES

Egyptian Behavior. The bargaining behavior of the Egyptian team deviated seriously from optimal strategy, although many members of the team were highly competent. Even before coming to Camp David many Egyptian diplomats complained that Sadat was revealing too much of his position unnecessarily. They argued, for example, that Sadat's unconditional trip to Jerusalem was a form of recognition of Israel that could have been better used as leverage; that his declaration of "no more war" at the Knesset was an unnecessary unilateral move; and that his expulsion of the Soviets was accomplished without first securing promises from the United States.[10] This pattern seemed to continue at Camp David.

To be sure, the Egyptian team arrived with a tough, professionally prepared opening position. But Sadat apparently revealed his real position as soon as the negotiations began. Sadat met with President Carter and handed him the opening Egyptian proposal. "As I read it," Carter wrote, "my heart sank; it was extremely harsh and filled with all the unacceptable Arab rhetoric." But almost as soon as Carter finished reading it, Sadat said that "he would like to offer me some modifications which could later be adopted as acceptable to him. He cautioned me not to reveal these to anyone because it would destroy his negotiating strength. . . . I saw for the first time that we might achieve substantial success. . . . [Sadat's] positions had a good chance of being acceptable to the Israelis."[11] Sadat apparently offered Carter a written document outlining Egypt's position, of which only one member of the Egyptian delegation was aware.[12]

By the fourth day Carter seemed willing to reveal much of Egypt's position to the Israelis. When Begin expressed frustration with the formal Egyptian position Carter states that he "tried to convince him that this was not the final Egyptian position, and that the Egyptians were willing to be accommodating within the limits previously explained to him. . . . I had been assured of this by Sadat." When Begin responded that "he did not see how honorable men could put forward one thing publicly and a different thing privately," Carter seemed to feel obliged to divulge more information.[13] "From then on," as William Quandt put it, "Begin adopted an unyielding position on settlements in the Sinai. . . . Unlike Sadat, he had no intention of telling Carter what his fallback position really was."[14] Sadat would occasionally threaten to walk out or reconsider his commitment,[15] but such threats rarely work. Once a bottom line is revealed it becomes, in effect, a new formal position and removes a great deal of the uncertainty. To be fair to Carter, Sadat may have given away his minimal position much earlier, during his visit to Egypt.[16]

The Egyptian team also lacked a meaningful hierarchy. It included competent lower-level officials who engaged in painstaking negotiating sessions, but their work was not sufficiently assimilated into Egypt's bargaining strategy. Both Israeli and American negotiators had easy access to President Sadat, and when reached he made his mind up without considering his aides' input. As Carter put it: "I never consulted Sadat's aides but always went directly to their leader."[17] Similarly, members of the Israeli negotiating team, especially Ezer Weizman and Moshe Dayan, went directly to Sadat, who was all too willing to make final decisions without consulting his aides.

Sadat's behavior was also predictable, especially in relation to President Carter. As his aide Butrus Ghali put it: "Sadat was a real amateur. He often moved hastily and predictably."[18] Carter proclaimed, as though he was burdened with a responsibility he could not meet, that Sadat "seemed to trust me too much."[19] This considerable deviation from optimal bargaining is particularly surprising since many of the Egyptians were competent bargainers. An explanation of Egyptian behavior will be considered later in this chapter.

Israeli Behavior. Israel's bargaining behavior at Camp David shows a close fit with optimal bargaining on all three points. The Israelis not only refrained from revealing their real position but also avoided introducing a formal position beyond the initial proposal at Ismailiyya. This tactic was applied to both Egypt and the United States. Recalled Carter: "The Israeli delegation was very reluctant to trust us with any revelation of its real ultimate desires or areas of possible compromise."[20] Moreover, the Israeli delegation seemed capable of exaggerating its position effectively, especially in the case of Israeli settlements in the Sinai. Coupled with the element of time, this gave Israel a decided advantage.

More time was expended over the issue of Israeli settlements in the Sinai than perhaps any other issue in the negotiations. The Israelis seemed unwilling to negotiate on this issue at all. Begin declared that "no Israeli leader could possibly advocate the dismantling of the Sinai settlements."[21] He maintained this stand until the very last day of the negotiations, when he was still "shouting words like 'ultimatum,' 'excessive demands,' and 'political suicide.' "[22]

Yet it is doubtful that this Israeli behavior was more than a tactic. The number of settlements and settlers in the Sinai was very small and there was no strong Israeli public opinion that insisted on maintaining them. Even Begin himself never appeared committed to them because, unlike the West Bank, the Sinai was not part of historic *Eretz Yisrael*. Indeed, on this issue Begin (while in the Israeli opposition) seemed more compromising than the Labor Party, which saw some security merit in maintaining parts of the Sinai. As Ezer Weizman pointed out, "Begin joined his fellow ministers in the cabinet of National Unity [in 1967] in agreeing to withdraw to the international boundaries in the Sinai and the Golan Heights."[23]

It is also clear from Israeli deliberations and from the observations of Camp David participants that the issue of the Sinai settlements was a tactic intended to prevent compromises on the West Bank and Gaza. Referring to Begin's insistence on this issue, Ezer Weizman concluded that "Begin was stating his most extreme position, with the intention of compromising later on."[24] He also told Carter that "keeping the Sinai settlements is important only as a precedent for the Golan and the West Bank."[25] Sadat apparently thought that the settlement issue was being used strictly to deflect American pressure from other issues. He told Carter that the "Israelis have urged us to exclude you Americans from any discussions. They want the West Bank, and are willing to give back the Sinai to me in exchange for the West Bank."[26] Carter confessed that "he shared the belief that the Israeli leader would do almost anything concerning the Sinai and other issues in order to protect Israel's presence in 'Judea and Samaria.'"[27]

It is also clear that when the issue of settlements was discussed by the Israeli government, several ministers proposed their employment as a bargaining tactic. Agriculture Minister Sharon, backed by Foreign Minister Dayan, "proposed that something be constructed in the Sinai without delay to create 'facts on the ground.' "[28] The prevailing view in the Israeli government supported Sharon on the grounds that: "if the Egyptians acquiesced to our 'colonization,' we would have pulled it off; if they refused to countenance the new 'settlements,' Israel could make a gesture and give them up in return for the right to retain the existing settlements."[29]

What the above indicates is that Israel used the issue of Sinai settlements as a successful bargaining chip, diverting attention (and thus American pressure) from more central issues. This tactic was particularly effective in that time seemed to work against the United States; the longer the negotiations lasted the more pressure the United States came under to end them successfully, and the more the American position softened toward an agreement for its own sake.

The Israeli team was also organized in a manner consistent with optimal bargaining. While Begin headed the team and made the final decisions, his aides played a central role. Moreover, his aides' opinions seemed to have some influence on him. When a proposal needed his approval it was usually taken up with him directly by his own aides, not by the Americans or the Egyptians. "It soon became obvious to all of us," wrote Carter, "that Dayan, Weizman, or Attorney General Barak could be convinced on an issue more quickly than the Prime Minister, and they were certainly more effective in changing Begin's mind than I was."[30]

Finally, the Israeli team pursued an effective mix of strategies that was not readily predictable. Begin was not generally inclined to compromise, and when he did the process was time and energy consuming; often the process was stalled over what the American team considered to be "semantics." Cyrus Vance wrote that Begin was "a formidable and at times, difficult negotiator . . . capable of endlessly adhering to the same positions while castigating the motives of his negotiating partners for failing to agree."[31] Carter "dreaded having to negotiate with Begin."[32] Under such circumstances, it was easier to get concessions from the Egyptian side; Carter concluded that "had both men [Begin and Sadat] been preoccupied with semantics or details, my job would have been much more difficult."[33] While part of this behavior by Begin could be attributed to what many students of his personality referred to as "stubbornness,"[34] there is little doubt that it was partly tactical. With no Arab country able to threaten Israel militarily, Begin "asked why Israel would have to even consider compromise."[35] Yet the Israeli team was not entirely uncompromising. Other members of the Israeli team seemed more forthcoming, and Begin himself seemed to know when to compromise. Vance concluded that Begin was "shrewd enough to know when he must adapt, and he can act with restraint when necessary."[36] In short, Israeli behavior seemed consistent with optimal bargaining.

American Behavior. The United States bargaining behavior was at best ambiguous; if anything the American team suffered from inconsistency and confusion about its role. While the Carter administration wanted to play the role of participant and assured Sadat of this intention, it also sought to assure Israel that it would be more of a broker. While Sadat "trusted" American "partnership," the role forced on the United States by its own priorities and the structure of the bargaining situation entailed the betrayal of Egypt's confidence and undermined the achievement of American objectives. Carter had agreed with Sadat that they would behave as "partners" and devise a plan that would lead to Israeli concessions, but he abandoned that agreement without informing Sadat.[37] And while Sadat seemed anxious to inform Carter, in confidence, of his real position, Carter sometimes revealed this position to the Israelis.

The organization of the American team was effectively hierarchal but less than optimal. To be sure, several American officials played a significant role in the negotiations, but Carter himself became too engaged in details to allow for a fallback position, even when the Israeli participants were low-ranking aides. This may have undermined the American position on several occasions.

Finally, American behavior was predictable on at least one significant issue: when Carter confronted Israeli steadfastness he almost always hurried to the Egyptian delegation, where he consistently found a responsive Sadat. Knowing that, the Israelis could afford to maintain their strategy.

Section C: Explaining Deviation from Optimal Behavior

It is intuitively appealing (and often correct) to ascribe deviation from optimal behavior to such things as misperception and incompetence. While such explanations are not without merit, they do not usually lend themselves to predictive generalization: one still needs to ask what makes misperceptions (or incompetence, etc.) important in some cases but not in others. For example it may be that, had the Carter administration not misperceived its leverage it may have behaved differently; had Sadat not misperceived Carter's weakness he might have used a different method. But questions remain as to when and why misperceptions occur and under what circumstances are they likely to have more impact on behavior.

If other causal variables could be specified, the entire issue of misperception might be sidestepped and a direct link between these variables and behavior could be made. Two such variables will be considered as they relate to optimal bargaining: the system of government and the leader's personality. What follows will attempt to consider them both in general terms and in terms of Camp David.

Before proceeding, however, it is useful to point out that the task here is to establish the relevance of these two variables to bargaining *given* the specified international constraints. That is to say, these measures address what are marginal differences in outcome. This is an important point, since in the process of isolating specific variables one takes the others for granted, and the impression may be given that these two variables have a dominant impact on behavior, which may not be the case.

SYSTEMS OF GOVERNMENT AND OPTIMAL BARGAINING BEHAVIOR

A good case can be made that, at least in relation to some important issues of foreign policy, centralized governments ("strong states") tend to serve the "national interest" better than decentralized governments ("weak states").[38] In situations of international bargaining, however, I will argue that the opposite is true.

Intuitively, one expects a straightforward hypothesis: the more decentralized a state is the larger the role of interest groups within the state, the less able the state is to defend the "national interest." The weakest state, the most decentralized, borders on Thomas Hobbes' state of nature; the "nation" hardly exists, so a national interest is almost impossible to define. But, as in Hobbes' defense of sovereign authority, there is a tension regarding the national interest that the state is supposed to serve. For Hobbes, sovereign authority is preferable to the state of nature because the quality of life of the community on the whole (and perhaps all individuals) is better under sovereign authority. Figuratively speaking, "national interest" is better served. Yet what guarantee do we have that the sovereign authority will not abuse its power; what enforcer do we have for the pact between the community and the sovereign authority? Are we not back in the state of nature at a different level? The point is that, if the concept of national interest is to encompass any concept of the constituents' welfare, the hypothesis linking national interest with centralized power will run into serious difficulties.

Yet, a concept of national interest that is independent from welfare is hollow; it also undermines the Hobbesian foundation of the modern concept of state. If having states is not better than their absence, why have them, why care about the "national interest?" The only way to save a meaningful concept of national interest along these lines is to transcend the Hobbesian explanation and to posit the concept in contingent international terms: in a world of other states, it is better for a given community of individuals to have a state than not; and it is better to have a comparatively strong state than a weak one. National interest can be defined as entailing the preservation of the state and the maximization of its power in relation to other states.

But this latest postulation of national interest, while it may be somewhat less problematic than the earlier one, does not resolve the tension: there is no guarantee that a strong government will serve the national interest; it may pursue policies that weaken the state in order to preserve itself in power. We are thus back to the same problem.

One way out of this dilemma is to avoid the concept of national interest. Instead, one can speak of "national preferences;" an agenda of ends that motivate a state's behavior. Those could be arrived at by deriving a state's international and domestic preferences, as attempted in chapter 6, and then, taking the system of government into consideration, developing an agenda of national priorities that may be called national preferences. This agenda can be taken as a given, without an assessment of values and without measurement of popular welfare. One could even call it "national interest," except that the latter term is often value-laden—understood to entail an "ought" whereas the purpose of deriving national preferences is strictly to explain and predict international relations.[39]

With this formulation my original question about the link between the system of government and optimal bargaining behavior boils down to the following: what system of government is most conducive to maximizing the chance of attaining the national agenda (preferences) in international bargaining? The quest thus pertains to the attainment of a given agenda rather than to the formation of an a priori preferable one; i.e., it does not deal with the question of which system of government is most conducive to the formation of a national agenda which is consistent with an a priori established "national interest."

SYSTEM OF GOVERNMENT AND THE BARGAINING HYPOTHESIS

Having defined my question in specific terms, I am now in a position to introduce the following hypothesis: decentralized systems of government are more conducive to optimal bargaining behavior than centralized ones.[40] Of the participants at Camp David, Egypt's system of government was least conducive to optimal bargaining, Israel's most conducive, and the American somewhere between the two.

A decentralized form of government minimizes the chance of misperception and leaders' mistakes. It also satisfies the requirements of prescriptive bargaining theory in several ways: it lends itself to a meaningful bargaining hierarchy, it permits the appearance of compromise even when the top leadership is steadfast, and it allows for better concealment of the bottom line position through proliferation of views. Figure 7.1 shows the possibilities of centralized and decentralized governments. The letters in the cells denote the payoffs to the horizontal actor, where $A > B + t > B > C$. In this matrix decentralized "dominates" centralized in that it performs better regardless of the opponent. The estimated payoff of two opposing nonoptimal strategies is, lacking additional information, equal to the payoff of opposing optimal strategies, with the possible exception of time. I have thus characterized the payoff in this category as $B + t$, since agreement may be reached sooner, thus enhancing the value of the agreement by some value t.

Time is significant in assessing bargaining behavior because a given

FIGURE 7.1. Governmental Centralization and Bargaining Payoffs

	Centralized	Decentralized
Centralized	B+t	C
Decentralized	A	B

agreement is generally worth less in the future than in the present.[41] Yet the optimal bargaining recommendations seem to entail a process of delay that sometimes appears to prevent agreement altogether. This time element should be taken into consideration, but it is a serious mistake to conclude that the benefits gained by optimal bargaining strategy are outweighed by the value of time, i.e., it is unlikely that $B+t > A$. Still, bargaining when at least one of the parties has a decentralized form of government generally consumes more time, though the value of this time is usually overestimated.

SYSTEM OF GOVERNMENT AND BARGAINING: THE CASE OF CAMP DAVID

The Egyptian Government. Egypt's system of government is highly centralized, with the president making all of the critical decisions. Other Egyptian officials owe their positions to the president, who may appoint and dismiss as he wishes. Moreover, with a government-controlled media and nominal elections, the president is not held accountable for his actions. As a result, the system allows for a considerable presidential role and potentially unchecked mistakes. At Camp David, therefore, the Egyptian system was not conducive to optimal bargaining behavior. Moreover, the system was conducive to what Irving L. Janis called "groupthink," which increased the chance of costly misperceptions.[42]

Competent Egyptian negotiators were often humiliated by Sadat, who overruled them casually in the presence of others; on critical issues Sadat preferred to negotiate without them.[43] The system did not allow for dissent since Egyptian officials lacked any independent power base. As former Egyptian Foreign Minister Ismail Fahmy put it: "if you disagreed with Sadat, you collapsed."[44]

While the leader's personality can make a noticeable difference in centralized governments, the system cannot protect itself against negative influences from this source. The system also imposes limitations on any leader that are difficult to overcome. For example, during one bargaining session Sadat attempted to use "Egyptian public opinion" as leverage, only to be told by Begin that "the people of Egypt could be easily manipulated by Sadat, and their beliefs and attitudes could be shaped by their leader." Begin went on to cite Sadat's ability to convince his people that the Soviets were their best friends, only to later cast them as their worst enemy.[45] While Sadat could rhetorically object to Begin's characterizations, his leverage was inevitably diminished.

Even similarly inclined leaders will behave differently in different systems of government. As Egyptian minister Butrus Ghali said: "both Carter and Sadat were amateurs [at bargaining], but whereas Carter was inclined to listen to his aides, Sadat was not."[46] Sadat simply did not have to. As I will show later, Begin's deference to other Israeli officials derived from the Israeli system of government, not from his personality.

The system of government also contributed to Sadat's overconfidence, which in turn increased the likelihood of misperceptions and policy mistakes.[47] Isolationism and lack of dissent were partly responsible for Sadat's feeling of invulnerability, so that when mistakes were committed his tendency was to rationalize them and chastise those who pointed them out; "he sustained the illusion of success by denying any one the right to challenge it."[48] The Egyptian system of government thus contributed to wishful thinking because, to use Robert Jervis' words, there was a "lack of incentive for accuracy."[49]

In conclusion, the centralized Egyptian system of government was not conducive to optimal bargaining behavior. Ironically, some Egyptian officials voiced their fear over this issue as far back as 1974, as Egypt was entering its first serious negotiations with Israel. In a commentary in the semi-official Egyptian newspaper *Al-Ahram* (translated in Appendix 7) Muhammad Haykal described the weakness of the Egyptian bargaining structure compared with Israel's and made a veiled call for participation in the negotiations by a wide spectrum of Egyptians. But the mere suggestion of decentralization was sufficiently threatening to Sadat that Haykal was dismissed from his positions as editor of the newspaper and advisor to the president and later jailed.

The Israeli Government. The Israeli pluralist-parliamentary system of government was more conducive to optimal bargaining. To be sure, the government was largely controlled by the Likud Party, which was dominated by Begin. But although Begin had a substantial hand in the ranking of individuals within the party (and, thus, their chances of being elected to the Knesset), several members of his team had independent standing and could run independently. Indeed, Foreign Minister Dayan was not a member of Likud, and another member, Ezer Weizman, later broke from Likud and was elected to the Knesset independently. Begin thus could not ignore at least some of his key aides, especially given his slim plurality in the Knesset.

Nor was Begin's deference to his aides' opinions due to his personality. If anything Begin was inclined to rule like a dictator and did not tolerate dissent; Ben-Gurion had once remarked that Begin would rule the way Hitler did.[50] As one biography notes: "it is Begin's voice that has consistently predominated. . . . not consensus among members of his government;" he was "leader of party" but not "party man."[51]

The involvement of the entire Israeli "lineup" made the team effective, especially given Begin's steadfastness and difficult bargaining style, which made him an effective final arbiter. Even if Begin felt pressured to make decisions he had several fallback positions. He could claim that he needed the approval of the full Israeli government, the Knesset, or Israeli public opinion. Indeed, on several occasions, Begin used these arguments to avoid making unwanted concessions.

The participation of top officials with independent political stature in the Israeli bargaining team was also conducive to the impression of a conciliatory attitude, even when no concessions were forthcoming. Positions hinted at by Dayan or Weizman gave Egyptian and American negotiators hope and incentive to make more concessions and to maintain the bargaining process, even if these concessions were later overruled by Begin. In short, the Israeli system of government improved the bargaining posture of the Israeli team.

The American Government. The American system of government proved somewhat less effective than the Israeli system. Although power is decentralized in the United States, the President still holds substantial power, especially in foreign affairs. He does have the fallback of congressional approval and deference to public opinion, but within the cabinet his authority is nearly absolute. All members of the cabinet and the national security staff owe their positions to him, and most have little independent political clout. The President's personality and inclinations can therefore greatly influence the team's performance; though some presidents allocate much responsibility to their staff, this need not be so. Carter's tendency to involve himself in the minutest details showed itself at Camp David. While he often listened to the advice of his aides, his decisions were final. And of course a president has a tendency to select those who agree with him, and those whom he selects have the tendency to tell him what he likes to hear.

Nonetheless, the diffused nature of the American political system, with an independent media and public opinion that must be taken into account, gives every official a degree of independence: he can weaken the president merely by resigning. Unlike the situation in Egypt, an official is not "finished" if he disagrees or resigns. Indeed, there were some serious differences of opinion between the Department of State and the National Security staff, although Carter was more inclined toward State Department positions.

In conclusion, the degree of governmental centralization seems to partly account for deviation from optimal bargaining; the Israeli structure, the most decentralized of the three at Camp David, is most conducive to optimal bargaining, the American system less so, and the highly centralized Egyptian system was least conducive to optimal bargaining.

Leaders' Personalities and Bargaining Behavior

The more centralized a government is, the larger the role of the leader in shaping policy, though leaders' personalities play some role in any system. What personality types are most conducive to optimal bargaining? How did Carter, Begin, and Sadat perform at Camp David?

The first task is to identify relevant personality characteristics. Students of the role of personality in politics have identified more than a dozen useful characteristics,[52] most of which are not directly related to bargaining. To avoid ad hoc analysis these characteristics should be derived from some general hypotheses about bargaining. I shall therefore start with the derivation of three characteristics that are relevant to the optimal bargaining prescriptions and that have support in the literature on personalities: the ability to separate roles, realism, and level of focus.[53]

PERSONALITY TRAITS AND OPTIMAL BARGAINING

Realism. Wishful thinking can influence bargaining. As Robert Jervis put it: "A statesman would like his enemies to be weak—or better yet, for them not to be his enemies at all—but if he believes this and it is not true, he will pay a high price."[54]

Wishful thinking could also lead to overestimation of one's capabilities, underestimation of the opponent, an overly trusting strategy, or the interpretation of failure as success. (If you perceive your opponent as not reciprocating your optimistic gestures, you may believe you have succeeded when in fact you have not.)

Separation of Roles. Robert Price has made a relevant distinction between leaders in various societies on the basis of the capacity to separate roles.[55] In experimental social psychology, Mark Snyder makes a relevant distinction between people who have high and low "self-monitoring," based on their ability to alter their self-presentation to accommodate different situations.[56] Low self-monitors are more readily predictable than high self-monitors, and, at least in this sense, they make better bargainers. But this distinction is relevant to situations of intense bargaining for several other reasons.

Bargaining situations are inherently both social and professional situations. A leader whose behavior is dominated by the social dimension will be less effective, hence the need to insulate the top decision maker from the initial process. Even a good bargainer may make mistakes to protect his social integrity. Further, the relations within a bargaining team are both those of the domestic social order and those of a professional team. This latter tension often accounts for what Irving Janis called "groupthink." Though Janis did not put it this way, his recommendations for minimizing groupthink seem designed for the better separation of roles.[57] Some leaders can separate these roles better than can others; the more successfully they can do so, the more successful their bargaining should be.

Level of Focus. Some leaders tend to focus on the highest levels of analysis, on broad relations and general categories (the forest), ignoring the details (the trees) within. Others tend to focus on details without being fully aware of the broader situation. Still others seem able to move comfortably from one level to the next as the situation demands. A similar distinction exists in social psychology between people who are "broad-categorizers" and those who are "narrows." Thomas Pettigrew found that: "Broad categorizers are superior on tasks that benefit from a more integrated, holistic strategy; narrows are superior when detailed or analytic processing is required."[58] He also found that narrows are more susceptible to cognitive dissonance.

These categories have particular relevance for bargaining situations. A leader with a lower level of focus is likely to perform well once structural constraints have been established, while a leader with a higher focus is likely to do well in setting up the structural constraints, but poorly in over-the-table bargaining. A leader who can focus at several levels may perform well in both tasks.

SADAT, BEGIN, AND CARTER: CHARACTERISTICS AND PERFORMANCE

Anwar Sadat. That Sadat was excessively inclined toward wishful thinking has been observed by most of those who knew him and studied his personality. Brzezinski wrote that Sadat "had the tendency to let himself be carried away by his own words, and I noted in my journal that 'my worry is that Sadat does not seem to differentiate clearly between fact and fiction.' "[59] Former Egyptian Foreign Minister Ibrahim Kamel observed that "Sadat lived in a world of fiction,"[60] and former chief of staff Saad el-Din Shazly noted that Sadat was usually overconfident in his assessment of such issues as the ceasefire, the peace talks, and the Egyptian initiative in the Sinai. During the final days of the 1973 war, "Sadat kept rejecting a ceasefire initially because he led himself to believe we were victors and could command next steps."[61] Two of his biographers observed that Sadat "chose to ignore diplomatic consequences [of his actions], to pretend before his people and perhaps even to himself, that it never really happened." His response to Arab outcry was "a mixture of wishful thinking and weird arithmetic . . . that most of the Arab world supported him."[62]

In his dealings with foreign leaders Sadat often failed to distinguish between personal (social) and state (professional) relations. He developed close personal relations with Henry Kissinger and was accused by many of his domestic critics of relying too much on Kissinger's "goodwill."[63] His personal relation with Carter also seemed to obscure relevant professional considerations. "Sadat seemed to trust me too much," remarked Carter, as though he was burdened with a responsibility that he could not meet; for while Carter truly liked Sadat and even agreed with his political objectives, Carter's own professional constraints as president inclined him to behave independently.[64] Cyrus Vance remarked that "above all, [Sadat] valued loyalty and friendship. Once trust was gained, he would stand with you unfailingly."[65] At the same time, aware of the dominance of social-cultural traits in Sadat's behavior, Carter used them to gain concessions from Sadat. Remarked Brzezinski: "He showed sensitivity to Sadat's pride, he appealed for his magnanimity, at no point did he make Sadat feel inferior or dependent, and yet he pressed steadily for more and more significant concessions."[66]

This inability to separate roles was particularly striking and detrimental to Egyptian bargaining. At the outset of the conference, in addition to Egypt's formal opening position Sadat offered Carter a written document describing Egypt's bottom-line positions. This document was prepared with the knowledge of only one Egyptian advisor, Usama al-Baz, who advised Sadat against revealing it to Carter. But Sadat apparently assumed that a personally frank relationship with

Carter was more beneficial than caution, oblivious to the professional pressures on Carter as president.

Sadat's level of focus was clearly high ("forest") level. Butrus Ghali said that: "Sadat had no interest in detail whatsoever."[67] Ibrahim Kamel concluded that: "Sadat was too lazy to deal with detail. He never read reports, and never displayed interest."[68] Sadat's behavior at Camp David clearly reflected this. He even considered it small-minded to be concerned with details, and "accused" Begin of being so inclined.[69]

This tendency served Sadat well in grasping overall relationships and relative leverage with the United States and Israel. His ability to perceive the potential competition between Israel and Egypt for alliance with the United States enabled him to maneuver toward a favorable bargaining situation. But even here, before the actual bargaining, Sadat's lack of attention to detail may have been partly responsible for his apparent failure to recognize that American domestic politics and the Middle East's ranking in American priorities would incline the American government toward an agreement for its own sake, negating much of Sadat's leverage.

In summary, Sadat's personality was not conducive to optimal bargaining behavior. A harsh and exaggerated, but nonetheless telling, conclusion about Sadat's personality is offered by Hirst and Beeson:

> . . . . [he] fit the definition of 'fahlawi':. . . . pain avoidance and pleasure seeking. . . . few dislike him, few trust him. . . . concept of manhood quixotic-idyllic and chivalric. . . . search for quickest means to end. . . . avoidance of discomfort. . . . important to complete task in way which enhances image. . . . behavior patterns of this type of personality force us to hide results, failure etc., in order to preserve appearances and save face. . . . one distinctive trait is propensity for sudden excitement, violent audacity, underestimating differences and excessive desire for self-affirmation and penchant for making a show of being able to manage affairs.[70]

Menachem Begin. Begin did not display the optimism and trust of the opponent that are entailed in wishful thinking. He was not inclined to rely on verbal agreements or gestures by other leaders, and appeared to examine the consequences of his actions very carefully. Carter wrote: "He reminded Sadat of the transient nature of our leadership but the permanent nature of the consequences of our decisions. He tried to convince Sadat that we had to be very careful not to make a mistake through undue haste."[71]

Begin was also capable of separating roles, clearly distinguishing between social and professional situations. Vance noted that while Begin was "a formidable and, at times, difficult negotiator, . . . When formal negotiations ceased, he could become charming and relaxed, speaking lovingly of his family and grandchildren."[72] Begin was always conscious that his role as prime minister did not put him on par with Presidents Carter and Sadat, who by protocol were heads of state. Begin was always properly attired in their presence, and went to their quarters for discussions.

Begin had a potentially serious conflict of roles which proved insignificant at Camp David. This conflict involved Begin's roles as both the leader of an ideological movement and prime minister of a nation-state. Although this tension was stronger for Begin than for other Israeli leaders, it derives from the very nature of Israel. This tension became clear in discussions by members of the Israeli government. Ezer Weizman recalls that chief of staff Motta Gur remarked: "Peace without Zionism is something I do not want. Zionism without peace? That's feasible. Sadat wants peace, but on his own terms and we can't accept those terms."[73] This tension, however, only minimized Israeli concessions and certainly did not prevent an agreement.

It is widely recognized that Begin was exceptionally inclined toward detail and semantics, and seems to fit the characteristics of someone with low-level ("tree") focus. Yet Begin was not unaware of the "forest," and he shifted to that level when necessary. Perhaps he can best be classified as one with variable focus. While some of this preoccupation with detail at Camp David was tactical, prompting Carter to conclude that Begin "was trying to postpone" decisions, there can be little doubt that this was part of Begin's personality.[74]

Such attention to detail can help bargainers once general parameters have been set. Thus, in over-the-table bargaining this behavior helped the Israelis, especially since in the end the letter of the agreement dominated whatever spirit may have prevailed during the negotiations. It could hurt a bargainer who loses sight of the larger picture, but Begin clearly kept the greater strategic picture in mind and was able to shift focus when necessary. For example, he was obviously aware of the implications of the negotiations for American-Israeli relations and, as Carter noted, was more interested in preserving Israel's relationship with the United States than in reaching an agreement with Egypt.[75]

Begin was also aware of the domestic constraints which made Carter's first priority at Camp David the achievement of success for its own sake. Thus, when Carter seemed to threaten Begin, the Prime Minister felt sufficiently confident to "counterthreaten" the President.[76] And when Israeli officials were concerned that Israel might be cornered at Camp David, Begin seemed to have the vision to see the Israeli advantage. Carter wrote that when he told Begin that "Sadat had expressed a concern about Begin's preoccupation with details at the expense of major issues," Begin replied that he could handle both. "I believed him," Carter continued, "and hoped he would be inclined to prove it."[77] In the end whatever obsession with detail that Begin had did not seem to prevent an agreement acceptable to Israel, and Begin's variable focus seemed to help his bargaining stance. Begin's personality was conducive to optimal bargaining strategy.

Jimmy Carter. Carter tended to be over-optimistic, inclined to trust the opponent, and usually predictable in persisting in a cooperative strategy—all of which are traits of wishful thinking. He also had some difficulty (though less than Sadat) in separating roles, and he was decidedly a man of low-level focus, making him a successful bargainer tactically, but a poor one strategically.[78]

In terms of role separation, Carter's personal values and his "chivalry," as Brzezinski put it, often dominated his professional role. In one case, when Brzezinski suggested wiretapping the Israeli and Egyptian quarters, Carter declined. Ironically, both the Egyptian and the Israeli delegations apparently assumed that their quarters were not secure, and typically conferred outside.[79] Carter also changed his mind, apparently on moral grounds, following an agreement with Sadat to advance a settlement plan that was seen as serving both American and Egyptian interests.[80] In the heat of bargaining Carter found it difficult to protect information confided to him by Sadat, as he felt it necessary to reassure Begin about the prospects for success of the negotiations. Carter was also predictable in his cooperative strategy; this was not limited to Camp David but seemed to color his entire foreign policy, and may have derived from his difficulty in separating roles. Carter's personal beliefs about moral and social norms were applied to international politics, even when inappropriate.

There is also a near consensus that Carter was interested in smaller details, and that he possessed great talent at comprehending the most intricate relations at that level. This gave Carter a strong edge in tactical bargaining, and he impressed many of his own aides. Whatever tactical weakness the American team had did not derive from this aspect of Carter's behavior but from the organization of the team. Had Carter not been head of the negotiating team but a negotiator his personal effectiveness would have been more visible.

Yet Carter lacked the capacity to shift his focus when necessary. This tendency manifested itself in his general lack of understanding of Washington politics, his apparent failure to perceive the prevailing norms of international relations (indicated by his surprise and "disappointment" at the Soviet invasion of Afghanistan), and his inability to correctly perceive his own dependence on domestic politics as he entered negotiations at Camp David. As a result, he lacked the ability to make full use of his potential strategic advantage.

EVALUATION

I have argued that Israeli bargaining behavior at Camp David corresponded more closely to optimal bargaining than did that of Egypt or the United States, and that this deviation seems to correspond well to differences in the system of government and in the personalities of the leaders. So far there has been no attempt to derive the effect of this deviation on the outcome. Indeed, what could have one expected as an outcome if all actors followed optimal bargaining strategy? One member of the Egyptian team suggested that the outcome could not have been substantially different in any case.[81] How, then, does one assess the possibilities?

The answer cannot be derived from prescriptive bargaining theory, which can state only that prescribed strategies will maximize the chance of attaining one's preferences. On that basis one can state only that Egypt (or Israel) may or not have been able to achieve more; the only way to find out is to behave optimally as each actor must test the limits of the opponent's position to the maximum.

Assessment of Outcome. The difficulty in assessing possible outcomes given optimal bargaining behavior derives from two sources, the actors' uncertainty about the positions of their opponents and the underdetermination of the model even with such information. Prescriptive bargaining theory cannot specify the exact outcome, but it does recommend that each actor test the limits of the opponent. At Camp David Israel tested the limits of the Egyptian position on relevant issues, while the Egyptians did not similarly press Israel.[82] In the end the outcome was closer to Israeli preferences than to Egypt's on all four of the bargaining issues that were defined elsewhere.[83]

Whether or not the outcome could have been different given optimal Egyptian behavior remains unclear. Butrus Ghali concluded that the outcome could not have been substantially different, and that the real Egyptian position couldn't be hidden through good tactics because: "objectively speaking, our relative weakness was out there for the whole world to see."[84] Sadat apparently shared this view. Moreover, since Sadat felt that "details" mattered little, once he concluded that an overall settlement was not possible he paid less attention to such issues as settlements and linkage.

But some "detail" does matter. According to Harold Saunders, who was dispatched to the Middle East following the accords to secure the approval of Arab states, several states would have accepted the agreements if they contained two specific changes: a freeze on Israeli settlements and recognition of the right of the Palestinians to self-determination. Whether or not Saunders' impressions were justified, his observations demonstrate the potential significance of these issues.[85]

An examination of the bargaining over these three issues is telling. Egypt demonstrated a virtual lack of interest in these issues, and certainly did not press the Israelis to test the limits of their position. This may have been due partly to Sadat's operating at a much high level of abstraction, but there seem to be other reasons. When asked about Egypt's apparent lack of attention to these issues, Butrus Ghali replied that: "we left these issues to the Americans to handle. We and the Americans had full agreement over them, and we simply trusted them to use their leverage to negotiate over them."[86]

Yet the Americans, who already faced a dilemma over their roles of mediator and partner (and the tension this dilemma brought between success of any sort and success for American objectives) faced another problem besides. While the U.S. positions which coincided with Egypt's were independently based on American preferences, the United States often appeared to be taking sides. Egypt's lack of involvement in negotiating some of the issues threatened to make Carter appear "more Arab than the Arabs," according to Saunders. America could not maintain such positions for long.

One issue where a different management of 'detail' may have made a difference in the outcome is the controversial agreement on the freezing of Jewish settlements on the West Bank and Gaza. The Egyptian delegation was largely absent from the negotiations over this issue, and discussions were generally conducted by the Israeli and American delegations. While there remains some ambiguity about what took place, accounts by members of the Israeli and American delegations and research by William Quandt make several facts clear.

First, most of the negotiations over this issue were conducted on the twelfth day, one day before the conclusion of the negotiations, after agreement had been reached on all other issues.

Second, both sides had agreed that the issue should not be addressed in the text of the accords, but in a public letter from Begin to Carter. The text was to read: ". . . . After the signing of the framework and during the negotiations, no new Israeli settlements will be established in this area. The issue of future Israeli settlements will be decided and agreed among the negotiating parties."[87]

Third, there is no doubt that the American delegation specifically understood this to refer to the negotiations for autonomy in the West Bank and Gaza and so stated during that session; there is also little doubt that the Israelis understood this to be the case.

Fourth, the Israelis apparently thought that the talks on autonomy would last two to three months, but that they could be extended.

Fifth, the Americans had the distinct impression that the Israelis fully approved the American interpretation of the agreement, while some Israeli members of the delegation understood that Begin's approval was only tentative, and that he was to give his final answer the next day. Quandt concluded that: "it seems most likely that on Saturday night Begin did not give Carter a firm agreement to a freeze on settlements for the duration of the autonomy negotiations. But he may have wanted to leave the president with the impression that such an agreement had almost been reached."[88]

Sixth, the letter handed to Carter by Begin the next day, after agreement had been reached on the text of the accords, stated that the freeze on settlement building applied to the *three months* envisaged for the negotiation of an Egyptian-Israeli peace treaty.

On Sunday, September 17, 1978, the final day of the negotiations, an "exhausted" American delegation suddenly discovered the discrepancy over the settlement issue.[89] As Quandt put it: "by then, they were so close to concluding the negotiations that they chose to overlook this 'misunderstanding.' It was a costly mistake."[90] Asked why the American delegation, which had clearly perceived the issue's significance, did not press it further, Harold Saunders replied: "You cannot imagine how difficult, how agonizing, it was to deal with Begin. It was so time and energy consuming. Carter dreaded having to deal with him. And we were all so exhausted, yet so thrilled that we finally had an agreement."[91]

From this it would appear that the Israeli use of this issue as a tactic (mentioned above) and the American desire for diplomatic success were responsible for the failure to press the central issue of settlements further. Yet while such pressure may have improved the chance of a favorable agreement for the American side, the fact remains that our analysis cannot state that this would have been likely. Further theoretical hypotheses are required to measure the likelihood of competing possible outcomes. For the purpose of accomplishing the latter task, I will now discuss abstractive bargaining theory.

Section E: Abstractive Bargaining Theory: Speculative Outcomes

As stated earlier, bargaining takes place because of uncertainty about two factors: the opponent's (and, perhaps, one's own) position, and the opponent's "rationality." Optimal bargaining strategy is designed in terms of the first factor, to test the limits of the opponent's position. For example, while Israeli preferences could be derived on "objective" grounds, i.e., on the basis of the behavior of states in general and the historical pattern of Israeli behavior in particular, one is nonetheless faced with the possibility that Begin was so committed to his ideology that he was willing to take more risks on security in order to attain it. Yet Begin's priorities may have been unique. For while general theoretical hypotheses may explain a phenomenon well in the aggregate, there is always the exceptional case; and while a theorist must always bet on the verified general hypothesis over the unique, the decision maker in a specific case may not be able to afford even the smallest risk. Thus while it is often the case that in the interest of maintaining maximum uncertainty a negotiator attempts to project his preferences as unique, the opponent cannot always tell the difference between the ploy and the serious, and may not be willing to take risks. Begin in particular was so apt at this game that he often kept his real position unknown to some of his closest aides.

Even if reasonable certainty about the actors' preferences could be established, however, a specific outcome cannot be predicted without the imposition of additional assumptions about the behavior of the actors. Even traditional game theory lacks determinate solutions for bargaining-like non-zero sum games. John Harsanyi has argued that game theory's inability to provide determinate solutions make it less useful for applications in the social sciences.[92] Thus several formal theorists have attempted to formulate abstractive theories for the purpose of providing determinate solutions to formal games.

But the empirical criteria for establishing abstractive theories as positive are either difficult to apply or in principle cannot be applied. The criterion for the acceptability of the theory is thus limited to establishing the reasonability of the additional axioms.[93] But this task is sometimes difficult because we are often confronted with alternative assumptions that appear equally reasonable.

IMPOSED AXIOMS OF RATIONALITY

Most of the assumptions imposed by mathematical theorists for the purpose of deriving determinate solutions to given games involve the expectation of "rational" behavior. And though these assumptions are stated mathematically, they can nonetheless be stated in ordinary language thereby becoming more accessible to the test of reasonableness.[94]

One pertinent assumption about rationality in complex bargaining games, for example, pertains to whether a "rational" player tries to maximize his gains (liberal rationality) or to minimize his losses (conservative rationality). The outcome is decidedly different depending on what assumption one chooses, yet the choice seems independent of any objective criterion. The matter seems strictly one of individual taste or inclination.

Yet if we employ either assumption in our model, those actors who adopt the other would be judged by the model to be "irrational." This should make it clear that the distinction is merely formal and cannot in itself be a basis for judging the desirability of the actor's approach. For example, it may be argued that Sadat adopted liberal rationality in risking a great deal in case of failure, but maximizing his chance in case of the success in the competition with Israel for alliance with the United States. His failure to attain his objective would not in itself be a reason to fault his approach, or to consider him "irrational."

It should be evident so far that it is difficult to usefully employ abstractive bargaining theory in real-world situations of political bargaining. Even if one chooses among the alternative assumptions, it remains extremely difficult to translate the real preference function and threat function of the actors into a mathematical form that lends itself to identifying a specific solution. Nonetheless, it may be useful to summarize Harsanyi's interpretations of a solution to the two-person general cooperative game with binding threats. The solution predicts that each player i will achieve a higher final payoff:

1. The greater his own willingness, and the less his opponent's, to risk a conflict in order to obtain better terms, as shown by the two player's cardinal utility functions....

2. The easier it is to transfer utility from the other player to player i, and the harder it is to transfer it the other way around. . . .

3. The greater the damage that player i could cause to his opponent in a conflict situation at a given cost to himself and the lesser damage that the opponent could cause to player i at a given cost to himself.[95]

It should be apparent that the last two conditions pertain to the actors' objective positions, while the first one pertains to their chosen strategies. It is thus useful to assess Israeli and Egyptian behavior in relation to the first condition.

While the overall strategic behavior of Egypt conformed to this strategy, the tactical behavior of Egypt on specific issues did not. Egypt seemed willing to risk a great deal in initiating the Camp David process in order to obtain its long-term regional objectives, but over such issues as Israeli settlements on the West Bank, Palestinian self-determination, and firm linkage between normalization of relations with Israel and an agreement on Palestinian autonomy, the Egyptians did not project any willingness to risk failure. The Israelis, on the other hand, were capable of projecting their willingness to risk failure for these issues. The model predicts that had the Egyptians behaved like the Israelis over these issues they would have been able to obtain more. How much more, and whether it would have been worth the effort, can be assessed only by less-formal methods. Two conclusions can be drawn with respect to these questions.

The first is that the failure to ensure firmer links between the two Camp David agreements is due largely to Egypt's ineffective bargaining, which resulted from a system of government that does not lend itself to optimal bargaining. The second is that the failure to attain a more specific agreement on settlement building in the West Bank and Gaza is due largely to Israel's superior bargaining, which, in this case, can be credited to the superior bargaining personality of Prime Minister Begin, especially in comparison to the personalities of Presidents Carter and Sadat. These conclusions require further elaboration.

It is important to note here that at the heart of the discrepancy over these two issues is the *absence of incentive* for Israel to move toward an eventual agreement on the West Bank and Gaza—not the final shape of a settlement over the occupied territories; Israel could not have been expected to acquiesce in the withdrawal from the West Bank and Gaza at Camp David even if Israeli leaders held no ideological commitment to these territories, since the Camp David agreements did not bind the most important parties for these issues, the Palestinians and Jordan. No one, for example, argued that the Camp David Accords could stipulate a final agreement over the Golan Heights in the absence of Syria.

Still, one could wonder: given Begin's strong ideological commitment to the West Bank, which few scholars doubt, would he have accepted a freeze on settlement building for the duration of the autonomy talks? Is it reasonable to expect that, given better Egyptian bargaining, Begin would have acquiesced in a firmer linkage between improved Israeli-Egyptian relations and progress on Palestinian autonomy? In essence, I have answered both questions affirmatively. But the grounds for my answers lay at the heart of the methodology employed in this work.

I have not discounted the relevance of individual-level variables, such as Begin's personal inclinations to international relations. What I have argued is that, since other variables also count, the only way to assess the relative weight of each is by comparing them in the context of a research program which employs them consistently.[96] These variables cannot be evaluated simply in isolation. Consequently, I have proposed a research program that evaluates the relevance of several variables at different levels of analysis. My conclusion is thus drawn on the basis of this overall assessment. An alternative conclusion would have to similarly account for the relative weight of relevant variables, before it could be comparatively assessed.

Still, is it intuitively unacceptable to have expected some compromises by Begin over these issues, given his strong ideological beliefs? International relations, especially in the Middle East, are rich with examples of leaders who have modified ideological positions to accommodate international and domestic constraints, and Begin himself, although always coveting the West Bank ideologically, was not an advocate, like some of his colleagues in the early 1960s, of Israeli military action to occupy the West Bank. As I have argued in this work, on the basis of important international and domestic variables, failure to achieve an agreement with Egypt would have been extremely costly to Begin, both internationally and domestically, regardless of the lack of concern that he tried to project.

In the end, however, acceptable methodologies and prescribed strategies are based on empirical corroboration *in the aggregate*. There are always exceptions. Begin could have been this exception, no doubt, although I almost always bet on the general. The key point is that the Egyptians could not really know what Begin's bottom line was unless they had persued optimal bargaining strategies that forced choices. Begin, the seasoned political bargainer, was fond of rhetorically asking his Israeli critics, why he should compromise when this was unnecessary!

APPENDIX 7

AN EGYPTIAN PERCEPTION OF ISRAEL'S BARGAINING STRATEGY

THE FOLLOWING is a translation by the author of a remarkable commentary written by Egypt's leading journalist and former presidential advisor, Muhammad Hasanein Haykal, published on January 18, 1974 in Egypt's semi-official newspaper *al-Ahram*. The article clearly envisions an upcoming period of long-term negotiations with Israel, continuing beyond the disengagement of forces. It emphasizes the importance of bargaining strategy in these negotiations and attempts to articulate several fundamental bargaining principles, most of which were clearly not adhered to by Egypt's negotiators at Camp David. It attempts, in addition, to warn against reading too much into Israel's statements of its bargaining position on the grounds that Israel is a good bargainer and would naturally exaggerate its minimal requirements. It argues that a decentralized system of government is more conducive to optimal bargaining than a centralized one; as such, both Israel and the United States have a bargaining advantage over Egypt. It seems to voice a veiled call for a public dialogue in Egypt about the upcoming negotiations. Within days of publishing this commentary, Haykal was dismissed from his position by presidential order.

Israel's Bargaining Method?

It is not apparent yet what the real value will be for the outcome of the ongoing intensive negotiations over what has been termed "the disengagement of the fighting forces on the Suez front." Until the results and their meaning become clear, I propose a brief review of the Israeli bargaining method, having observed it this week in full gear, as Israel negotiated with—perhaps collaborated with—Dr. Henry Kissinger in a fashion that deserves a careful study.

Bargaining has always been a diplomatic art, but it has recently been elevated to a near science; several great universities that are concerned with the study of politics have assigned a full professorial chair to this subject.

We have benefited a great deal in the past from dealing with the Israeli fighting method; indeed we have learned how to confront it. Similarly, it may also be useful to study the Israeli bargaining method, for we may be able to learn how to confront that as well.

Lest there be any misunderstanding, let me specify that what I speak of today is not negotiations with Israel but the method of Israeli bargaining, using the examples of the past week as a sample for analysis. My concern, therefore, is simply the Israeli bargaining method in the context of the extensive Israeli diplomatic operations following the 1973 war.

Israel realized that given the outcome of the October war, a stage of bargaining was forthcoming. Even if she intended to return to war once more, she would have to confront a stage of negotiations first. Even if Israel intended to freeze the situation at a given point, she would not be able to reach that point without a stage of negotiations. Israel thus began preparing the stage in ways conducive to the type of negotiations that she desired.

The first question that Israel asked herself was: "With whom shall we negotiate. . . . regardless of the objective?" An answer was found, but in order to get at it, it is useful to consider the steps that Israel undertook in preparation:

1. To start with, we find that the ceasefire was achieved by means of a UN resolution that was co-sponsored by both superpowers—the United States and the Soviet Union—and was passed in the Security Council unanimously with the exception of Chinese abstention. In other words, the resolution was an international one.

2. When talks proceeded for implementing the ceasefire, it is note-

worthy that the role of the UN declined, the role of the Soviet Union disappeared in the shadows. The six-point proposal for implementing the ceasefire was solely an American attempt, resulting in the negotiations at the Kilometer 101 on the Cairo-Suez road. Henry Kissinger merely informed UN Secretary General Waldheim about the proposal, letter by letter: "Dear Secretary General, under the guidance of the United States. . . ." so and so was agreed upon. Then he asked him to arrange for a conference in Geneva to discuss the steps to follow.

3. Before the Geneva conference, Dr. Waldheim did not know what role he or the UN would play, but felt obliged to go along in the hope of getting some results. But then, Israel insisted on excluding France and Britain, who had been expected to attend. Israel insisted on keeping away any other party representing countries interested in resolving the conflict justly. It was finally decided that Waldheim would only play the role of honorary chairman during the opening session. The United States and the Soviet Union would then chair the conference jointly.

4. Then matters proceeded in such a way that Syria, a major party in the war, was excluded. The attendance was limited to only two participants in the war: Israel and Egypt. Jordan, which was not a party to the war, attended only the opening session. The first stage of the Geneva conference finally ended with the establishment of an Egyptian-Israeli military committee to discuss the separation of the fighting forces on the Suez front, a matter which was supposed to have been discussed and resolved during the negotiations at Kilometer 101 on the Cairo-Suez road.

Israel adamantly opposed the participation of the Soviet Union in the military committee in Geneva, angering the Soviets to such a degree that the Soviet representative threatened to "send a high ranking Soviet officer to the meeting hall of the military committee, with instructions to force his way into the meeting, and to wait and see who could stop him." This of course did not occur, as diplomatic efforts succeeded in convincing the Soviets to stay out of the meeting. Soviet and American military representatives were to be briefed daily.

5. The military committee in Geneva finally reached a deadlock as a result of the intransigence of the Israeli delegation headed by General Gur, who would one day state that he was not authorized to negotiate beyond certain boundaries, and on another day would state that he must await the results of Israeli elections, and on yet another, declare that if the Egyptian delegation had a prepared proposal then he was ready to listen. . . . and so on and so forth, leading to a deadlock.

When Israeli elections were over, Dr. Henry Kissinger made his dramatic appearance on the Middle Eastern stage shuttling back and forth between Aswan and Jerusalem. This meant that the entire process had disintegrated, at least temporarily, leaving only Dr. Kissinger flying between Aswan and Jerusalem.

The question Israel first asked herself, "with whom shall we negotiate. . . . whatever the objectives?" was finally answered: with Egypt solely, through the mediation of Dr. Henry Kissinger. An attempt was made to exclude the UN, to exclude the other Great Powers, and to keep the Soviets away. Even the Geneva conference was slated to be left naked in the cold, as they say.

There is more. An attempt was made to separate the oil crisis from the Middle East crisis, so that the oil crisis became strictly a problem of setting prices, and the Middle East crisis became something else entirely. Then there was an attempt, through suggestions and accusations, to maintain that Egypt's position was unique and separate from the rest of the Arab world. These suggestions at best await realization.

This is not to say that the Israeli negotiator was responsible for both of these attempts. There is no doubt that other forces were responsible for them; but the Israeli negotiator has benefited, as usual, from the efforts of others.

In the end, Israel obtained an outcome very close to its desired end, even if only in form: Egypt alone, Israel alone, and Kissinger in between. Of course, we must not forget, Kissinger represented the policy of the United States of America.

We follow the Israeli bargaining strategy one more step. The first stage ended with the Israeli negotiator facing Dr. Henry Kissinger; indeed, Israel continued unceasingly to pursue her bargaining strategy in the United States.

The Israeli bargaining method made Dr. Henry Kissinger—and I wouldn't say imposed on him—negotiate with several parties in the United States before coming to negotiate in Israel:

1. Dr. Kissinger had to negotiate with the American Jewish community, which constituted a political force capable of exerting heavy pressure, especially toward an American president totally weakened by the Watergate scandal. Kissinger himself said: "I have spent long nights with American Jewish leaders, especially in New York, in order to assure them that I would not undertake any step that would undermine the security and future of Israel."

2. Dr. Kissinger had to negotiate with groups of congressmen known for their support of Israel. While it is true that the foreign policy

decisions of the United States belong to the resident of the White House, things are much more complicated, especially given the weakened position of the American president in relation to Congress as a result of Watergate.

3. Dr. Henry Kissinger had to "negotiate" with elements within the Pentagon, because there were groups in the U.S. military that had become convinced that Israel was the single stable base for the protection of American interests in the Middle East; and that Israel was the focal point of the defense system in the region against "Soviet infiltration attempts," to use their expression, and against "the forces of national revolution," that, like a ghost, threaten their sweet dreams.

4. Dr. Henry Kissinger had to "negotiate" with many of those who influenced American public opinion; specifically, those in the American media, most of whom sympathized with Israel. Moreover, the media had succeeded, especially given Arab incompetence, in portraying Israel as a democratic oasis of progress in the midst of a vast desert of Arab backwardness.

5. Dr. Henry Kissinger even had to "negotiate" with some of the journalists accompanying him during his travels, on the same plane, shuttling between Aswan and Jerusalem. Some of the news conferences on the airplane turned into confrontations, as Henry Kissinger himself described it, with Kissinger constantly forced to defend U.S. actions by repeating that he "will do only that which will guarantee Israel's security and future."

All the above adds up to the fact that Henry Kissinger was negotiating for his own political future. Put differently, whether or not Henry Kissinger wanted it that way, he found himself in such a position that considerations for "his personal future" and concerns for "the security and future of Israel" could be easily confused. This was the second step in Israel's negotiating strategy.

The third step of Israel's bargaining strategy was realized when, upon his arrival in Jerusalem, Dr. Henry Kissinger found that he had to negotiate on many different, and often competing, levels:

1. There was no single man or woman with whom Dr. Henry Kissinger was able to conclude a deal; rather, there were organizations and forces, groups and even individuals with whom Kissinger had to negotiate. Prime Minister Golda Meir, on the other hand, was ill in the hospital, and Kissinger could only meet with her for no more than half an hour during which time he could merely try to catch her inaudible speech. What Golda Meir said was that the Labor party, which she headed, was holding on to a small majority which did not

enable her to move far. Moreover, she went on to state that she had yet to form a new government following the general elections, and would therefore have to take the views of other parties into account. If major decisions had to be made, she might be forced to call new elections with the hope that the public would grant her a greater majority allowing her a greater degree of maneuverability. Then Golda Meir added the clincher: "I am already over seventy-five and I am not ready to go down in history with the responsibility of having reduced Israeli borders. . . . to a degree that threatened its security."

2. Dr. Henry Kissinger then "negotiated" with Golda Meir's cabinet, whose authority had expired and would have to replaced following the elections. At any rate, most members of the cabinet had differing opinions: Allon had an opinion, Galili had an opinion, Eban had another, Sapir yet another, and Dayan held his own.

3. Henry Kissinger then "negotiated" with the leaders of the other blocks and parties. . . . even if they had no chance of joining the new government, for each one of them was able to make the Israeli Knesset a theater of confrontation even over a procedural matter. Israeli public opinion is particularly vulnerable to these internal debates especially after the experience of the October war, which demonstrated weaknesses in Israel's security system.

4. Next, Dr. Henry Kissinger had to "negotiate" with the Israeli military establishment, which managed to retain its influence despite its failure in the October war. Although Kissinger had already met several weeks before in Washington with the head of this establishment, General Moshe Dayan, he still had to negotiate with many other generals.

5. Then Dr. Henry Kissinger had to "negotiate" with Israeli public opinion, which is a key party over the issue of security, because the question of security is a matter of life for Israel, and because voters in Israel, given Israel's small size, are also the ones who bear arms. In this case, the negotiations were public, so that Dr. Henry Kissinger made public declarations, and public commitments, every time he entered and left Israel.

All this meant that Dr. Henry Kissinger negotiated not just on one, but on several levels, on each of which he made specific requests and obtained specific commitments. This is the third step in Israel's bargaining strategy.

Following Israel's negotiating strategy a fourth step will make it clear how Israel mastered the modern science of negotiations and put it to practical application.

The following are some of the basic principles of the modern science of negotiations:

1. There must be several ideas proposed at the same time, because the more ideas there are, spread between moderation and extremism, the more the impression is given of the sincerity of the negotiating party's position, since it allows all the differing views to be professed freely. Moreover, negotiators find that they have a greater space for negotiating. This procedure also permits the final decision to be acceptable to broad segments, since each would be inclined to feel that it played a role in the process.

2. The negotiation process must begin with the presentation of extreme positions, both strategically and tactically. In this regard it is likely that Israel has learned from Dr. Henry Kissinger, who wrote that "the success of a given party at the negotiations depends on its ability to exaggerate its demands and their vital importance. Only those who are naive begin the negotiating process by proposing their minimally acceptable requirements. . . . In doing so, they leave themselves no space to retreat . . . which would inevitably portray them as extremists who, instead of negotiating, simply attempt to dictate their conditions."

3. Among the scientific principles of negotiations is that a person with wide authority should not be engaged in the details, or the final decision, of the negotiations; otherwise, he would become the target of concerted efforts demanding concessions, since every one would know that the decisions lay with him. Therefore, any negotiator should have limited authority, and should not be ashamed to declare at some point: "this matter extends beyond my authority, and, therefore, I must consult with my superiors to receive instructions."

4. The negotiations should be a collective effort by various institutions that can, through dialogue, present several proposals for the settlement of any aspect of the problem under consideration; these proposals must be prepared rationally, leaving emotions aside.

In Geneva, for example, the Israeli military delegation presented, in one session, three different possible proposals for the separation of forces; within a short time, the negotiations were derailed by "from point 1 of proposal A to Point 2 of proposal C," etc. Had it not been for the alertness of the Egyptian delegation, the negotiations would have remained stuck on words and numbers.

When proposals emanate from several institutions, emotional involvement by individuals may be avoided. One of the old principles of European diplomacy in the eighteenth century is a well known proverb: "Emotions of princes sometimes overwhelm their interests. . . . for humans behave according to fixed norms, as they often succumb, in their judgment, to emotions of the moment."

Consequently, alternative proposals in Israel are not prepared by Golda Meir or Eban but by collective institutions, from the prime minister's office to the foreign ministry and intelligence to security committees in the Knesset to several centers for strategic studies in universities and outside. These institutions are staffed with dozens of experts who specialize in political science, conflict, and bargaining.

5. Public opinion, in any country, must be a participant in any negotiations dealing with its future and security. What Morgenthau wrote still holds true: public opinion in democratic states makes the negotiators' task more difficult because it demands that they be heroes who do not succumb to the enemy even if war is at stake, and because it portrays as weak those who compromise even if for the sake of peace. Yet, public participation, if only through observation, gives the negotiator real power of determination outside, and the ability to persuade inside.

The upshot of the above is that when Dr. Henry Kissinger negotiated with Israel, he found he was facing moderation and extremism simultaneously, confronting an intransigent position from the first moment, and facing limited space for movement at every level; confronting several alternative positions presented by various institutions, while facing a public opinion that had real weight, even if it tended to delude itself. This is the practical application of a science—the fourth step in Israel's negotiating strategy.

Proceeding to the fifth step in Israel's negotiating strategy, it can be summarized in one expression: "at what price?" Every movement has a price, every whisper deserves compensation; even when the move is strictly procedural, and even when the whisper is mere gibberish beyond coherent translation.

The precedents are many, but what is yet to come will be even more telling. Henry Kissinger himself, for example, justified the size of American military aid to Israel, which was around $2.3 billion, saying: "this was necessary to convince Israel to accept the cease fire, without making her feel that her security and future are in danger." This was in October 1973. Today, as Kissinger negotiates the separation of forces with Israel, the news from Tel Aviv is beginning to speak about "what Israel will receive in return for its acceptance of the separation of forces."

It is justified, therefore, if we ask ourselves the following: if Israel received $2.3 billion worth of weapons for the cease fire, what will Israel get in exchange for the separation of forces? More importantly, what will Israel receive for evacuating the territories occupied in June of 1967, and in return for fulfilling the legitimate rights of the Palestinian people?

8

Conclusion

IN THE process of answering some perplexing questions pertaining to the Camp David accords, I set out to develop a general framework for the study of cases in international relations, particularly those involving formal bargaining. From the outset I have argued that any such framework must avoid two serious problems facing the theorist of international relations: the confusion of theories according to both their intended purpose and their level of analysis. It was hoped that such a framework would be capable of assessing the relative explanatory power of relevant variables in given cases, in a consistent manner.

The method that I introduced accomplished several important tasks. It reconciled two theoretical traditions in international relations: realist theory and bargaining theory. It also demonstrated the explanatory power of both traditions in empirical situations: The distribution of military and economic power, a key realist variable, was shown to be central in understanding the behavior of Egypt, Israel, and the superpowers; bargaining theory helped explain various behavioral tendencies of the actors, and accounted for some specific components of the Camp David accords. In addition, the proposed method provided a consistent means for evaluating the relative weight of variables at different levels of analysis: by focussing on the identification of the actors' preferences this method permitted the employment of variables at both the state and international levels. The employment of the bargaining framework, on the other hand, permitted the evaluation of outcomes as well as preferences and behavior.

In addition, some interesting conclusions were reached about the suitability of particular systems of government to efficient bargaining. It was theoretically argued, and empirically corroborated by the three political systems interacting at Camp David, that *decentralized* systems of government are more conducive to optimal bargaining than centralized systems; these conclusions support recent works in international political economy.

The procedure avoided ad hoc explanation, especially in the identification of preferences, in several ways: the theoretical assumptions about the behavior of the actors were shown to be consistent with a more general research program; and the hypotheses derived from these assumptions were shown to explain the behavior of the actors not only in the specific case at hand, but also across time.

Empirically the framework allowed interesting and sometimes surprising conclusions about the Camp David accords. The framework provided not only a systematic explanation for the accords themselves, but also some general hypotheses about the foreign policies of Egypt, Israel, and the United States. Furthermore, propositions about general patterns in inter-Arab relations were advanced, and a method for evaluating bargaining performance and bargaining outcomes in general was proposed.

The Empirical Conclusions

The first general conclusion is that one does not need to rely on the exotic, the unique, or the arbitrary to explain the surprising outcome of Camp David. Generally accepted variables provide more convincing, and certainly more useful, explanations that allow some preliminary predictions about future patterns in Arab-Israeli relations.

At the outset, two specific questions about the accords were raised:

why did Egypt and Israel conclude a bilateral peace treaty, and what explains the specific terms of the final agreement? Given the assumptions about the preferences of Egypt and Israel, a single variable explained much of the first question: change in the distribution of military and economic power among states, both at the international and regional levels. The second question was best explained through bargaining theory, personalities of the leaders, and the systems of government of the three states.

Specifically, I have argued that Egypt's relations with the superpowers were largely a function of incremental changes in the balance of military power, between the United States and Soviet Union in general and in the Middle East region in particular. As rough parity was attained by the early 1970s, Egypt was forced to make choices between semi-nonalignment and alignment; the inclination to choose one superpower over the other was a function partly of superpower relations, and partly of Egypt's regional preferences. Ideology, personal inclinations, and domestic politics in Egypt appear to have played a less significant role.

More telling was the conclusion about Egypt's regional behavior leading to the Camp David accords. To begin with, it was argued that the common explanations of Egypt's behavior are implausible, not only on theoretical grounds, but also for lack of empirical fit and logical consistency. In particular, explanations linking the general Egyptian policy with cultural and individual characteristics were shown to be ad hoc, inconsistent, and empirically inaccurate. The apparently more plausible explanations, linking Egypt's economic problems with the change in its foreign policy, were also shown to be inadequate: Egypt had other means of relieving the immediate economic crisis; and it is unlikely that Sadat, in his attempt to quell domestic unrest, as indicated in the "food riots," would embark on a most controversial journey to Jerusalem.

An alternative explanation was proposed employing one variable, change in the regional distribution of power, given some identified, enduring preferences of Israel and Egypt. In particular, it was argued that, given major shifts in the distribution of military and political capabilities in the Middle East from the 1950s to the 1970s, Egypt's enduring drive for leadership of the Arab world could no longer be met through the active advocacy of Pan-Arabism; on the contrary, Egypt's commitment to this cause, and therefore to the confrontation of Israel, eventually reduced Egypt's regional influence instead of enhancing it.

Ironically, the objective of leading the Arab world could be met only by the temporary abandonment of the Pan-Arabist cause. By making peace with Israel, Egypt would receive economic aid from the United States that would free Egypt from dependence on other Arab states. By forging strategic relations with the United States, Egypt would prevent Israel's regional hegemony, and would eventually return to a position of leadership in the Arab world; leadership comes from independence and relative strength, not from ideology.

An examination of the impact of the international environment on the preferences of Israel ended with the conclusion that, ever since its creation, Israel has sought two enduring international objectives that derived from its inherent vulnerability and the nature of its environment: the consolidation of relations with the United States and the prevention of other regional actors from competing with these relations; and the separation of Egypt from the rest of the Arab world. These two objectives were shown to endure throughout the short history of Israel, and to consistently account for much of its behavior. The Egyptian peace initiative thus posed a serious dilemma for Israel. While it promised the attainment of Israel's regional objective, by isolating Egypt from the rest of the Arab world, it also had the potential of undermining the more important international objective, by permitting Egyptian competition with the strategic relations between Israel and the United States. Israel's behavior at Camp David was designed largely to protect its relations with the United States, while maximizing the chance of attaining the regional objective.

An assessment of American international and domestic preferences showed how the resolution of the Arab-Israeli conflict is essential for removing an inherent tension among American preferences in the Middle East: minimizing Soviet influence, securing the flow of oil at reasonable prices, and maintaining the security and well being of Israel. The realization of this inherent tension, especially following the Arab oil embargo, led the Carter administration to intensify the drive for a settlement of the Arab-Israeli conflict.

But while the international preferences of the United States recommended a role of an active participant in the negotiations, the domestic priorities pushed toward a mediating role, and thus an agreement for its own sake. Given the priorities in American foreign policy, the domestic preferences dominated American behavior.

In summary, the distribution of military and economic power among states was shown to be a primary variable in explaining the behavior of states. Changes in that distribution, both at the overall international level, and at the regional level, explain much of the desires of Israel and Egypt to end hostility between them. But this variable failed to account for the specific terms of the concluded agreements at Camp David, including components that were highly relevant to the future of Israeli-Egyptian relations.

The assessment of the specific terms of the final agreements reached at Camp David was accomplished through the use of the basic form of bargaining theory which allowed the employment of positive, prescriptive, and abstractive theories, without overlap. Specifically, I have argued that comparing the actual outcome to the opening bargaining positions of the actors is not a good method of evaluation, and that derived preferences in themselves are insufficient for predicting a specific outcome. Instead, I proposed that the bargaining behavior of the actors be assessed on the basis of its deviation from prescriptive bargaining theory. While prescriptive theory is incapable of predicting determinate solutions, it recommends optimal strategies, i.e., strategies that maximize the given actor's chance of attaining his preferences. Accordingly, several general strategies recommended by prescriptive bargaining were set forth, and the actual behavior of the actors was compared to them.

It was shown that Israel's behavior coincided most with optimal bargaining strategy, Egypt's deviated from it most, and American behavior fell somewhere in between. The next task was to explain why one state behaved optimally while another did not. The variables used to explain the extent of fit were primarily two: the domestic system of government and the leader's personality. On the basis of proposed general criteria, it was argued that the Israeli system of government was more conducive to optimal bargaining than the Egyptian and the American systems, and that Begin's personality was more conducive to optimal bargaining than Sadat's or Carter's.

While the employment of prescriptive bargaining theory revealed which actor was likely to maximize the chances of a favorable outcome, it did not inform us about what specific objectives were likely to be attained. Thus, although in the case of Camp David more optimal bargaining by Egypt would have led to a more favorable outcome, the exact terms of this optimal outcome cannot be specified on the basis of prescriptive theory alone.

Through analysis of the actors' preferences and their relative power, I specified several issues that could be called "bargaining issues," that is, issues over which the exact outcome could be determined only through bargaining. Two primary bargaining issues that were relevant to the future of Israeli-Egyptian relations were identified: the extent of linkage between normalization of relations between Egypt and Israel on the one hand, and progress on the West Bank and Gaza on the other; and the agreements regarding Jewish settlements on the West Bank and Gaza. On both issues, the outcome decidedly favored Israeli preferences, thus begging the question if Egypt could have attained more. Prescriptive theory essentially informed us that Egypt did not try enough, that it did not sufficiently test the limits of Israeli compromise; but it did not tell us what may have occurred had Egypt tried its best. It may have still turned out that not much more could have been achieved, as at least one top Egyptian negotiator believed.

The help of abstractive bargaining theory was sought to evaluate the specific outcome. While speculative, in that it has not been established as positive theory, abstractive theory has the capacity to predict determinate solutions. Yet, even if one is to accept the axioms of abstractive bargaining theory as reasonable, its application in the empirical case is limited since the actual preferences of actors cannot be easily translated mathematically. Through a less formal analysis of the bargaining issues and the actors' preferences, I concluded that two primary issues were highly affected by bargaining strategies: the absence of a firm agreement on the building of Jewish settlements in the West Bank and Gaza, and the lack of a firm link between the normalization of Egyptian-Israeli relations and progress on Palestinian autonomy. Both issues, it was found, could have been settled in a manner favoring Egyptian preferences, and that Sadat's personality and the Egyptian system of government were largely responsible for the Egyptian failure in this regard.

Given the contingency of the later conclusion about the relevance of domestic variables to the outcome of the negotiations (despite the availability of much information about these variables), and given the more confident conclusion about the central impact of change in the distribution of power, the historical focus on power as an explanatory variable in international affairs appears justified, even in this peculiar case of Camp David.

The Patterns and the Future

What conclusions can be derived about the future of Israeli-Egyptian relations and Middle East politics in general? Given Egypt's and Israel's enduring international preferences, and given the changes that occurred regionally as a result of the Camp David accords some likely trends can be predicted, especially if the other aspects of the Israeli-Arab conflict are not resolved. Much of these predictions derive from Egypt's inability, through the Camp David accords, to fully achieve its long standing regional objectives, despite improving relations with the rest of the Arab world.

Egypt's early failure to achieve its long term regional objectives through the Camp David accords was especially visible following the Israeli invasion of Lebanon: Egypt lacked the ability to influence, not to mention check Israel's regional hegemony; its influence in the Arab world declined to a new low, since most Arab states assessed that only the neutralization of the Egyptian military threat through the Camp David accords made it possible for Israel to carry out the invasion; Egypt was forced to cool off its relations with the United States because of the perceived collusion between the United States and Israel; and Israeli-American relations, despite the tension during the invasion emerged stronger than ever, since, given the new facts on the ground created by the invasion, it was better for the United States to cooperate with Israel than not.

The situation has improved for Egypt since then, as Egypt has been re-admitted to the Arab League and has regained some of its influence in the Arab world. But in the long run, Egypt's ability to be the dominant influence on Arab politics is contingent on one of two things: either maintaining friendly relations with Israel, but projecting the capacity to use these relations to help other actors attain a favorable peace; or returning to the Arab fold at the expense of Egyptian-Israeli relations. In other words, through peace or through war, Egyptian influence in the Arab world could not increase substantially without delivering some leverage in favor of the Arabs in relation to Israel. Egyptian-Israeli relations cannot therefore withstand a protracted stalemate on the Arab-Israeli conflict. Indeed, the recent improvement in Egypt's relations with key Arab actors stem from the increased hope for a political settlement. As soon as these hopes dissipate, Egyptian-Israeli relations will be seriously threatened. To be sure, Egypt has attempted, with partial success, to return to the Arab fold by offering badly needed support in the confrontation with Iran (and thus avoiding concessions to the other Arabs on Israel). But the Palestinian uprising in the occupied territories, and the ceasefire between Iran and Iraq, have refocused attention on the Arab-Israeli conflict. Syria and the Palestinians are likely to make sure that this conflict remains at center stage.

Fouad Ajami has argued that Pan-Arabism is forever dead. That it has declined there can be little doubt; but that this decline is forever is rather doubtful. Ajami's conclusion can be reached only if one posits that Arabism, while it prevailed, was an end-in-itself for Arab states. But I have argued that Arabism, while psychologically "real" and prevelant at the popular level, was largely instrumental at the state level, pursued by Arab states only when its advancement served their national interests; its decline was merely the result of its reduced utility. As the winds shift again, and its utility once again emerges, Arabism can be resurrected. Egypt may once again be one of its advocates.

If Egypt should return to the helm of a new Arabist movement, at the expense of its relations with Israel, the Camp David accords will likely be rationalized as a mistake committed by a treacherous Sadat; the likelihood of a similar course under any Egyptian president facing Egypt's situation in the 1970s, and the fact that many in Egypt were all too glad to have Sadat perform what they had viewed as a necessary task, will, of course, not be admitted. Nor will the instrumental nature of Arabism be recognized, as it will, no doubt, be advocated as an end in itself. But the patterns speak for themselves: enduring and recognizable forces of history seem responsible for the birth, death, and the likely resurrection of Arabism; leaders, perceptions, and slogans seem less significant.

For Israel, *if* the remaining unresolved issues in the Arab-Israeli conflict endure, the prospects are not promising. This should give far-sighted Israeli leaders the incentive to move quickly to resolve the conflict, and to create new possibilities. But the domestic realities in Israel, and its short term impressive military superiority, make the chances of movement slim. As a consequence, Israel is likely to grow ever more protective of its relations with the United States, diminishing America's ability to influence events in the region in the process. This would make Israeli-American relations increasingly vulnerable to events that highlight the tension between the commitment to Israel and other American interests; a backlash detrimental to Israeli-American relations could result.

Aside from the moral considerations that have become even more compelling in the wake of the Palestinian uprising, an enduring settlement to the Arab-Israeli conflict is in the interest of all three Camp David actors. Sadly, the prospects of this remain small; the costs may be tragic for all concerned.

Documentary Appendix

Opening Bargaining Positions Compared with Final Accords

A Comparison of the Camp David Peace Proposals

ISSUE	BEGIN'S AUTONOMY PLAN FOR THE OCCUPIED TERRITORIES, DECEMBER 1977.	CAMP DAVID FRAMEWORK FOR PEACE, SEPTEMBER 1978.
Self-governing authority	. . . introduction of an administrative authority for the Arab residents . . . . . . administration of the military rule . . . will be abolished. . . . adm. autonomy of, by, and for the Arab residents will be established. . . . every resident will be allowed to vote for the administrative council. . . . council will issue regulations pertaining to (the said departments). . . . (residents) will have free option to receive either Israeli or Jordanian citizenship. . . . (responsibility of Israeli, Jordan and adm. council . . . to examine law . . . determine which will remain . . . (decisions) will be adopted unanimously.	. . . transnational arrangements for the orderly transfer of authority . . . to provide full autonomy to the inhabitants of West Bank and Gaza. . . . Israeli military government and civilian adm. will be withdrawn as soon as a self-governing authority has been freely elected by the inhabitants of those (areas). . . . Egypt, Israel and Jordan will agree on the modalities for establishing the elected self-governing authority . . . will negotiate an agreement . . . define power and responsibilities of the self-governing authority.
Security	. . . security and public order . . . entrusted to the Israeli authorities. . . . (no) military withdrawal. . . . (IDF) deployed in (those areas). . . . issue for the Arabs of Eretz Israel is an administrative	. . . withdrawal of Israel's armed forces will take place . . . redeployment of remaining Israeli forces into specified security locations. . . . police force may include Jordanian citizens. . . . measures taken to assure security of Israel.

	authority . . . for Jews of EI . . . genuine security.	. . . strong local police force will be constituted by the self-governing authority . . . composed of the inhabitants of the WB and G.
Land Purchase	. . . Israeli residents will be entitled to purchase land and settle in areas of Judea, Samaria and Gaza . . . Arab residents (of said areas) who become Israeli citizens . . . will be entitled to purchase land and settle in Israel.	
Palestinians	. . . committee of representatives of Israel, Jordan, and adm. council will be established to determine immigration rules for (those areas) . . . will postulate those rules which will permit the Palestinian refugees outside (those areas) immigration. . . . will be assured free movement of economic activity. . . . one member to represent council before the government of Israel . . . one before the gov. of Jordan . . . on common issues.	. . . (negotiations) . . . to determine the final status of WB and G . . . to recognize the legitimate rights of the Palestinian people . . . among Egypt, Israel, Jordan and representatives of the inhabitants of the WB and G . . . (said reps) will decide on the modalities of administration of persons displaced from the WB and G in 1967.
Jerusalem	. . . free access to holy places.	
Refugees		. . . Egypt and Israel agreed . . . to achieve . . . solution of the problem of Palestinian and *Jewish refugees*.
Sovereignty	. . . (Israeli) right over said territories . . . (other demands) open . . . free admission to holy places.	. . . (negotiations) to decide how they shall govern themselves consistent with the provisions of the agreement.

A Comparison of the Camp David Peace Proposals, *continued*

ISSUE	EGYPTIAN PROPOSAL AT CAMP DAVID	FIRST DRAFT OF THE AMERICAN PROPOSAL AT CAMP DAVID, SEPTEMBER 10, 1978.
Self-Governing Authority	. . . upon signing of the treaty Israeli military government in the West Bank and Gaza shall be abolished and authority transferred to the Arab side . . . transitional period (5 yrs.) . . . during which Jordan shall supervise the administration of the WB and Egypt shall supervise the adm. of the Gaza strip. . . . Egypt and Jordan shall carry out responsibilities in cooperation with freely elected representatives of the Palestinian people who shall exercise direct authority over the adm. of the WB and G. . . . joint municipal council . . . equal number of Palestinian and Israeli members . . . shall be entrusted with regulating and supervising . . . (adm. matters mentioned.) . . . representatives of the Palestinian people shall take part in the peace talks . . . after the signing of the "Framework."	. . . Egypt, Israel and Jordan will determine the modalities for establishing the elected self-governing authority . . . . . . delegates may include Palestinians from the WB and G. . . . (agreements) will define responsibilities of the self-governing authority. . . . during transitional period (Egypt, Israel, Jordan and self-governing authority) . . . to reach agreements on . . . interpretations of unforseen issues . . . return of an agreed number of displaced persons . . . . . . (Jerusalem) shall not be divided . . . all peoples must have free access to it.
Security	. . . security measures shall be introduced . . . to meet the Parties' legitimate concerns for security.	. . . (Egypt, Israeli) propose . . . that Jordan and Egypt assign personnel to police forces in WB and G . . . maintain liaison (with Israel) on internal security matters. . . . nature of Israeli security presence during the transition

		period . . . will be agreed in the negotiations. . . . will provide for the withdrawal of Israeli armed forces and redeployment of some of them to specified security points . . . arrangements for internal and external security . . . including . . . roles of Israeli armed forces and local police.
Palestinians	. . . six months before the end of the transition period the Palestinian people shall exercise their fundamental rights to self-determination and shall be enabled to establish their national identity . . . (Egypt and Jordan) recommend that the entity be linked with Jordan . . . Palestinian refugees should be enabled to return or receive compensation. . . . (Israel) . . . to pay . . . compensation for the damage which resulted from the operations of its armed forces . . . as well as its exploitation of natural resources in occupied territories.	. . . solution must recognize the legitimate rights of the Palestinian people and enable the Pales. to take part in the determination of their own future. . . . (stages or autonomy) . . . Israeli military government will be abolished as soon as a self-governing authority can be freely elected by the inhabitants of the area . . . (Jordan) to join the negotiations . . . . . . arrangements should give due consideration both to the principle of self-government by the inhabitants and their territories and to the legitimate security concerns of Egypt, Israel, Jordan and the inhabitants of the WB and G.
Sovereignty	. . . Arab sovereignty and administration shall be restored to the Arab sector.	. . . within three years (Parties) negotiation . . . to settle the final status of the WB and G . . . including withdrawal of Israeli forces . . . just settlement of the refugee problem and establishment of boundaries.

SELF-RULE FOR PALESTINIAN ARABS, RESIDENTS OF JUDAEA, SAMARIA AND THE GAZA DISTRICT, WHICH WILL BE INSTITUTED UPON THE ESTABLISHMENT OF PEACE

*T*HE FOLLOWING programme was submitted by Prime Minister Begin to President Sadat, as announced by Mr. Begin in the Knesset on 28 December 1978:

1. The administration of the Military Government in Judaea, Samaria and the Gaza District will be abolished.
2. In Judaea, Samaria and the Gaza District administrative autonomy of the residents, by and for them, will be established.
3. The residents of Judaea, Samaria and the Gaza District will elect an Administrative Council composed of eleven members. The Administrative Council will operate in accordance with the principles laid down in this paper.
4. Any resident, 18 years old and above, without distinction of citizenship, or if stateless, will be entitled to vote in the elections to the Administrative Council.
5. Any resident whose name is included in the list of candidates for the Administrative Council and who, on the day the list is submitted, is 25 years old or above, will be entitled to be elected to the Council.
6. The Administrative Council will be elected by general, direct, personal, equal, and secret ballot.
7. The period of office of the Administrative Council will be four years from the day of its election.
8. The Administrative Council will sit in Bethlehem.
9. All the administrative affairs relating to the Arab residents of the areas of Judaea, Samaria and the Gaza District will be under the direction and within the competence of the Administrative Council.
10. The Administrative Council will operate the following Departments:
    (a) The Department of Education;
    (b) The Department of Religious Affairs;
    (c) The Department of Finance;

(d) The Department of Transportation;
(e) The Department for Construction and Housing;
(f) The Department for Industry, Commerce, and Tourism;
(g) The Department of Agriculture;
(h) The Department of Health;
(i) The Department for Labour and Social Welfare;
(j) The Department for Rehabilitation of Refugees;
(k) The Department for the Administration of Justice and the Supervision of Local Police Forces; and promulgate regulations relating to the operation of these Departments.

11. Security and public order in the areas of Judaea, Samaria and the Gaza District will be the responsibility of the Israeli authorities.
12. The Administrative Council will elect it own chairman.
13. The first session of the Administrative Council will be convened 30 days after the publication of the election results.
14. Residents of Judaea, Samaria and the Gaza District, without distinction of citizenship, or if stateless, will be granted free choice (option) of either Israeli or Jordanian citizenship.
15. A resident of the areas of Judaea, Samaria and the Gaza District who requests Israeli citizenship will be granted such citizenship in accordance with the citizenship law of the State.
16. Residents of Judaea, Samaria and the Gaza District who, in accordance with the right of free option, choose Israeli citizenship, will be entitled to vote for, and be elected to, the Knesset in accordance with the election law.
17. Residents of Judaea, Samaria and the Gaza District, who are citizens of Jordan will elect, and be eligible for election to, the Parliament of the Hashemite Kingdom of Jordan in accordance with the election law of that country.
18. Questions arising from the vote to the Jordanian Parliament by residents of Judaea, Samaria and the Gaza District will be clarified in negotiations between Israel and Jordan.
19. A committee will be established of representatives of Israel, Jordan and the Administrative Council to examine existing legislation in Judaea, Samaria and the Gaza District, and to determine which legislation will continue in force, which will be abolished, and what will be the competence of the Administrative Council to promulgate regulations. The rulings of the committee will be adopted by unanimous decision.
20. Residents of Israel will be entitled to acquire land and settle in the areas of Judaea, Samaria and the Gaza District. Arabs, residents

of Judaea, Samaria and the Gaza District who, in accordance with the free option granted them, will become Israeli citizens, will be entitled to acquire land and settle in Israel.
21. A committee will be established of representatives of Israel, Jordan and the Administrative Council to determine norms of immigration to the areas of Judaea, Samaria and the Gaza District. The committee will determine the norms whereby Arab refugees residing outside Judaea, Samaria and the Gaza District will be permitted to immigrate to these areas in reasonable numbers. The rulings of the committee will be adopted by unanimous decision.
22. Residents of Israel and residents of Judaea, Samaria and the Gaza District will be assured freedom of movement and freedom of economic activity in Israel, Judaea, Samaria and the Gaza District.
23. The Administrative Council will appoint one of its members to represent the Council before the Government of Israel for deliberation on matters of common interest, and one of its members to represent the Council before the Government of Jordan, for deliberation on matters of common interest.
24. Israel stands by its right and its claim of sovereignty to Judaea, Samaria and the Gaza District. In the knowledge that other claims exist, it proposes, for the sake of the agreement and the peace, that the question of sovereignty in these areas be left open.
25. With regard to the administration of the holy places of the three religions in Jerusalem, a special proposal will be drawn up and submitted that will include the guarantee of freedom of access to members of all the faiths to the shrines holy to them.
26. These principles will be subject to review after a five-year period.

EGYPTIAN PROPOSAL AT CAMP DAVID FRAMEWORK FOR THE COMPREHENSIVE PEACE SETTLEMENT OF THE MIDDLE EAST PROBLEM

*F*OLLOWING: THE historic initiative of President SADAT which rekindled the hopes of all nations for a better future for mankind.

FROM DAYAN, BREAKTHROUGH.

In view of the firm determination of the peoples of the Middle East, together with all peace-loving nations, to put an end to the unhappy past, spare this generation and the generations to come the scourge of War and open a new chapter in their history ushering in an era of mutual respect and understanding.

Desirous to make the Middle East, the cradle of civilization and the birthplace of all Divine missions, a shining model for coexistence and cooperation among nations.

Determined to revive the great tradition of tolerance and mutual acceptance free from prejudice and discrimination.

Determined to conduct their relations in accordance with the provisions of the Charter of the United Nations and the accepted norms of international law and legitimacy.

Committed to adhere to the letter and spirit of the Universal Declaration of Human Rights.

Desirous to develop between then good-neighborly relations in accordance with the Declaration of Principles of International Law Concerning Friendly Relations and Cooperation Among States in Accordance with the Charter of the United Nations.

Bearing in mind that the establishment of peace and good-neighborly relations should be founded upon legitimacy, justice, equality and respect for fundamental rights and that good neighbors should demonstrate, in their acts and claims, a strict adherence to the rule of law and a genuine willingness to assume their mutual obligation to refrain from any infringement upon each other's sovereignty or territorial integrity.

Convinced that military occupation and/or the denial of other peoples' rights and legitimate aspirations to live and develop freely are incompatible with the spirit of peace.

Considering the vital interests of all the peoples of the Middle East as well as the universal interest that exists in strengthening World Peace and security.

Article 1

The Parties express their determination to reach a comprehensive settlement of the Middle East problem through the conclusion of peace treaties on the basis of the full implementation of Security Council Resolutions 242 and 338 in all their parts.

Article 2

The Parties agree that the establishment of a just and lasting peace among them requires the fulfillment of the following:

First: Withdrawal of Israel from the occupied territories in accordance with the principle of the inadmissibility of the acquisition of territory by War.

In Sinai and the Golan, withdrawal shall take place to the international boundaries between mandated Palestine and Egypt and Syria respectively.

In the West Bank, Israel shall withdraw to the demarcation lines of the 1949 Armistice Agreement between Israel and Jordan with such insubstantial alterations as might be mutually accepted by the Parties concerned. It is to be understood that such alterations should not reflect the weight of conquest. Security measures shall be introduced in accordance with the provisions below mentioned with a view to meeting the Parties' legitimate concern for security and safeguarding the rights and aspirations of the Palestinian people.

Withdrawal from the Gaza Strip shall take place to the demarcation lines of the 1949 Armistice Agreement between Egypt and Israel.

Israeli withdrawal shall commence immediately after the signing of the peace treaties and shall be completed according to a time-table to be agreed upon within the period referred to in Article 6.

Second: Removal of the Israeli settlements in the occupied territories according to a time-table to be agreed upon within the period referred to in Article 6.

Third: Guaranteeing the security, sovereignty, territorial integrity and inviolability and the political independence of every State through the following measures:

(a) The establishment of demilitarized zones astride the borders.
(b) The establishment of limited armament zones astride the borders.
(c) The stationing of United Nations forces astride the borders.
(d) The stationing of early warning systems on the basis of reciprocity.
(e) Regulating the acquisition of arms by the Parties and the type of their armament and weapons systems.
(f) The adherence by all Parties to the Treaty on the Non-Proliferation of nuclear weapons. The Parties undertake not to manufacture or acquire nuclear weapons or other nuclear explosive devices.
(g) Applying the principle of innocent passage to transit through the Straits of Tiran.

(h) The establishment of relations of peace and good-neighborly cooperation among the Parties.

Fourth: An undertaking by all the Parties not to resort to the threat or the use of force to settle disputes. Any disputes shall be settled by peaceful means in accordance with the provisions of Article 33 of the Charter of the United Nations.

The Parties also undertake to accept the compulsory jurisdiction of the International Court of Justice with respect to all disputes emanating from the application or the interpretation of their contractual arrangements.

Fifth: Upon the signing of the peace treaties, the Israeli military Government in the West Bank and Gaza shall be abolished and authority shall be transferred to the Arab side in an orderly and peaceful manner. There shall be a transitional period not to exceed five years from the date of the signing of the "Framework" during which Jordan shall supervise the administration of the West Bank and Egypt shall supervise the administration of the Gaza Strip.

Egypt and Jordan shall carry out their responsibility in cooperation with freely elected representatives of the Palestinian people who shall exercise direct authority over the administration of the West Bank and Gaza simultaneously with the abolition of the Israeli military government.

Six months before the end of the transitional period, the Palestinian people shall exercise their fundamental right to self-determination and shall be enabled to establish their national entity. Egypt and Jordan by virtue of their responsibility in the Gaza Strip and the West Bank, shall recommend that the entity be linked with Jordan as decided by their peoples.

Palestinian refugees and displaced persons shall be entitled to exercise the right to return or receive compensation in accordance with relevant United Nations resolutions.

Sixth: Israel shall withdraw from Jerusalem to the demarcation lines of the Armistice Agreement of 1949 in conformity with the principle of the inadmissibility of the acquisition of territory by war. Arab sovereignty and administration shall be restored to the Arab sector.

A joint municipal council composed of an equal number of Palestinian and Israeli members shall be entrusted with regulating and supervising the following matters:

(a) Public utilities throughout the City.
(b) Public transportation and traffic.

(c) Postal and telephone services.
(d) Tourism.

The Parties undertake to ensure the free exercise of worship, the freedom of access, visit and transit to the holy places without distinction or discrimination.

Seventh: Synchronized with the implementation of the provisions related to withdrawal, the Parties shall proceed to establish among them relationships normal to States at peace with one another. To this end, they undertake to abide by all the provisions of the Charter of the United Nations. Steps take in this respect include:

(a) Full recognition.
(b) Abolishing economic boycott.
(c) Ensuring the freedom of passage through the Suez Canal in accordance with the provisions of the Constantinople Convention of 1888 and the Declaration of the Egyptian Government of April 24, 1957.
(d) Guaranteeing that under their jurisdiction the citizens of the other Parties shall enjoy the protection of the due process of law.

Eight: Israel undertakes to pay full and prompt compensation for the damage which resulted from the operations of its armed forces against the civilian population and installations, as well as its exploitation of natural resources in occupied territories.

Article 3

Upon the signing of this "Framework," which represents a comprehensive and balanced package embodying all the rights and obligations of the Parties, other parties shall be invited to adhere to it under the Middle East Peace Conference in Geneva.

Article 4

The representatives of the Palestinian people shall take part in the peace talks to be held after the signing of the "Framework."

Article 5

The United States shall participate in the talks on matters related to the modalities of the implementation of the agreements and working out the time-table for the carrying out of the obligations of the Parties.

Article 6

Peace treaties shall be concluded within three months from the signing of this "Framework" by the Parties concerned, thus signalling the beginning of the peace process and setting in motion the dynamics of peace and co-existence.

Article 7

The Security Council shall be requested to endorse the Peace Treaties and ensure that their provisions shall not be violated. The Council shall also be requested to guarantee the boundaries between the Parties.

Article 8

The Permanent members of the Security Council shall be requested to underwrite the Peace Treaties and ensure respect for their provisions. They shall also be requested to conform their policies and actions with the undertakings contained in this Framework.

Article 9

The United States shall guarantee the implementation of this "Framework" and the peace treaties in full and good faith.

FIRST DRAFT OF THE AMERICAN PROPOSAL AT CAMP DAVID, SEPTEMBER 10, 1978

A Framework for Peace in the Middle East Agreed at Camp David

MUHAMMAD ANWAR al-Sadat, President of the Arab Republic of Egypt, and Menachem Begin, Prime Minister of Israel, met with Jimmy Carter, President of the United States of America, at Camp David from September 5 to —, 1978, and have agreed on the following framework for peace in the Middle East. They invite other parties to the Arab-Israeli conflict to adhere to it.

Preamble

The search for peace in the Middle East must be guided by the following:

— After four wars during thirty years, despite intensive human efforts, the Middle East, which is the cradle of civilization and the birthplace of three great religions, does not yet enjoy the blessings of peace. The people of the Middle East yearn for peace so that the vast human and natural resources of the region can be turned to pursuits of peace and so that this area can become a model for coexistence and cooperation among nations.
— The historic initiative of President Sadat in visiting Jerusalem and the reciprocal visit of Prime Minister Begin to Ismailia, the constructive peace proposals made by both leaders, as well as the warm reception of these missions by the peoples of both countries, have created an unprecedented opportunity for peace which must not be lost if this generation and future generations are to be spared the tragedies of war.
— The provisions of the Charter of the United Nations and the other accepted norms of international law and legitimacy now provide accepted standards for the conduct of relations among all states.
— The only agreed basis for a peaceful settlement of the Arab-Israeli conflict is United Nations Security Council Resolution 242, supplemented by Resolution 338. Resolution 242 in its preamble emphasizes the obligation of Member States in the United Nations to act in accordance with Article 2 of the Charter. Article 2, among

other points, calls for the settlement of disputes by peaceful means and for Members to refrain from the threat or use of force. Egypt and Israel in their agreement signed September 4, 1975, agreed: "The Parties hereby undertake not to resort to the threat or use of force or military blockade against each other." They have both also stated that there shall be no more war between them. In a relationship of peace, in the spirit of Article 2, negotiations between Israel and any neighbor prepared to negotiate peace and security with it should be based on all the provisions and principles of Resolution 242, including the inadmissibility of the acquisition of territory by war and the need to work for a just and lasting peace in which every state in the area can live in security within secure and recognized borders. Negotiations based on these principles are necessary with respect to all fronts of the conflict—the Sinai, the Golan Heights, the West Bank and Gaza, and Lebanon.

— Peace is more than the juridical end of the state of belligerency. It should encompass the full range of normal relations between nations. Progress toward that goal can accelerate movement toward a new era of reconciliation in the Middle East marked by cooperation in promoting economic development, in maintaining stability, and in assuring security.

— Security is enhanced by a relationship of peace and by cooperation between nations which enjoy normal relations. In addition, under the terms of peace treaties, the sovereign parties can agree to special security arrangements such as demilitarized zones, limited armaments areas, early warning stations, special security forces, liaison, agreed measures for monitoring, and other arrangements that they agree are useful.

Agreement

Taking these factors into account, Egypt and Israel are determined to reach a just, comprehensive, and durable settlement of the Middle East conflict through the conclusion of peace treaties on the basis of the full implementation of Security Council Resolutions 242 and 338 in all their parts. Their purpose is to achieve peace and good neighborly relations. They recognize that, for peace to endure, it must involve all those who have been principal parties to the Arab-Israeli conflict; it must provide security; and it must give the people who have been most deeply affected by the conflict, including the Palestinians, a sense that they have been dealt with fairly in the peace agreement. They therefore agree that this Framework as appropriate is intended by them to constitute a basis for peace not only between Egypt and Israel, but also between Israel and each of its other neighbors which is prepared to negotiate peace with Israel on this basis. With that objective in mind, they have agreed to proceed as follows:

A. EGYPT-ISRAEL

1. Egypt and Israel undertake not to resort to the threat or the use of force to settle disputes. Any disputes shall be settled by peaceful means in accordance with the provisions of Article 33 of the Charter of the United Nations. In the event of disputes arising from the application or interpretation of their contractual agreements, the two parties will seek to reach a settlement by direct negotiations. Failing agreement, the parties accept the compulsory jurisdiction of the International Court of Justice with respect to all disputes emanating from the application or the interpretation of their contractual arrangements.

2. In order to achieve peace between them, they have agreed to negotiate without interruption with a goal of concluding within three months from the signing of this Framework a peace treaty between them, while inviting the other parties to the conflict to proceed simultaneously to negotiate and conclude similar peace treaties with a view to achieving a comprehensive peace in the area. Israel has agreed to the restoration of the exercise of full Egyptian sovereignty in the Sinai up to the internationally recognized border between Egypt and Israel, and Egypt has agreed to establish full peace and normal relations with Israel. Security arrangements, the timing of withdrawal of all Israeli forces from the Sinai, and the elements of a normal, peaceful relationship between them have been discussed and will be defined in the peace treaty.

3. Egypt and Israel agree that freedom of passage through the Suez Canal, the Strait of Tiran, and the Gulf of Suez should be assured for ships of all flags, including Israel.

B. WEST BANK AND GAZA

1. Egypt and Israel will participate in negotiations on resolution of the Palestinian problem in all its aspects. The solution must recognize the legitimate rights of the Palestinian people and enable the Palestinians to participate in the determination of their own future.

2. To this end, negotiations relating to the West Bank and Gaza should provide for links between these areas and Jordan and should proceed in three stages:

(a) Egypt and Israel hereby agree that the following should be the main elements of a settlement in the West Bank and Gaza: In order to ensure a peaceful and orderly transfer of authority, there should be transitional arrangements for the West Bank and Gaza for a period not exceeding five years. In order to provide full autonomy to the inhabitants, under these arrangements the Israeli military government and administration will be abolished and withdrawn as soon as a self-governing authority can be freely elected by the inhabitants of these areas to replace the existing military government. This transitional arrangement should derive its authority for self-government from Egypt and Israel, and Jordan, when Jordan joins the negotiations. To negotiate the details of a transitional arrangement, the Government of Jordan will be invited to join the negotiations on the basis of this Framework. These new arrangements should give due consideration both to the principle of self-government by the inhabitants of these territories and to the legitimate security concerns of Egypt, Israel, Jordan, and the inhabitants of the West Bank and Gaza.

(b) Egypt, Israel, and Jordan will determine the modalities for establishing the elected self-governing authority in the West Bank and Gaza. The delegations may include Palestinians from the West Bank and Gaza. The parties will negotiate an agreement which will define the powers and responsibilities of the self-governing authority. The agreement will provide for the withdrawal of Israeli armed forces and the redeployment of some of them to limited and specified security points. It will also include arrangements for assuring internal and external security and public order, including the respective roles of Israeli armed forces and local police.

(c) When the self-governing authority in the West Bank and Gaza is inaugurated, the transitional period will begin. Within three years after the beginning of the transitional period, Egypt, Israel, Jordan and the self-governing authority in the West Bank and Gaza will undertake negotiations for a peace treaty which will settle the final status of the West Bank and Gaza after the transitional period and its relationship with its neighbors on the basis of all of the principles of UN Security Council Resolution 242, including the mutual obligations of peace, the necessity for security arrangements for all parties concerned following the transitional period, the withdrawal of Israeli forces, a just settlement of the refugee problem, and the establishment of secure and recognized boundaries. The boundaries and security arrangements must both satisfy the aspirations of the Palestinians and meet Israel's security needs. They may incorporate agreed minor modifications in the temporary armistice lines which existed between 1949 and 1967. The peace treaty will define the rights of the citizens of each of the parties to do business, to work, to live, and to carry on other transactions in each other's territory on a reciprocal basis.

3. All necessary measures will be taken and provisions made to assure Israel's security during the transitional period and beyond. To assist in providing security during and beyond the transitional period:

(a) Egypt and Israel propose that Jordan and Egypt assign personnel to the police forces of the self-governing authority in the West Bank and Gaza, respectively. They will also maintain continuing liaison on internal security matters with the designated Israeli authorities to ensure that no hostile threats or acts against Israel or its citizens originate from the West Bank or Gaza. The numbers, equipment, and responsibilities of such Egyptian and Jordanian personnel will be defined by the agreement. By mutual agreement, United Nations forces or observers may also be introduced during the transitional period.

(b) The nature of the Israeli security presence during the transitional period and beyond will be agreed in the negotiations described in paragraphs B2 (b) and (c) above.

4. During the transitional period, the negotiating parties (Egypt, Israel, Jordan, the self-governing authority) will constitute a continuing committee to reach mutual agreements applicable during that period on:

(a) issues involving interpretation of the agreement or issues unforseen during the negotiation of the agreement, if not resolvable by the self-governing authority.

(b) the return of agreed numbers of persons displaced from the West Bank in 1967 and of Palestinian refugees together with necessary measures in connection with their return to prevent disruption and disorder.

5. Jerusalem, the city of peace, shall not be divided. It is a holy city to Jew, Muslim, and Christian and all peoples must have free access to it and enjoy the free exercise of worship and the right to visit and transit to the holy places without distinction or discrimination. The holy places of each faith will be under the administration of their representatives. For peace to endure, each community in Jerusalem must be able to express freely its cultural and religious values in an acceptable political framework. A representative municipal council shall supervise essential functions in the city. An agreement on relationships in Jerusalem should be reached in the negotiations dealing with the final status of the West Bank and Gaza.

6. Egypt and Israel agree to work with each other and with other interested parties to achieve a just and permanent solution of the problems of Palestinian and Jewish refugees.

7. If Jordan is unable to join these negotiations, Egypt, Israel, and the inhabitants of the West Bank and Gaza will proceed to establish and administer the self-governing authority.

C. SETTLEMENTS

(Language to be inserted)

D. ASSOCIATED PRINCIPLES

1. Egypt and Israel believe that the principles and provisions described below should apply to peace treaties on all fronts.

2. Synchronized with the implementation of the provisions related to withdrawal, signatories shall proceed to establish among themselves relationships normal to states at peace with one another. To this end, they should undertake to abide by all the provisions of the Charter of the United Nations. Steps to be taken in this respect include:

(a) full recognition, including diplomatic, economic, and cultural relations;
(b) abolishing economic boycotts and barriers to the free movement of goods and people;
(c) guaranteeing that under their jurisdiction the citizens of the other parties shall enjoy the protection of the due process of law.

3. Signatories should agree to provide for the security and respect the sovereignty, territorial integrity and inviolability and the political independence of each state negotiating peace through measures such as the following:

- (a) the establishment of demilitarized zones;
- (b) the establishment of limited armament zones;
- (c) the stationing of United Nations forces or observer groups as agreed;
- (d) the stationing of early warning systems on the basis of reciprocity;
- (e) regulating the size of their armed forces and the types of their armament and weapons systems.

4. Signatories should explore possibilities for regional economic development in the context of both traditional arrangements and final peace treaties, with the objective of contributing to the atmosphere of peace, cooperation and friendship which is their common goal.

5. Claims Commissions may be established for the mutual settlement of all financial claims.

6. The United States shall be invited to participate in the talks on matters related to the modalities of the implementation of the agreements and working out the timetable for the carrying out of the obligations of the parties.

7. The United Nations Security Council shall be requested to endorse the peace treaties and ensure that their provisions shall not be violated. The permanent members of the Security Council shall be requested to underwrite the peace treaties and ensure respect for their provisions. They shall also be requested to conform their policies and actions with the undertakings contained in this Framework.

For the Government of the
Arab Republic of Egypt:

For the Government of
Israel:

Witnessed by:

Jimmy Carter, President of
the United States of America

THE CAMP DAVID ACCORDS, SEPTEMBER 17, 1978

A Framework for Peace in the Middle East Agreed at Camp David

MUHAMMAD ANWAR al-Sadat, President of the Arab Republic of Egypt, and Menachem Begin, Prime Minister of Israel, met with Jimmy Carter, President of the United States of America, at Camp David from Sepember 5 to September 17, 1978, and have agreed on the following framework for peace in the Middle East. They invite other parties to the Arab-Israeli conflict to adhere to it.

Preamble

The search for peace in the Middle East must be guided by the following:

— The agreed basis for a peaceful settlement of the conflict between Israel and its neighbors is UN Security Council Resolution 242, in all its parts.

— After four wars during thirty years, despite intensive human efforts, the Middle East, which is the cradle of civilization and the birthplace of three great religions, does not yet enjoy the blessings of peace. The people of the Middle East yearn for peace, so that the vast human and natural resources of the region can be turned to pursuits of peace and so that this area can become a model for co-existence and co-operation among nations.

— The historic initiative of President Sadat in visiting Jerusalem and the reception accorded to him by the parliament, government and people of Israel, and the reciprocal visit of Prime Minister Begin to Ismailia, the peace proposals made by both leaders, as well as the warm reception of these missions by the peoples of both countries, have created an unprecedented opportunity for peace which must not be lost if this generation and future generations are to be spared the tragedies of war.

— The provisions of the Charter of the United Nations and the other accepted norms of international law and legitimacy now provide accepted standards for the conduct of relations between all states.

- To achieve a relationship of peace, in the spirit of Article 2 of the United Nations Charter, future negotiations between Israel and any neighbor prepared to negotiate peace and security with it, are necessary for the purpose of carrying out all the provisions and principles of Resolutions 242 and 338.
- Peace requires respect for the sovereignty, territorial integrity and political independence of every state in the area and their right to live in peace within secure and recognized boundaries free from threats or acts of force. Progress toward that goal can accelerate movement toward a new era of reconciliation in the Middle East marked by cooperation in promoting economic development, in maintaining stability, and in assuring security.
- Security is enhanced by a relationship of peace and by cooperation between nations which enjoy normal relations. In addition, under the terms of peace treaties, the parties can, on the basis of reciprocity, agree to special security arrangements such as demilitarized zones, limited armaments areas, early warning stations, the presence of international forces, liaison, agreed measures for monitoring, and other arrangements that they agree are useful.

Framework

Taking these factors into account, the parties are determined to reach a just, comprehensive, and durable settlement of the Middle East conflict through the conclusion of peace treaties based on Security Council Resolutions 242 and 338 in all their parts. Their purpose is to achieve peace and good neighborly relations. They recognize that, for peace to endure, it must involve all those who have been most deeply affected by the conflict. They therefore agree that this framework as appropriate is intended by them to constitute a basis for peace not only between Egypt and Israel, but also between Israel and each of its other neighbors which is prepared to negotiate peace with Israel on this basis. With that objective in mind, they have agreed to proceed as follows:

A. WEST BANK AND GAZA

1. Egypt, Israel, Jordan and the representatives of the Palestinian people should participate in negotiations on the resolution of the Pal-

estinian problem in all its aspects. To achieve that objective, negotiations relating to the West Bank and Gaza should proceed in three stages:

(a) Egypt and Israel agree that, in order to ensure a peaceful and orderly transfer of authority, and taking into account the security concerns of the parties, there should be transitional arrangements for the West Bank and Gaza for a period not exceeding five years. In order to provide full autonomy to the inhabitants, under these arrangements the Israeli military government and its civilian administration will be withdrawn as soon as a self-governing authority has been freely elected by the inhabitants of these areas to replace the existing military government. To negotiate the details of a transitional arrangement, the government of Jordan will be invited to join the negotiations on the basis of this framework. These new arrangements should give due consideration to both the principles of self-government by the inhabitants of these territories and to the legitimate security concerns of the parties involved.
(b) Egypt, Israel and Jordan will agree on the modalities for establishing the elected self-governing authority in the West Bank and Gaza. The delegations of Egypt and Jordan may include Palestinians from the West Bank and Gaza or other Palestinians as mutually agreed. The parties will negotiate an agreement which will define the powers and responsibilities of the self-governing authority to be exercised in the West Bank and Gaza. A withdrawal of Israeli armed forces will take place and there will be a redeployment of the remaining Israeli forces into specified security locations. The agreement will also include arrangements for assuring internal and external security and public order. A strong local police force will be established, which may include Jordanian citizens. In addition, Israeli and Jordanian forces will participate in joint patrols and in the manning of control posts to assure the security of the borders.
(c) When the self-governing authority (administrative council) in the West Bank and Gaza is established and inaugurated, the transitional period of five years will begin. As soon as possible, but not later than the third year after the beginning of the transitional period, negotiations will take place to determine the final status of the West Bank and Gaza and its relationship with its neighbors, and to conclude a peace treaty between Israel and Jordan by the end of the transitional period. These negotiations will be con-

ducted among Egypt, Israel, Jordan, and the elected representatives of the inhabitants of the West Bank and Gaza. Two separate but related committees will be convened, one committee, consisting of representatives of the four parties which will negotiate and agree on the final status of the West Bank and Gaza, and its relationship with its neighbors, and the second committee, consisting of representatives of Israel and representatives of Jordan to be joined by the elected representatives of the inhabitants of the West Bank and Gaza, to negotiate the peace treaty between Israel and Jordan, taking into account the agreement reached on the final status of the West Bank and Gaza. The negotiations shall be based on all the provisions and principles of UN Security Council Resolution 242. The negotiations will resolve, among other matters, the location of the boundaries and the nature of the security arrangements. The solution from the negotiations must also recognize the legitimate rights of the Palestinian people and their just requirements. In this way, the Palestinians will participate in the determination of their own future through:

(1) The negotiations among Egypt, Israel, Jordan and the representatives of the inhabitants of the West Bank and Gaza to agree on the final status of the West Bank and Gaza and other outstanding issues by the end of the transitional period.
(2) Submitting their agreement to a vote by the elected representatives of the inhabitants of the West Bank and Gaza.
(3) Providing for the elected representatives of the inhabitants of the West Bank and Gaza to decide how they shall govern themselves consistent with the provisions of their agreement.
(4) Participating as stated above in the work of the committee negotiating the peace treaty between Israel and Jordan.

2. All necessary measures will be taken and provisions made to assure the security of Israel and its neighbors during the transitional period and beyond. To assist in providing such security, a strong local police force will be constituted by the self-governing authority. It will be composed of inhabitants of the West Bank and Gaza. The police will maintain continuing liaison on internal security matters with the designated Israeli, Jordanian, and Egyptian officers.

3. During the transitional period, the representatives of Egypt, Israel, Jordan, and the self-governing authority will constitute a continuing committee to decide by agreement on the modalities of admission of persons displaced from the West Bank and Gaza in 1967,

together with necessary measures to prevent disruption and disorder. Other matters of common concern may also be dealt with by this committee.

4. Egypt and Israel will work with each other and with other interested parties to establish agreed procedures for a prompt, just and permanent implementation of the resolution of the refugee problem.

B. EGYPT-ISRAEL

1. Egypt and Israel undertake not to resort to the threat or the use of force to settle disputes. Any disputes shall be settled by peaceful means in accordance with the provisions of Article 33 of the Charter of the United Nations.

2. In order to achieve peace between them, the parties agree to negotiate in good faith with a goal of concluding within three months from the signing of this Framework a peace treaty between them, while inviting the other parties to the conflict to proceed simultaneously to negotiate and conclude similar peace treaties with a view to achieving a comprehensive peace in the area. The Framework for the Conclusion of a Peace Treaty between Egypt and Israel will govern the peace negotiations between them. The parties will agree on the modalities and the timetable for the implementation of their obligations under the treaty.

C. ASSOCIATED PRINCIPLES

1. Egypt and Israel state that the principles and provisions described below should apply to peace treaties between Israel and each of its neighbors—Egypt, Jordan, Syria and Lebanon.

2. Signatories shall establish among themselves relationships normal to states at peace with one another. To this end, they should undertake to abide by all the provisions of the Charter of the United Nations. Steps to be taken in this respect include:

(a) full recognition;
(b) abolishing economic boycotts;
(c) guaranteeing that under their jurisdiction the citizens of the other parties shall enjoy the protection of the due process of law.

3. Signatories should explore possibilities for economic development in the context of final peace treaties, with the objective of con-

tributing to the atmosphere of peace, cooperation and friendship which is their common goal.

4. Claims Commissions may be established for the mutual settlement of all financial claims.

5. The United States shall be invited to participate in the talks on matters related to the modalities of the implementation of the agreements and working out the timetable for the carrying out of the obligations of the parties.

6. The United Nations Security Council shall be requested to endorse the peace treaties and ensure that their provisions shall not be violated. The permanent members of the Security Council shall be requested to underwrite the peace treaties and ensure respect for their provisions. They shall also be requested to conform their policies and actions with the undertakings contained in this Framework.

For the Government of the
Arab Republic of Egypt: A. Sadat

For the Government of Israel: M. Begin

Witnessed by: *Jimmy Carter*
                  JIMMY CARTER, PRESIDENT OF
                  THE UNITED STATES OF AMERICA

EXCHANGE OF LETTERS

ALL LETTERS FROM MR. CARTER ARE DATED 22 SEPTEMBER 1978, ALL OTHERS ARE DATED 17 SEPTEMBER, 1978.

His Excellency
Anwar El-Sadat
President of the Arab Republic of Egypt
Cairo

22 September 1978

Dear Mr. President:

I transmit herewith a copy of a letter to me from Prime Minister Begin setting forth how he proposes to present the issue of the Sinai settlements to the Knesset for the latter's decision.

In this connection, I understand from your letter that Knesset approval to withdraw all Israeli settlers from Sinai according to a timetable within the period specified for the implementation of the peace treaty is a prerequisite to any negotiations on a peace treaty between Egypt and Israel.

Sincerely yours,
Jimmy Carter

Enclosure:
Letter from Prime Minister Begin.

The President
Camp David
Thurmont, Maryland

17 September 1978

Dear Mr. President:

I have the honour to inform you that during two weeks after my return home I will submit a motion before Israel's Parliament (Knesset) to decide the following question:

If during the negotiations to conclude a peace treaty between Israel and Egypt all outstanding issues are agreed upon, 'are you in favour of the removal of the Israeli settlers from the northern and southern Sinai areas or are you in favour of keeping the aforementioned settlers in those areas?'

The vote, Mr. President, on this issue will be completely free from the usual Parliamentary Party discipline to the effect that although the coalition is being now supported by 70 members out of 120, every member of the Knesset, as I believe, both of the Government and the Opposition benches, will be enabled to vote in accordance with his own conscience.

Sincerely yours,
Menachem Begin

His Excellency
Menachem Begin
Prime Minister of Israel

22 September 1978

Dear Mr. Prime Minister:

I have received your letter of 17 September 1978, describing how you intend to place the question of the future of Israeli settlements in the Sinai before the Knesset for its decision. Enclosed is a copy of President Sadat's letter to me on this subject.

Sincerely,
Jimmy Carter

Enclosure:
Letter from President Sadat

His Excellency Jimmy Carter
President of the United States

17 September 1978

Dear Mr. President:

In connection with the "Framework for a Settlement in Sinai" to be signed tonight, I would like to reaffirm the positions of the Arab Republic of Egypt with respect to the settlements:

1. All Israeli settlers must be withdrawn from Sinai according to a timetable within the period specified for the implementation of the peace treaty.

2. Agreement by the Israeli Government and its constitutional institutions to the basic principle is therefore a prerequisite to starting negotiations for concluding a peace treaty.

3. If Israel fails to meet this commitment, the 'framework' shall be void and invalid.

Sincerely,
Mohamed Anwar El-Sadat

The President
Camp David
Thurmont, Maryland

17 September 1978

Dear Mr. President:

I have the honour to inform you, Mr. President, that on 28 June 1967 Israel's parliament (The Knesset) promulgated and adopted a law to the effect: "the Government is empowered by a decree to apply the law, the jurisdiction and administration of the State to any part of Eretz Israel (land of Israel - Palestine), as stated in that decree."

On the basis of this law, the government of Israel decreed in July 1967 that Jerusalem is one city indivisible, the Capital of the State of Israel.

Sincerely,
Menachem Begin

His Excellency Jimmy Carter
President of the United States

17 September 1978

Dear Mr. President:

I am writing you to reaffirm the position of the Arab Republic of Egypt with respect to Jerusalem.

1. Arab Jerusalem is an integral part of the West Bank. Legal and historical Arab rights in the city must be respected and restored.

2. Arab Jerusalem should be under Arab sovereignty.

3. The Palestinian inhabitants of Arab Jerusalem are entitled to exercise their legitimate national rights, being part of the Palestinian People in the West Bank.

4. Relevant Security Council resolutions, particularly Resolutions 242 and 267, must be applied with regard to Jerusalem. All the measures taken by Israel to alter the status of the City are null and void and should be rescinded.

5. All peoples must have free access to the City and enjoy the free exercises of worship and the right to visit and transit to the holy places without distinction or discrimination.

6. The holy places of each faith may be placed under the administration and control of their representatives.

7. Essential functions in the City should be undivided and a joint municipal council composed of an equal number of Arab and Israeli members can supervise the carrying out of these functions. In this way, the city shall be undivided.

Sincerely
Anwar El-Sadat

His Excellency
Anwar El-Sadat
President of the Arab Republic of Egypt
Cairo

22 September 1978

Dear Mr. President:

I have received your letter of 17 September, setting forth the Egyptian position on Jerusalem. I am transmitting a copy of that letter to Prime Minister Begin for his information.

The position of the United States on Jerusalem remains as stated by Ambassador Goldberg in the United Nations Assembly on 14 July 1967, and subsequently by Ambassador Yost in the United Nations Security Council on 1 July 1969.

Sincerely,
Jimmy Carter

His Excellency
Jimmy Carter
President of the United States
The White House
Washington, D.C.

17 September 1978

Dear Mr. President:

In connection with the 'Framework for Peace in the Middle East,' I am writing you this letter to inform you of the position of the Arab Republic of Egypt with respect to the implementation of the comprehensive settlement.

To ensure the implementation of the provisions related to the West Bank and Gaza and in order to safeguard the legitimate rights of the Palestinian People, Egypt will be prepared to assume the Arab role emanating from these provisions, following consultations with Jordan and the representatives of the Palestinian People.

Sincerely,
Mohamed Anwar El-Sadat

His Excellency
Menachem Begin
Prime Minister of Israel

22 September 1978

Dear Mr. Prime Minister:

I hereby acknowledge that you have informed me as follows:

A. In each paragraph of the Agreed Framework Document the expressions "Palestinians" or "Palestinian People" are being and will be construed and understood by you as "Palestinian Arabs."

B. In each paragraph in which the expression "West Bank" appears it is being, and will be, understood by the Government of Israel as Judea and Samaria.

Sincerely,
Jimmy Carter

ABOVE DOCUMENTS AND LETTERS FROM QUANDT, CAMP DAVID (MOST ALSO IN DAYAN, BREAKTHROUGH.).

LETTER FROM SECRETARY OF DEFENSE HAROLD BROWN TO ISRAELI DEFENSE MINISTER EZER WEIZMAN, ACCOMPANYING THE DOCUMENTS AGREED TO AT CAMP DAVID.

(RELEASED SEPTEMBER 29, 1978)

September 28, 1978

Dear Mr. Minister:

The U.S. understands that, in connection with carrying out the agreements reached at Camp David, Israel intends to build two military airbases at appropriate sites in the Negev to replace the airbases at Eitam and Etzion which will be evacuated by Israel in accordance with the peace treaty to be concluded between Egypt and Israel. We also understand the special urgency and priority which Israel attaches to preparing new bases in light of its conviction that it cannot safely leave the Sinai airbases until the new ones are operational.

I suggest that our two governments consult on the scope and cost of the two new airbases as well as on related forms of assistance which the United States might appropriately provide in light of the special problems which may be presented by carrying out such a project on an urgent basis. The President is prepared to seek the necessary Congressional approvals for such assistance as may be agreed upon by the U.S. side as a result of such consultations.

Harold Brown

FROM DAYAN, BREAKTHROUGH.

MEMORANDUM OF AGREEMENT BETWEEN THE GOVERNMENTS OF THE UNITED STATES AND ISRAEL - OIL

26 March 1979

The oil supply arrangements of 1 September 1975, between the Governments of the United States and Israel, annexed hereto, remain in effect. A memorandum of agreement shall be agreed upon and concluded to provide an oil supply arrangement for a total of 15 years, including the 5 years provided in the 1 September 1975 arrangement.

The memorandum of agreement, including the commencement of this arrangement and pricing provisions, will be mutually agreed upon by the parties within sixty days following the entry into force of the Treaty of Peace between Egypt and Israel.

It is the intention of the parties that prices paid by Israel for oil provided by the United States hereunder shall be comparable to world market prices current at the time of transfer, and that in any event the United States will be reimbursed by Israel for the costs incurred by the United States in providing oil to Israel hereunder.

Experts provided for in the 1 September 1975 arrangement will meet on request to discuss matters arising under this relationship. The United States administration undertakes to seek promptly additional statutory authorization that may be necessary for full implementation of this agreement.

M. Dayan
For the Government of Israel

Cyrus Vance
For the Government of the United States

ANNEX TO THE MEMORANDUM OF AGREEMENT CONCERNING OIL

ANNEX

ISRAEL WILL make its own independent arrangement for oil supply to meet its requirements through normal procedures. In the event Israel is unable to secure its needs in this way, the United States Government, upon notification of this fact by the Government of Israel, will act as follows for five years, at the end of which period either side can terminate this arrangement on one year's notice.

(a) If the oil Israel needs to meet all its normal requirements for domestic consumption is unavailable for purchase in circumstances where no quantitative restrictions exist on the ability of the United States to procure oil to meet its normal requirements, the United States Government will promptly make oil available for purchase by Israel to meet all of the aforementioned normal requirements of Israel. If Israel is unable to secure the necessary means to transport such oil to Israel, the United States Government will make every effort to help Israel secure the necessary means of transport.

(b) If the oil Israel needs to meet all of its normal requirements for domestic consumption is unavailable for purchase in circumstances where quantitative restrictions through embargo or otherwise also prevent the United States from procuring oil to meet its normal requirements, the United States Government will promptly make oil available for purchase by Israel in accordance with the International Energy Agency conservation and allocation formula, as applied by the United States Government, in order to meet Israel's essential requirements. If Israel is unable to secure the necessary means to transport such oil to Israel, the United States Government will make every effort to help Israel secure the necessary means of transport.

Israeli and United States experts will meet annually, or more frequently at the request of either party, to review Israel's continuing oil requirement.

FROM DAYAN, BREAKTHROUGH.

Notes

1. Overview

1. One may understandably question the separation of the two questions, since, in reality, no such easy separation actually exists; both questions are related. My reason for doing this is very simple, and coincides with my methodological arguments presented in the next chapter. Specifically, I view the *conceptual* separation as a pragmatic tool. The issue becomes whether or not this conceptual separation provides more explanatory power than other forms of conceptualization. This book argues that it does.

2. Kurth, "A Widening Gyre," p. 373.

3. Collinearity is fully defined in chapter 2.

4. Three aspects of this problem are treated in chapter 2: the choice of the appropriate level of analysis; the problem of collinearity; and the "cross-level fallacy."

5. These theory types are defined in chapter 2. Briefly, positive theories are intended to explain and predict; prescriptive theories are intended to prescribe, given assumed ends; and abstractive theories are preliminary, speculative, and intended to break new ground in the absence of good positive theories.

6. Preferences are defined as the agenda of ends that states are assumed to pursue. They are established by satisfying two criteria: they must be consistent with a given research program, and they must be shown to explain the behavior of the given state, *across time*, better than alternative assumptions.

7. See appendix 1.

8. Quoted by Weizman, *Battle for Peace*, p. 50.

9. This phrase was a favorite in Nasser's speeches.

10. See Documentary Appendix.

11. See, for example, Cooper, *The Transformation of Egypt*.

12. Examples of these offers are given in chapter 4.

13. *Infitah* was the new economic policy that encouraged the private sector and sought to attract foreign investments. A version of this argument is provided by Walid Kazzia who argues that "Sadat's objectives were geared to satisfying the newly emerging bourgeoisie" (Kazzia, *Palestine in the Arab Dilemma*, London, 1979, pp. 87–107). Others, like Jake Wien, combine the economic-need argument with Sadat's inclination to open up the economic system because of the failure of the socialist experiment (Wien, "Saudi-Egyptian Relations: The Political and Military Dimensions of Saudi Financial Flows to Egypt," Rand Paper P-6327, Santa Monica, January 1980, pp. 21–31).

14. *Egypt Report*, May, 1977, p. 24.

15. Quoted by *The Economist*, June 28, 1975.

16. One proponent of *infitah* as an explanation for Egypt's policy to settle the conflict with Israel, Jake Wien, also argues that attracting Saudi funds was central to Egypt's policy, although he does not adequately explain why the Egyptians persisted even when this policy jeopardized Saudi-Egyptian relations (Ibid.).

17. See, for example, Israeli, *Man of Defiance*, pp. 74–76. Several other analysts have, to varying degrees, focused on Sadat's personality in explaining at least some aspects of Egypt's foreign policy. See, for example, Mohamed Heikal, *Autumn of Fury* (New York, 1983); Ismail Fahmy, *Negotiating for Peace in the Middle East* (Baltimore, 1983); and David Hirst and Irene Beeson, *Sadat* (London, 1981), among others.

18. *Ibid.*, p. 76.

19. See, for example, Martin Indykk, *To the End of the Earth: Sadat's Jerusalem Initiative*, Harvard Middle East Papers, Modern Series, number 1, Cambridge, 1984.

20. Carter, *Keeping Faith*, p. 366.

21. Personal interview, Cairo, August 28, 1983.

22. According to Carter's National Security Advisor, Zbigniew Brzezinski, when Sadat threatened to leave Camp David on the eleventh day of the negotiations, Carter warned him that "it will mean first of all an end to the relationship between the United States and Egypt." Sadat quickly reversed his plans (Brzezinski, *Power and Principle*, p. 272).

23. By "domestic" preferences I mean those that derive from domestic

politics; by "international" preferences, I mean those deriving from international politics.

24. See chapter 7 for a discussion of this issue.

25. I remain committed to the *analytical* separation of the "ought" from the "is," in the absence of a more useful alternative.

2. *A Framework for the Study of Cases in International Politics*

1. See, for example, James Rosenau's treatment of this question in his article "National Interest."

2. Telhami, "International Bargaining and the Level of Analysis Problem: The Case of Camp David," chapter 11.

3. One example of missing this point is to be found, once again, in the treatment of national interest. Krasner, in *Defending the National Interest*, p. 13, distinguishes his concept of national interest from those of E. H. Carr, Robert Gilpin, Hans Morgenthau, Robert Tucker, Kenneth Waltz, and Arnold Wolfers. He assumes that national interest as employed by these thinkers is a "basic assumption in constructing a logical-deductive model of international politics." In contrast, Krasner's national interest "is defined inductively as the preferences of American central decision makers" (which must, among other things, persist over time). In doing so, Krasner denies "positive" status to both approaches; while, at least in the case of Waltz and Morgenthau, the concept is an analytic assumption in a logical-deductive system, its acceptability can be established only by empirically corroborating the hypotheses derived from that system (after all, Waltz agrees with Lakatos). On the other hand, Krasner's definition amounts to an attempt to empirically establish axioms.

4. Most notably John Searle (1964), by means of "speech acts" analysis.

5. John Harsanyi, *Rational Behavior and Bargaining Equilibrium*, p. 12.

6. *Ibid.*, p. 4.

7. The requirement of consistent ends is standard in formal theories of behavior, although other rationality postulates vary. See chapter 7.

8. One of the things that is least understood about Axelrod's work is that his computer simulation is not a test of the acceptability of the model but a substitute for a purely deductive solution to the proposed axioms. If a convincing deductive solution were available there would be no need for the simulation. In that sense, the model is purely abstractive.

9. Harsanyi, *Rational Behavior and Bargaining Equilibrium*.

10. Jervis, *Perception and Misperception*, p. 14.

11. Timothy McKeown has argued that "although the distinction among explanations in terms of between-state processes and within-state processes seems to be popular among students of international politics, it is not obvious that it serves as more than a cataloging scheme for classifying existing studies in terms of their research emphasis. It certainly ought not to inhibit the

development of theories that incorporate influence processes of both types" (McKeown, "Firms and Tariff Regime Change.").

12. Examples of this argument are provided by Alker, "Dialectical Thinking and World Order," and Biersteker, "Dialectical Thinking about the World."

13. The reason for this is that the abstraction of variables at different levels almost inevitably entails abstraction of part of the same reality in each of these variables: while a state is a unit, for example, it also includes people and institutions as component parts (although it is not equal to the sum of these parts); the arbitrary combination of variables like states, individual actors, and institutions leads to an "overlap," unless an a priori mechanism of separation is provided. A conceptual overlap occurs when combining any units with others that subsume them. Such overlap in mathematical set theory leads to the so-called "Russell Paradox," named after Bertrand Russell. Russell considered classes (or sets) that were not members of themselves. When he asked whether "the class of all classes" was a member of itself, it turned out that it *was* a member of itself if and only if it *was not*, which is obviously paradoxical. Russell resolved this paradox by advancing the "ramified theory of types," distinguishing different *types* of hierarchical classes which, if combined arbitrarily, would lead to nonsense (see Edwards, "Bertrand Russell, pp. 245–246, 250–251).

14. W. S. Robinson, "Ecological Correlations and the Behavior of Individuals."

15. See, for example, Leo Goodman, "Some Alternatives to Ecological Correlation."

16. Alker, "Dialectical Thinking about World Order."

17. James Lee Ray, *Global Politics*, 3rd ed., Boston: Houghton Mifflin, 1987, p. 429.

18. The test in the specific case is not intended as a general evaluation of the research program. Rather, it is intended to measure the explanatory power of the a priori assumed research program in the specific case.

19. Based on the work of Herbert Simon, the concept of nesting was employed in international relations by Vinod Aggarwal and Robert Keohane (see Simon, "The Architecture of Complexity"; Aggarwal, *Liberal Protectionism;* and Keohane, *After Hegemony*).

20. For example, see Alker, "Dialectical Thinking about World Order," and Biersteker, "Dialectical Thinking About the World."

21. Waltz, *Man, The State, and War.*

22. Telhami, "International Bargaining and the Level of Analysis Problem: The Case of Camp David."

23. Aggarwal, *Liberal Protectionism.*

24. John Harsanyi makes an important distinction between two types of formal theories: decision theory and game theory. Individual decision theory "deals primarily with rational behavior in situations in which the outcome depends on an individual's (the decision maker's) own behavior." In contrast, game theory (and "ethics") deals with behavior in a social setting, where the

outcome depends not only on the preferences of an individual player but also on the preferences and decisions of other players (Harsanyi, *Rational Behavior and Bargaining Equilibrium*, p. 11). Bargaining theory is a subset of game theory with the specific stipulation that all the players seek to maximize their defined interests (in contrast with "arbitration theory," where the outcome depends on the additional moral notion of "fairness").

25. For a discussion of this issue, see chapter 4.

26. Snyder and Diesing, *Conflict Among Nations*, p. 22.

27. Snyder and Diesing argue that while generalized formal bargaining theory, based on utility maximization, can be useful, it has some major limitations because it fails to capture several important characteristics (they specify five) in the real world of bargaining (Snyder and Diesing, *Conflict Among Nations*, p. 11).

28. For example, Harsanyi has formalized a general solution to the bargaining problem, capturing the variability of the O point, based on Nash's solution to the simple game. I have similarly generalized a solution based on alternative assumptions made by Raiffa (see Harsanyi, *Rational Behavior and Bargaining Equilibrium*; Nash, "The Bargaining Problem;" and Raiffa, "Arbitration Schemes for Two-Person Games").

3. The Superpowers and the Preferences of States

1. It is *not* my argument that change in the distribution of power is the only variable affecting the superpowers' policies in the Middle East, but that this variable explains some major shifts in these policies. Some important domestic variables are taken into account in chapter 6.

2. Several analysts have reached similar conclusions. Martin Indyk has argued for example that Egypt's situation in the 1970s was such that the path of "positive" neutralism was closed (Indyk, *To the End of the Earth: Sadat's Jerusalem Initiative*, Harvard Middle East Papers, Modern Series, number 1, Cambridge, 1984, p. 8). Galal Amin concluded that "as a result of détente, countries of the Third World were suddenly deprived of their ability to take neutral stand vis-á-vis the superpowers." (Amin, "External Factors in the Reorientation of Egypt's Economic Policy" in Malcolm H. Kerr and Sayed Yassin, eds., *Rich and Poor States in the Middle East*, Boulder, 1982, p. 301). And Ismail Fahmy noted that some within the Soviet leadership knew that "Egypt needed an ally more than ever, and that it would turn to the United States if the Soviet Union drew back" (Fahmy, *Negotiating for Peace*, p. 186).

3. The argument for close American-Israeli relations as an enduring component of Israeli foreign policy is fully articulated in chapter 5.

4. Brown, *International Politics and the Middle East*, p. 5.

5. Heikal, *The Sphinx and the Commissar*, p. 243.

6. From a realist point of view, it can be argued that, in pursuing détente with the U.S., the Soviet Union was motivated by the need to get economic

and technological help from the West; as a result of détente, the Soviets subordinated their relation with Egypt to the objective of preserving détente, thus acceding to U.S. requests for holding back on military aid to Egypt. Détente is thus posited as a dependent intermediate variable, largely explained by the distribution of economic power. In addition, relative economic weakness prevented the Soviets from providing Egypt with badly needed economic aid.

7. Chapter 4 constitutes a full articulation of the regional component of Egypt's foreign policy.

8. For example, see Kenneth Waltz, "International structure, national force, and the balance of world power" (1967); Morton Kaplan, *System and Process in International Politics* (New York, 1964); and Karl Deutsch and J. David Singer,"Multipolar Power Systems and International Stability" (1964).

9. See Stephen Krasner, "Introduction: International Regimes and Structural Constraints" (1982); Robert Keohane, "The Theory of Hegemonic Stability and Changes in International Economic Regimes, 1967–1977" (1980); and Vinod Aggarwal, "The Unraveling of the Multi-Fiber Arrangement, 1981: An Examination of International Regime Change" (1983).

10. It is useful to note once more that while change in the distribution of power in itself does not necessarily explain all U.S. policies in the Middle East, it does explain the general tendencies across time. In chapter 6 I show how and why domestic variables explain historical deviations from these tendencies.

11. Lenczowski, *Soviet Advances in the Middle East*, p. 76.

12. For a discussion of this issue see Gerson, *John Foster Dulles*, pp. 241–245.

13. *Ibid.*

14. *Ibid.*

15. The "Eisenhower Doctrine" is articulated in a presidential policy statement issued on January 5, 1957. It was aimed at reducing Soviet advances and local Communist activity in the Middle East.

16. See Appendix 3B.

17. Kissinger, *The White House Years*, p. 560.

18. Sheehan, *The Arabs, Israelis, and Kissinger*, p. 199.

19. Quoted by Lenczowski, *Soviet Advances in the Middle East*, pp. 12–13.

20. Quoted by Whiting, "Foreign Policy of China," p. 259.

21. Cf. note 4, which posits détente itself as a dependent variable.

22. See page 92 above, which describes how Soviet influence was minimal despite the large amounts of military and economic aid provided to Egypt.

23. *Rus al-Yusuf* (Arabic), Cairo, February 7, 1978.

24. Shazly, *The Crossing of the Suez*, pp. 100–101.

25. It is worth noting once more that Soviet acquiescence in "linkage politics," in the context of détente with the United States, is itself posited as a function of strategic parity coupled with economic disparity. In this sense, détente is not the explanatory variable but an intermediate dependant variable.

26. Quoted by Israeli, *Man of Defiance*, p. 44.
27. *Ibid.*
28. Shazly, *The Crossing of the Suez*, p. 105.
29. Personal interview, Cairo, August 28, 1983.
30. *Ibid.*
31. Shazly, *The Crossing of the Suez*, p. 94.
32. *Ibid.*
33. *Ibid.*, p. 100.
34. Israeli, *Man of Defiance*, p. 73.
35. Shazly, *The Crossing of the Suez*, p. 103. This seems consistent with Sadat's later behavior toward the United States. Having decided to forge closer ties with the U.S., Sadat unilaterally offered Egyptian facilities to the American Rapid Deployment Force.
36. *Ibid.*
37. *Ibid.*, p. 127.
38. *Ibid.*, p. 129.
39. Fahmy, *Negotiating for Peace in the Middle East*, pp. 6–7.
40. Shazly, *The Crossing of the Suez*, p. 175.
41. This view was shared by former Egyptian Foreign Minister, Ibrahim Kamel (personal interview, Cairo, August 25, 1983).
42. This view was unanimously shared by Sayyed Yasin, Ali Dessouki, and Ibrahim Kamel (personal interviews, Cairo, August 1983).
43. Fahmy, *Negotiating for Peace in the Middle East*, p. 172.
44. See chapter 5 for a full argument in support of this proposition.
45. Quandt, *Camp David*, p. 171.
46. Personal interview, Cairo, August 28, 1983.
47. *Ibid.*
48. Personal interview, Cairo, August 25, 1983.
49. Economic disparity affected decisions in two ways: it contributed to the elevation of détente to the top of Soviet priorities to enable the Soviet Union to receive Western technology and capital; and the economic superiority of the United States made the U.S. more attractive to Egypt in the absence of urgent Egyptian military needs following the 1973 war.
50. Libyan trade figures, as reported by the IMF, are taken from Libyan sources and should be used with some caution. These figures presumably include arms tranfers; any inaccuracies should be consistent across time.
51. Stockholm International Peace Research Institute, *SIPRI Yearbook: 1972*, p. 259.
52. On the characteristics and significance of Soviet treaties of this type, see Zafar Imam, "Soviet Treaties with Third World Countries."

4. Regional Politics and the Preferences of Egypt

1. A discussion of this argument is to be found in chapter 1.
2. See Joseph Schumpeter, *Imperialism and Social Classes*, pp. 128–130; and Dimitri K. Simes, "Disciplining Soviet Power," pp. 40–43.
3. See Adam Ulam, "Russian Nationalism," pp. 3–17; and Richard Pipes, *Survival is Not Enough*, pp. 12, 37–48.
4. Jervis, "Cooperation Under the Security Dilemma."
5. For a full discussion of Israel's international strategy, see chapter 5.
6. Fahmy, *Negotiating for Peace in the Middle East*, p. 175.
7. While Egypt did not become totally dependent on other Arab states, there can be little doubt that, at a minimum, there emerged increasing interdependence which resulted in diminished Egyptian influence in favor of other Arab states.
8. Consider, for example the early days of modern Egypt, beginning with the dynasty of Muhammad Ali (1811) whose dynasty ruled Egypt until the Free Officers overthrew the monarchy in 1952. The prevalent interpretations of that period are that Egypt sought regional control. For example, L. Carl Brown notes that "The Egypt of Muhammad Ali and his successors was an expansionist political system, conquering the Sudan, intervening for a time in the Arabian peninsula, Greece, Syria, and even Ethiopia, until state bankruptcy during Khedive Ismail's reign ended such ambitions" (Brown, *International Politics and the Middle East*, p. 75). Since I have argued in the theoretical section that a state's drive for domination may, under some specifiable environmental circumstances, be security based, Brown's interpretation may be consistent with that of Afaf al-Sayyid Marsot. Marsot sees Egypt's eventual attack on Ottoman-controlled Syria as being security motivated: "While the Ottomans looked on Egypt as a prey, the Mamluks also had plundered it. . . . Caught as they were between the devil and the deep blue sea, the Egyptians found little to look forward to. . . . These circumstances catapulted Muhammad Ali from a position of relative obscurity into a position of power. . . ." (Marsot, *Egypt in the Reign of Muhammad Ali*, p. 38). Marsot goes on to argue that Syria was seen as a buffer between Mohammed Ali and the Ottomans (p. 222).
9. Vatikiotis, *Nasser and His Generation*, pp. 243–244.
10. Dekmejian, *Egypt Under Nasir*, pp. 100–101.
11. For a discussion of this point, see the section on the level of analysis problem in chapter 2.
12. For support of this argument, see Stephen M. Walt, *The Origins of Alliances*, chapter 6.
13. International regimes are generally defined as norms, rules, and procedures governing a given area of international relations; they can be formal or informal (for a good discussion of regimes, see the special issue of *International Organization*, vol. 36 [2], Spring 1982). The Pan-Arabist movement can be

viewed as a regime represented by some inter-Arab institutions such as the Arab League and, more importantly, some implicit rules and norms pertaining to inter-Arab relations. Most notable of these are the commitment to some collective positions on Israel and Palestine, and the objective of attaining a united Arab world. Egypt's commitment to these collective positions in the 1950s and 1960s legitimized its Pan-Arab credentials; its clear violation of this commitment in the late 1970s signified the abandonment of the norms and rules of the regime.

14. As Oran Young put it, "imposed orders are deliberately established by dominant actors who succeed in getting others to conform to the rules of these orders through some combination of coercion, cooperation and the manipulation of interests" (Young, "Regime Dynamics," p. 284).

15. Stein, "Coordination and Collaboration," p. 323.

16. Krasner, "Regimes and the Limits of Realism," p. 499.

17. In the three years immediately following the Suez attack, Egyptian influence in the region reached impressive proportions. The pro-British monarchy in Iraq was overthrown, a pro-Nasser Baathist government emerged in Syria, and most regimes that opposed Egypt faced serious pro-Nasser uprisings at home. The results were crowned with the establishment of the United Arab Republic which joined Syria and Egypt (with Egypt as the dominant partner), and which promised to encompass other Arab states.

18. While Arabism was advocated in the Arab East, it is striking that aside from the King and the Wafd (whose priorities were Egyptian nationalism), the only other real political force in Egypt was the Muslim Brotherhood, which although anti-British, did not advocate Arabism. Nasser and the Free Officers also professed Egyptian nationalism and secularism, their declared objectives being "emancipation from imperialism and feudalism" and the achievement of social justice and economic progress.

19. As pointed out in note 8, many scholars interpret Egypt's behavior in the nineteenth century along these lines. The same could be said of Egypt in the 1940s, before the Free Officers came to power. Aside from its anti-colonial objectives, Egypt was also fearful of Arab competition for regional influence, as manifested in its rivalry with Iraq.

20. Two examples of this are telling. The first is Egypt's relations with Iraq *after* the overthrow of the pro-British monarchy. The new regime of Abd al-Kareem Qasim was fervently anti-colonial, advocated pan-Arabism and social justice, and seemed even more populist than Nasser's. Qasim, unwilling to subordinate himself to Nasser, quickly became Egypt's most targeted opponent. Nasser adamantly opposed Qasim's plan to control Kuwait following British withdrawal, a plan consistent with Nasser's pan-Arabist ideals. So sharp was Egypt's opposition to the incorporation that it was willing to reconcile its differences with its ideological opponent Saudi Arabia in the political fight against Iraq. More embarrassingly, Egypt found itself unable to attack the deployment of British troops in Kuwait to defend against potential Iraqi attacks.

The second example pertains to the unity talks between Egypt, Syria and Iraq in 1963–64, when the issue of leadership was a major obstacle to real unity. The following discussion between Nasser and the Baathist leaders of Syria and Iraq illustrates this point:

> "SHA'R: Why don't we have a Union Council, as in the USSR?. . .
> "NASSER: But this would change nothing. The basic problem remains, namely, of whom shall this council be composed? If it happens that you have an Iraqi Baathist, a Syrian Baathist and an Egyptian, then the Baath would actually be running the state" (quoted by Kerr, *The Arab Cold War*, p. 63).

21. One example of this is Egypt's military intervention in Yemen. Although Egypt was the most powerful state in the Arab world, its superiority was negated by U.S. aid to Saudi Arabia and to the Yemeni Royalists.

22. Egypt's military preoccupation with Israel and its failure in Yemen neutralized the military component as a means of influence in the Arab world.

23. Dessouki, "The New Arab Political Order," p. 326.

24. Al-Aqqad, *Al-Sadat and Camp David*, p. 31.

25. Israeli, *Man of Defiance*, p. 88.

26. Dessouki, "The New Arab Political Order," p. 326.

27. While Egypt may have been inclined to pursue these ends in any case, the fact that the Saudis would interfere was resented. Moreover, if Egypt were to pursue these ends on its own, leading to closer relations with the United States, it would no longer need Saudi help.

28. Personal interview, Cairo, August 25, 1983.

29. Bruzonsky, "Interview with Mohamed Ibrahim Kamel," p. 86.

30. Butrus Ghali (personal interview, Cairo, August 28, 1983).

31. Israeli, *Public Diary of President Sadat*, Part III, p. 1333.

32. Ibrahim Kamel (personal interview, Cairo, August 25, 1983).

33. Weizman, *Battle for Peace*, p. 89.

34. Al-Aqqad, *Al-Sadat and Camp David*, p. 31.

35. Former Israeli Defense Minister Ezer Weizman remarked that "in driving the Russians from Egypt [Sadat] brought the West closer to him, necessarily diluting its loyalty to us. His campaign was successful, costing us our position as the cosseted godchild of the Western world. Our situation went from bad to worse" (Weizman, *The Battle for Peace*, p. 18).

36. See note 34, p. 254.

37. Butrus Ghali, for example, called the Egyptian competition with Israel for strategic alliance with the United States "the most important leverage" that Egypt held, and "the secret weapon" that Israel feared most (personal interview, Cairo, August 28, 1983).

38. Apparently anticipating failure, Sadat prepared key Egyptian envoys for a massive information campaign following such failure, that would blame Israeli intransigence for missing a historic moment for peace. (Personal interview with former Egyptian advisor Tahseen Bashir, Princeton, March 1984).

39. Quoted by Zbigniew Brzezinski, *Power and Principle: Memoirs of the National Security Adviser, 1977–1981* (New York, 1983), p. 272.

5. International Politics and the Preferences of Israel

1. Selten, "The Chain-Store Paradox."
2. The chain-store paradox can be described as follows. Consider a sequential game with the following players: a chain store with branches in 20 towns (player A) and a local potential competitor in every town (player K), who might be able to raise just enough money to open a second store in one town. If player K raises the amount required to open a store, he must choose between opening the store or some other investment. If K opens a store, then A has to decide between two pricing policies: cooperation or aggression. Cooperation yields higher profits in town K for both players. Player A's profits in town K, however, are even higher if player K does not open the store in the first place. Player K's profits in case of an aggressive response are such that it is better for him not to open the store if player A responds in this way.

In the situation described above, it is apparent that while player K is interested only in his profits in town K, player A must be concerned with his cumulative profits in all 20 towns. Even though it would be more profitable for player A to cooperate in town K, when all 20 towns are taken into account, it is more profitable if other potential competitors do not open other stores in other towns. He is, therefore concerned with deterrence, that is, how well his actions in town K will serve to deter others from opening stores to compete with his own.

A deductive solution to this game could be found by adding the assumption of assessed probability. If we assume that player K has an assessment P of the probability that player A will be aggressive, a solution can be found. David Kreps and Robert Wilson employ such an approach, yielding impressive results. Even if P is *very small*, it turns out it is better for player K not to compete with the chain store, and better for the chain store to be aggressive if player K decides to compete. Kreps and Wilson also propose a systematic method to assess probability based on the history of player A. See Kreps and Wilson, "Reputation and Imperfect Information."

3. Knapp, "The United States and the Middle East: How Many Special Relationships?" p. 20.
4. Israel's strong opposition to the AWACS sale to Saudi Arabia, for example, may have been motivated partly by this consideration.
5. Kenan, "The Labor Party is to Blame," p. 359.
6. *New York Times*, March 9, 1986.
7. This consideration inclines Israel toward preemption and the pursuit of an offensive military strategy in which the air force plays a dominant role, since it requires less manpower and can be more efficient. The 1967 war was an example of Israel's success.

8. This idea played a part in Egypt's designs for a "war of attrition" against Israeli forces in 1969–70.
9. Quoted by David Hirst, *The Gun and the Olive Branch*, p.258.
10. Ariel Sharon, Israel's defense minister at the time, strongly believed that Israel could project itself as a regional superpower. For a discussion of this see Telhami, "The Israeli Invasion of Lebanon."
11. For a theoretical discussion of the "level of analysis" question, see chapter 2.
12. Quoted by Louis, *British Empire in the Middle East*, p. 615.
13. Ibid.
14. Ibid., pp. 613–620.
15. Ibid., p. 614.
16. Ibid., p. 615.
17. Ibid., p. 617.
18. Ben-Gurion, "Principles for the Jewish State," p. 80.
19. Ben-Gurion, *Ba-ma'arakhah*, vol. 3, pp. 27–28.
20. Ben-Gurion, *Ba-ma'arakhah*, vol. 2, pp. 260–261.
21. Quoted by Krammer, *The Forgotten Friendship*, p. 141.
22. Ibid., p. 143.
23. Eddy, *F.D.R. Meets Ibn Saud*, p. 37.
24. Krammer, *The Forgotten Friendship*, p. 143.
25. Louis, *British Empire in the Middle East*, p. 607.
26. Ibid.
27. Chomsky, *Fateful Triangle*, p. 467.
28. Dayan, *Diary of the Sinai Campaign*, p. 206.
29. See chapter 3 for a discussion of American policy in the Middle East in the 1950s.
30. There are several good studies of the Israeli decisions leading to the 1976 war that focus on the level of decision-making, many of them attributing the decision to irrational escalation by Egypt, failure of Israeli deterrence, or uncertainty about Egyptian capabilities. Examples include Michael Brecher and Benjamin Geist, *Decisions in Crisis: Israel, 1967 and 1973;* Nadav Safran, *From War to War;* and Janice Stein and Raymond Tanter, *Rational Decision-Making: Israel's Security Choices, 1967*, among others.
31. While some parties in Israel have always advocated a greater Israel along the lines of historic Eretz Yisrael, there was hardly a consensus on this in the Israeli government. Moreover, the public mood in Israel was not supportive of this objective.
32. For an elaboration of this general point see Jervis, "Cooperation Under the Security Dilemma," pp. 186–189.
33. Quandt, *Decade of Decisions*, p. 50. It should be noted however that Nadav Safran states that the Israeli military told Prime Minister Ashkol that every day Israel waited to preempt would increase the Israeli casualty rate by 200, and that failure to respond would "invite new pressures and eventual war" (Safran, *Israel: The Embattled Ally*, p. 411).

5. International Politics

34. It is useful to emphasize once more that the focus here is on one set of variables at one level of analysis, while ignoring others, such as the actual perception of policy makers, which may or may not completely coincide with this analysis. The theoretical case for this approach is made in chapter 2, especially the sections on "positive theories," and "the level of analysis."

35. These actions included closing the Straits of Tiran to Israeli shipping, removing United Nations forces from the Sinai, and publicly exhibiting his military strength.

36. Significantly, former Israeli Foreign Minister Abba Eban saw the signing of the Egyptian Jordanian pact, not the blockade of the Tiran Straits, to be the most threatening act to Israel: "by his journey to Cairo on May 30, Hussein made it certain that war would break." (Eban, *An Autobiography*, p. 380).

37. See pages 116–117 for a discussion of the 1956 war.

38. A good example of this point is the Israeli invasion of Lebanon. Before the war the U.S. had more regional options, and its interests did not recommend an Israeli invasion. Yet even though the invasion substantially limited American options, the new facts recommended closer cooperation with Israel as the best of the available options. For a discussion of this see Telhami, "American Foreign Policy: The Lessons of Beirut."

39. See chapter 3 and appendix 3 for patterns of Soviet influence in the Middle East.

40. Weizman, *Battle for Peace*, p. 18.

41. For example, General George Brown, then-chairman of the Joint Chiefs of Staff, declared: "From a purely military point of view, Israel has just got to be considered a burden for the U.S." (*Washington Post*, October 19, 1976).

42. Quoted by Stephen M. Wait, *The Origins of Alliances*, p. 239.

43. Quoted by Stork, "Israel as a Strategic Asset," p. 36.

44. *New York Times*, September 4, 1980.

45. Feldman, "Peacemaking in the Middle East: The Next Step," p. 763.

46. *JTA Daily News Bulletin*, June 16, 1980.

47. Avineri, "Beyond Camp David," pp. 35–36.

48. Weizman, *Battle for Peace*, pp. 115–116.

49. See chapter 4 for a discussion of Egyptian preferences.

50. See chapter 6 for a discussion of this point.

51. Carter, *Keeping Faith*, p. 414.

52. *Ibid.*

53. Telhami, "The Israeli Invasion of Lebanon."

54. The "success" of the strategy refers here only to the general ends of Israeli policy articulated in this chapter. One can make a good case that, in the last decade, Israel's regional environment has substantially changed, making these ends no longer optimal for Israel interest. For example, one can argue that the game between Israel and at least some Arab states is no longer zero-sum, so that there is now some room for cooperation. Such considerations, however, are beyond the scope of this work.

6. Preferences, Perceptions, and the Structure of Bargaining

1. In particular his *Perception and Misperception in International Politics* and "Cooperation Under the Security Dilemma."
2. Tahseen Bashir (personal interview, Princeton, March 1984).
3. *Ibid.*
4. Carter, *Keeping Faith*, p. 345.
5. *Ibid.*, p. 283.
6. *Ibid.*, p. 327.
7. *Ibid.*, p. 317.
8. William Quandt (personal interview, Princeton, February 21, 1984).
9. See pages 149–153 below.
10. Kerr, *The Arab Cold War*, p. 155.
11. Fahmy, *Negotiating for Peace in the Middle East*, p. 256.
12. Ibrahim Kamel (personal interview, Cairo, August 25, 1983).
13. Bruzonsky, "Interview with Mohamed Ibrahim Kamel," pp. 86–87.
14. Ibrahim Kamel (personal interview, Cairo, August 25, 1983).
15. Butrus Ghali (personal interview, Cairo, August 28, 1983).
16. Harsanyi, *Rational Behavior and Bargaining Equilibrium*, p. 11.
17. A discussion of possible definitions of rationality and their implications for behavior is presented in chapter 7.
18. See chapter 3 for a discussion of American foreign policy.
19. See note 34 to chapter 5 for a statement by General George Brown.
20. See appendix 3B for patterns of Soviet influence.
21. See chapter 7 for a full discussion of this issue.
22. See, for example, Krasner, *Defending the National Interest*.
23. See note 17, chapter 5.
24. Examples of tactical diplomatic successes include the agreements on PLO withdrawal from Beirut following the Israeli invasion of Lebanon in 1982, and the Israeli-Lebanese treaty, which was soon abrogated by Lebanon.
25. Carter, *Keeping Faith*, p. 317.
26. *Ibid.*, p. 356.
27. *Ibid.*, p. 315.
28. *Ibid.*, p. 392.
29. Dessouki, "Transformation of the Party System in Egypt," p. 8.
30. Shazly, *The Crossing of the Suez*, p. 182.
31. *Ibid.*, p. 101.
32. Carter, *Keeping Faith*, p. 358.
33. The visit to Egypt was undertaken in November of 1976.
34. Carter, *Keeping Faith*, p. 366. See chapter 1, note 20 for complete text of quotation.
35. The "Allon Plan" was advanced by then-deputy prime minister of Israel, Yigael Allon, in 1972.

36. Quoted by Yuran Nimrod, *Al Hamishmar* (Hebrew), Tel Aviv, April 16, 1984.
37. Butrus Ghali, for example, did not believe that the Israelis had much incentive for an agreement (personal interview, Cairo, August 28, 1983).
38. Carter, *Keeping Faith*, p. 328.
39. *Ibid*.
40. *Ibid*.
41. *Ibid.*, p. 365.
42. William Quandt (personal interview, Princeton, February 21, 1984).
43. Carter, *Keeping Faith*, p. 392.
44. *Ibid.*, p. 364.
45. Allan, *Crisis Bargaining and the Arms Race*, p. 23.
46. Carter, *Keeping Faith*, p. 317.
47. *Ibid.*, p. 391.

7. Bargaining Performance

1. It is useful to note once again that the purpose of conceptual separation of the issues into two questions (one pertaining to general inclinations, the other to specific terms) is strictly pragmatic. Obviously, in the real world these issues are interconnected. The question for the theorist, however, is what conceptualizations and aggregations provide the most powerful and consistent explanations. This has been my methodological position as articulated in Chapter 2. In this case, I believe that such separation of the issues lends itself best to the employment of existing theoretical literature and provides a consistent set of explanations that are more powerful than the alternatives.
2. See appendix 7.
3. Weizman, *Battle for Peace*, p. 119.
4. Carter, *Keeping Faith*, p. 307.
5. *Ibid*.
6. See chapter 6 for a discussion of perceptions.
7. For general treatments of the topic of international bargaining, see the works by Lockhart, Raiffa, Fisher, Zartman, and Snyder & Diesing listed in the bibliography.
8. This is the case, for example, in the iterated Prisoner's Dilemma game.
9. On this fourth point Egypt also sought to secure a role in future negotiations and to prevent unilateral Israeli decisions, as a way of ensuring future influence in the Arab world.
10. This view was conveyed by Ibrahim Kamel and Sayyid Yasin (personal interviews, Cairo, August 25–28, 1983).
11. Carter, *Keeping Faith*, p. 340.
12. William Quandt (personal interview, London, April 14, 1988).
13. Carter, *Keeping Faith*, p. 365.

14. Quandt, *Camp David*, p. 225.
15. See Quandt, pp. 354–5.
16. Weizman, *Battle for Peace*, pp. 87–88.
17. Carter, *Keeping Faith*, p. 356. See also p. 342 for Sadat's relations with his staff.
18. Butrus Ghali (personal interview, Cairo, August 28, 1983).
19. Carter, *Keeping Faith*, p. 322.
20. *Ibid.*, p. 356.
21. *Ibid.*, p. 351.
22. *Ibid.*, p. 396.
23. Weizman, *Battle for Peace*, p. 122.
24. *Ibid.*, p. 129.
25. Carter, *Keeping Faith*, p. 361.
26. *Ibid.*
27. *Ibid.*, p. 348.
28. Weizman, *Battle for Peace*, p. 142.
29. *Ibid.*
30. Carter, *Keeping Faith*, p. 356.
31. Vance, *Hard Choices*, p. 181.
32. Harold Saunders (personal interview, Princeton, February 15, 1984).
33. Carter, *Keeping Faith*, p. 356.
34. Aronoff, "Political Polarization," p. 56.
35. *Ibid.*, p. 83.
36. Vance, *Hard Choices*, p. 181.
37. Quandt, *Camp David*, pp. 171, 218–219.
38. See for example Stephen Krasner, *Defending the National Interest*, pp. 56–61. My analysis of the broad outline of American policy in the Middle East, and the relevance of "issue-publics" (chapter 6), also supports this view in some respects.
39. For examples of different postulations of national interest, see chapter 2, notes 1 and 3.
40. There is support for this hypothesis in recent literature on international political economy. See, for example, Lake, "The State and American Trade Strategy in the Pre-Hegemonic Era"; Ikenberry, "The Irony of State Strength"; and Putnam, "Diplomacy and Domestic Politics: The Logic of Two-Level Games," which builds on Thomas Schelling, *The Strategy of Conflict* (1960). Migdal, *Strong Societies and Weak States* is also relevant to this issue.
41. For a discussion of this issue see Allan, *Crisis Bargaining and the Arms Race*, pp. 23–32.
42. See Janis, *Groupthink*, pp. 7–13.
43. Carter, *Keeping Faith*, p. 342.
44. Fahmy, *Negotiating for Peace*, p. 277.
45. Carter, *Keeping Faith*, p. 358.
46. Butrus Ghali (personal interview, Cairo, August 18, 1983).
47. Fahmy, *Negotiating for Peace*, p. 25.

48. Hirst & Beeson, *Sadat*, p. 324.
49. Jervis, *Perception and Misperception*, p. 357.
50. Habec, *Menachem Begin*, p. 255.
51. Hirschler & Eckman, *Menachem Begin*, p. 9.
52. For general works on the subject of personality in politics, see Margaret C. Hermann and Thomas Milburn, eds., *A Psychological Examination of Political Leaders* (New York, 1977); Lloyd S. Etheredge, "Personality Effects on American Foreign Policy: 1898–1968: A Test of Interpersonal Generalization Theory" (1985); James D. Barber, *The Presidential Character: Predicting Performance in the White House* (Englewood Cliffs, 1985); and David C. McClelland, *Human Motivation* (Glenview, 1985). For specific applications in bargaining situations, see Dean G. Pruitt, *Negotiation Behavior* (New York, 1981); and Jeff Rubin and Burt Brown, *The Social Psychology of Bargaining and Negotiations* (New York, 1975).
53. It should be clearly understood that the these characteristics are not intended to be comprehensive, nor are they claimed "to capture" fully the personalities of the three leaders studied in this chapter. This is simply an attempt to identify, theoretically and empirically, some variables that are relevant to bargaining.
54. Jervis, *Perception and Misperception*, p. 357.
55. Price, *Society and Bureaucracy in Contemporary Ghana*, pp. 24–25.
56. A person with high self-monitoring has the ability to alter his self-presentation, while a person with low self-monitoring does not (Snyder, "Self-Monitoring Processes").
57. Janis, *Groupthink*, pp. 260–276.
58. Pettigrew, "Cognitive Style and Social Behavior," p. 202.
59. Brzezinski, *Power and Principle*, p. 93.
60. Ibrahim Kamel (personal interview, Cairo, August 25, 1983).
61. Shazly, *The Crossing of the Suez*, p. 282.
62. Hirst & Beeson, *Sadat*, p. 310.
63. Polk, *The United States and the Arab World*, p. 401.
64. Carter, *Keeping Faith*, p. 322.
65. Vance, *Hard Choices*, p. 174.
66. Brzezinski, *Power and Principle*, p. 93.
67. Butrus Ghali (personal interview, Cairo, August 28, 1983).
68. Personal interview, Cairo, August 25, 1983.
69. Carter, *Keeping Faith*, p. 330.
70. Hirst & Beeson, *Sadat*, p. 355.
71. Carter, *Keeping Faith*, p. 357.
72. Vance, *Hard Choices*, p. 191.
73. Weizman, *Battle for Peace*, p. 75.
74. Carter, *Keeping Faith*, p. 357.
75. *Ibid.*, p. 366.
76. Touval, *The Peace Brokers*, p. 315.
77. Carter, *Keeping Faith*, p. 330.

78. William Quandt, a participant in the negotiations, concurs in these observations (personal interview, Princeton, February 21, 1984).
79. Brzezinski, *Power and Principle*, p. 254.
80. Quandt, *Camp David*, pp. 235–236.
81. Butrus Ghali (personal interview, Cairo, August 28, 1983).
82. For example, the Israelis pressed hard for retaining some control in the Sinai, for maximal demilitarization, for Jewish settlements in the Sinai, for maximal normalization of relations, and for separation between the Egyptian-Israeli agreements and the question of the West Bank and Gaza. The Egyptians, on the other hand, while they pressed the Israelis on the issue of the Sinai, did not test the limits of the Israeli position on linkage with the West Bank and Gaza, their future role in the negotiations, and Jewish settlements on the West Bank.
83. Telhami, "International Bargaining and the Level of Analysis Problem," pp. 401–404.
84. Butrus Ghali (personal interview, Cairo, August 28, 1983).
85. Harold Saunders (personal interview, Princeton, February 15, 1984).
86. Personal interview, Cairo, August 28, 1983.
87. Quandt, *Camp David*, p. 248.
88. *Ibid.*, p. 250.
89. William Quandt (personal interview, Princeton, February 15, 1984).
90. Quandt, *Camp David*, p. 251.
91. William Quandt (personal interview, Princeton, February 15, 1984).
92. Harsanyi, *Rational Behavior and Bargaining Equilibrium*, p. 3.
93. See the section on abstractive theory in chapter 2.
94. As an example, I will set out the most commonly held assumptions in formal bargaining theory, those advanced by John Nash ("The Bargaining Problem"), with some interpretations. First, Nash excludes interpersonal comparisons of utility; that is, Nash assumes that a single 'unit' of utility is worth the same to a poor actor as to a rich one. Second, Nash assumes that the solution to the game is Pareto-optimal: that there exists only one solution point where neither bargainer is better off than the other. Third, Nash assumes that the solution is independent of irrelevant alternatives: if a new alternative point is added to the solution point without changing the point of disagreement, that point either provides the new solution to the game or it has no impact on it. Fourth, Nash adds the assumption of symmetry: if both actors change places, the solution remains the same. Given these assumptions Nash was able to find a unique solution to the simple bargaining game. Later Nash also provided a solution to bargaining games where the disagreement payoffs change during the game as a result of threats and escalations. John Harsanyi stated the solution for such games mathematically (*Rational Behavior and Bargaining Equilibrium*).

Every one of Nash's assumptions has been challenged. And although alternative assumptions were provided in some cases, questions were also raised about all the alternatives. No convincing tests have been conducted to date

7. Bargaining Performance

that have established the adequacy of the alternative assumptions in social situations, which leaves the solution tentative. Even if we accept the predicted solution to the simple game, it should be apparent that most bargaining games are not "simple": in most bargaining situations the process itself changes the costs of failure to both sides. Consequently, the variable-threat games are more relevant, but these games require even more assumptions for their solution.

95. Harsanyi, p. 179.
96. This was one of my central arguments in chapter 2.

Bibliography

Primary Sources

BOOKS

Brzezinski, Zbigniew. *Power and Principle: Memoirs of the National Security Adviser, 1977–1981*. New York: Farrar, Straus & Giroux, 1983.
Carter, Jimmy. *The Blood of Abraham*. Boston: Houghton Mifflin Company, 1985.
——*Keeping Faith: Memoirs of a President*. New York: Bantam Books, 1982.
Carter, Rosalynn. *First Lady From Plains*. Boston: Houghton Mifflin Company, 1984.
Dayan, Moshe. *Breakthrough: A Personal Account of the Egypt- Israel Peace Negotiation*. London: Weidenfeld and Nicolson, 1981.
Israeli, Raphael. *The Public Diary of President Sadat. Part I: The Road to War. October 1970–October 1973*. Leiden: E.J. Brill, 1978.
——*The Public Diary of President Sadat. Part III: The Road of Pragmatism. June 1975–October 1976*. Leiden: E.J. Brill, 1979.
Kissinger, Henry. *The Years of Upheaval*. Boston: Little, Brown & Company, 1982.
——*White House Years*. Boston: Little, Brown & Company, 1979.

Quandt, William. *Camp David: Peacemaking and Politics*. Washington: The Brookings Institution, 1986.
Rabin, Yitzhak. *The Rabin Memoirs*. Boston: Little, Brown & Company, 1979.
Sadat, Anwar el. *In Search of Identity*. New York: Harper & Row, 1977.
——*Those I Have Known*. New York: Continuum, 1984.
Saunders, Harold. *The Other Walls*. Washington: American Enterprise Institute, 1985.
Shazly, Saad El, Lt. Gen. *The Crossing of the Suez*. San Francisco: American Mideast Research, 1980.
Sullivan, William H. *Mission to Iran*. New York: W.W. Norton & Co., 1981.
Vance, Cyrus. *Hard Choices: Critical Years in America's Foreign Policy*. New York: Simon & Schuster, 1983.
Weizman, Ezer. *The Battle for Peace*. New York: Bantam Books, 1981.

DOCUMENTS, U.S.

"A Framework for Middle East Peace." *Department of State Bulletin* 78 (2019), October 1978.
The Camp David Summit - September 1978. Department of State Publication 8954. Washington, DC: U.S. Government Printing Office, 1978.
Carter, James E. "Cairo, Egypt: Address Before the People's Assembly. March 10, 1979." *Weekly Compilation of Presidential Documents* 15 (11), March 19, 1979, pp. 412–414.
——"Jerusalem, Israel: Address Before the Knesset. March 12, 1979." *Weekly Compilation of Presidential Documents* 15 (11), March 19, 1979, pp. 424–428.
The Egyptian-Israeli Peace Treaty - March 26, 1979. Department of State Publication 8976. Washington DC: U.S. Government Printing Office, 1979.
President Carter's Trip to the Middle East: March 7–14, 1979, Department of State Publication 8971. Washington DC: U.S. Government Printing Office, 1979.
Public Papers of the Presidents of the United States: Jimmy Carter, 1977, Book I. Washington DC: U.S. Government Printing Office, 1977.
——1978, Book I. Washington DC: U.S. Government Printing Office, 1979.
The Quest for Peace: Principal United States Public Statements and Documents Relating to the Arab-Israeli Peace Process, 1967–1983. Department of State Publication 9373. Washington D.C: U.S. Government Printing Office, 1983.
Saunders, Harold. "Middle East: Camp David Agreements." *Department of State Bulletin* 78 (2020), November 1978.

OTHER DOCUMENTS

"A Framework for Peace in the Middle East Agreed at Camp David." *Middle East Journal* 32 (4), Autumn 1978.
The Egyptian Position in Negotiations Concerning the Establishment of Transitional Arrangements for the West Bank and Gaza. Cairo: Ministry of Foreign Affairs, 1980.

"The Israeli-Egyptian Peace Negotiations: Main Documents." *Hamizrah Hehadash* 30, 1981. Tel Aviv: Shiloah Center, Tel Aviv University.
White Paper on Treaty of Peace between Egypt and Israel. Cairo: Ministry of Foreign Affairs, 1979.
White Paper on the Peace Initiative Undertaken by Anwar Sadat, 1971–1979. Cairo: Ministry of Foreign Affairs, 19??.

Secondary Sources

BOOKS

Aggarwal, Vinod. *Liberal Protectionism: The International Politics of Organized Textile Trade*. Berkeley: University of California Press, 1985.
Ajami, Fouad. *The Arab Predicament: Arab Political Thought and Practice Since 1967*. London: Cambridge University Press, 1981.
Allan, Pierre. *Crisis Bargaining and the Arms Race: A Theoretical Model*. Cambridge: Ballinger Publishing Company, 1983.
Al-Aqqad, Salah. *Sadat and Camp David* (in Arabic). Cairo: Maktabat Madboli, 1984.
Arad, Ruth. *The Economics of Peacemaking: Focus on the Egyptian-Israeli Situation*. London: Macmillan Press, 1983.
Aronson, Shlomo. *Conflict and Bargaining in the Middle East: An Israeli Perspective*. Baltimore: The Johns Hopkins University Press, 1978.
Axelrod, Robert. *The Evolution of Cooperation*. New York: Basic Books, 1983.
Barber, James D. *The Presidential Character: Predicting Performance in the White House*. 2d. edition. Englewood Cliffs: Prentice-Hall, 1985.
Bell, J. Bowyer. *Terror Out of Zion: Irgun Zvai Leumi, LEHI, and the Palestine Underground, 1948–1949*. New York: St. Martin's Press, 1977.
Ben-Gurion, David. *Ba-ma'arakhah* (in Hebrew), vols. 2 and 3. Tel Aviv: Am Oved Publishers, Ltd., 1957.
Benvenisti, Meron. *The West Bank Data Project: A Survey of Israel's Policies*. Washington DC: American Enterprise Institute for Public Policy Research, 1984.
Benziman, Uzi. *Prime Minister Under Siege* (in Hebrew). Jerusalem: Adam Publishers, 1981.
Berger, Monroe. *Islam in Egypt Today: Social and Political Aspects of Popular Religion*. London: Cambridge University Press, 1970.
Binder, Leonard. *In a Moment of Enthusiasm: Political Power and the Second Stratum in Egypt*. Chicago: University of Chicago Press, 1978.
Bradley, C. Paul. *The Camp David Peace Process: A Study of Carter Administration Policies 1977–1980*. Grantham, NH: Tompson & Rutter, 1981.
Brecher, Michael. *Decision in Israel's Foreign Policy*. New Haven: Yale University Press, 1975.

Brecher, Michael and Geist Benjamin. *Decisions in Crisis: Israel, 1967 and 1973.* Berkeley: University of California Press, 1980.

Brown, L. Carl. *International Politics and the Middle East.* Princeton: Princeton University Press, 1984.

Burrell, R. Michael and Abbas R. Kelidar. *Egypt: The Dilemmas of a Nation — 1970-1977.* Beverly Hills: Sage Publications, 1977.

Chomsky, Noam. *The Fateful Triangle.* Boston: South End Press, 1983.

Cobban, Helena. *The Palestinian Liberation Organization: People, Power and Politics.* New York: Cambridge University Press, 1984.

Cooper, Mark. *The Transformation of Egypt.* London: Croom Helm, 1982.

Dayan, Moshe. *Diary of the Sinai Campaign.* New York: Harper & Row, 1966.

Dekmejian, R. Hrair. *Patterns of Political Leadership, Egypt Israel, Lebanon.* Albany: State University of New York Press, 1975.

———*Egypt Under Nasir: A Study in Political Dynamics.* Albany: State University of New York Press, 1971.

Donovan, Hedley. *Roosevelt to Reagan: A Reporter's Encounters with Nine Presidents.* New York: Harper & Row, 1985.

Eban, Abba. *An Autobiography.* New York: Random House, 1977.

Eddy, William Alfred. *F.D.R. Meets Ibn Saud.* New York: American Friends of the Middle East, 1954.

Elazar, Daniel J. *The Camp David Framework for Peace: A Shift Toward Shared Rule.* Washington DC: American Enterprise Institute for Public Policy Research, 1979.

Fahmy, Ismail. *Negotiating for Peace in the Middle East.* Baltimore: Johns Hopkins University Press, 1983.

Friedlander, Melvin A. *Sadat and Begin: The Domestic Politics of Peacemaking.* Boulder, CO: Westview, 1983.

Gerson, Louis L. *John Foster Dulles.* New York: Cooper Square Publishers, 1967.

Ghanem, Joseph R. *The Complete Texts of the Camp David Agreements: Arabic and English Versions.* Beirut: Lebanese University. 1981.

Habec, Eitan. *Menachem Begin: The Legend and the Man.* New York: Delacorte Press, 1978.

Harsanyi, John. *Rational Behavior and Bargaining Equilibrium in Games and Social Situations.* Cambridge: Cambridge University Press, 1977.

Heikal, Mohammed. *The Sphinx and the Commissar: The Rise and Fall of Soviet Influence in the Middle East.* New York: Harper & Row, 1978.

———*Autumn of Fury: The Assassination of Sadat.* New York: Random House, 1983.

Hermann, Margaret C. and Thomas Milburn. *A Psychological Examination of Political Leaders.* New York: Free Press, 1977.

Hirschler, Gertrude, and Lester S. Eckman. *Menachem Begin: From Freedom Fighter to Statesman.* New York: Shengold Publishers, 1979.

Hirst, David. *The Gun and the Olive Branch.* London: Faber and Faber, 1977.

Hirst, David and Irene Beeson. *Sadat*. London: Faber and Faber, 1981.
Israeli, Raphael. *Man of Defiance: a Political Biography of Anwar Sadat*. London: Wiedenfeld & Nicolson, 1985.
Ikle, Fred. *How Nations Negotiate*. New York: Harper & Row, 1964.
Janis, Irving L. *Groupthink: Psychological Studies of Policy Decisions and Fiascoes*, 2d ed., revised. Boston: Houghton Mifflin Company, 1982.
Jervis, Robert. *Perception and Misperception in International Politics*. Princeton: Princeton University Press, 1976.
Jordan, Hamilton. *Crisis: The Last Year of the Carter Presidency*. New York: Putnam Publishing Group, 1982.
Kamel, Muhammad Ibrahim. *The Lost Peace in the Camp David Accords* (in Arabic). Jidda: Saudi Research and Marketing Company, 1984.
Keohane, Robert. *After Hegemony: Cooperation and Discord in the World Political Economy*. Princeton: Princeton University Press, 1984.
Kerr, Malcolm. *The Arab Cold War: Gamal 'Abd al-Nasir and His Rivals, 1958–1970*. London: Oxford University Press, 1971.
Kosman, William Yousef. *Sadat's Realistic Peace Initiative*. New York: Vantage Press, 1981.
Krammer, Arnold. *The Forgotten Friendship: Israel and the Soviet Bloc, 1947–1953*. Urbana: University of Illinois Press, 1974.
Krasner, Stephen. *Defending the National Interest: Raw Materials Investments and U.S. Foreign Policy*. Princeton: Princeton University Press, 1979.
Lakatos, Imre. *The Methodology of Scientific Research Programmes*. Cambridge: Cambridge University Press, 1978.
Leeden, Michael and Lewis, William. *Debacle: The American Failure in Iran*. New York: Alfred A. Knopf, 1981.
Lenczowski, George. *Political Elites in the Middle East*. Washington DC: American Enterprise Institute for Public Policy Research, 1975.
———*Soviet Advances in the Middle East*. Washington DC: American Enterprise Institute for Public Policy Research, 1972.
———*The Middle East in World Affairs*, 3rd ed. New York: Cornell University Press, 1962.
Lilienthal, Alfred. *The Zionist Connection: What Price Peace?*. New York: Middle East Perspective, Inc., 1979.
Louis, William Roger. *The British Empire in the Middle East: 1945–1951*. Oxford: Clarendon Press, 1984.
Marsot, Afaf al-Sayyid. *Egypt in the Reign of Muhammad Ali*. Cambridge: Cambridge University Press, 1984.
McClelland, David C. *Human Motivation*. Glenview: Scott, Foresman, 1985.
McLaurin, R.D., Mohammed Mughisuddin, and Abraham Wagner. *Foreign Policy Making in the Middle East*. New York: Praeger, 1977.
Medzini, Meron, ed. *Israel's Foreign Relations: Selected Documents, 1977–1979*, vols. 4 and 5. Jerusalem: Ministry for Foreign Affairs, 1981.
Migdal, Joel S. *Strong Societies and Weak States*. Princeton: Princeton University Press, 1988.

O'Conner, Patricia. *The Middle East: U.S. Policy, Israel, Oil and the Arabs*, 4th ed. Washington DC: Congressional Quarterly, 1980.
Pipes, Richard. *Survival is Not Enough: Soviet Realities and America's Future*. New York: Simon & Schuster, 1984.
Polk, William R. *The United States and the Arab World*. Cambridge: Harvard University Press, 1965.
Powell, Jody. *The Other Side of the Story*. New York: William Morrow and Company, 1984.
Price, Robert M. *Society and Bureaucracy in Contemporary Ghana*. Berkeley: University of California Press, 1975.
Pruitt, Dean G. *Negotiation Behavior*. New York: Academic Press, 1981.
Quandt, William B. *Decade of Decisions: American Policy Toward the Arab-Israeli Conflict, 1967-1976*. Berkeley: University of California Press, 1977.
——"U.S. Policy in the Jordan Crisis, 1970." In *Force without War: U.S. Armed Forces as a Political Instrument*, Barry M. Blechman and Stephen S. Kaplan, eds., pp. 257-288. Washington DC: Brookings Institution, 1978.
Rabinowich, Oscar K. *Vladimir Jabotinsky's Conception of a Nation*. New York: Beechhurst Press, 1946.
Reich, Bernard. *The United States and Israel: Influence in the Special Relationship*. New York: Praeger Publishers, 1985.
Rubin, Jeff and Burt Brown. *The Social Psychology of Bargaining and Negotiations*. New York: Academic Press, 1975.
Sachar, Howard. *Egypt and Israel*. New York: Richard Marek, 1981.
Safran, Nadav. *Israel: The Embattled Ally*. Cambridge: Harvard University Press, 1978.
Schelling, Thomas C.. *The Strategy of Conflict*. Cambridge: Harvard University Press, 1960.
Schiff, Ze'ev, and Ehud Ya'ari. *Israel's Lebanon War*. New York: Simon & Schuster, 1984.
Schumpeter, Joseph. *In Imperialism and Social Classes*, Paul M. Sweezy, ed. New York: Augustus M. Kelley, Inc., 1951.
Sheehan, Edward R. F. *The Arabs, Israelis, and Kissinger: a Secret History of American Diplomacy in the Middle East*. New York: Readers Digest Press, 1976.
Sick, Gary. *All Fall Down: America's Tragic Encounter with Iran*. New York: Random House, 1985.
Silver, Eric. *Begin: The Haunted Prophet*. New York: Random House, 1984.
Snyder, Glenn, and Paul Diesing. *Conflict Among Nations*. Princeton: Princeton University Press, 1977.
Spiegel, Steven L. *The Other Arab-Israeli Conflict: Making America's Middle East Policy, from Truman to Reagan*. Chicago: University of Chicago Press, 1985.
Springborg, Robert. *Family, Power and Politics in Egypt: Sayed Bey Marei; His Clan, Clients and Cohorts*. Philadelphia: University of Pennsylvania Press, 1982.

Sullivan, George. *The Man Who Changed Middle East History*. New York: Walker and Co., 1981.
Talbott, Strobe. *Endgame: The Inside Story of SALT II*. New York: Harper & Row, 1979.
Touval, Saadia. *The Peace Brokers: Mediators in the Arab-Israeli Conflict, 1948–1979*. Princeton: Princeton University Press, 1982.
Vatikiotis, P. J. *The History of Egypt*, 2d ed. Baltimore: Johns Hopkins University Press, 1980.
——*Nasser and His Generation*. London: Billing and Sons, 1978.
Walt, Stephen M. *The Origins of Alliances*. Ithaca: Cornell University Press, 1987.
Waltz, Kenneth. *Man, the State and War: A Theoretical Analysis*. New York: Columbia University Press, 1959.
Waterbury, John. *Egypt: Burdens of the Past, Options for the Future*. Bloomington: University of Indiana Press, 1978.
Wien, Jake. *Saudi-Egyptian Relations: The Political and Military Dimensions of Saudi Financial Flows to Egypt*, RAND Paper P-6327. Santa Monica: The Rand Corporation, January 1980.
Yanai, Nathan. *Party Leadership in Israel: Maintenance and Change*. Ramat Gan: Turtledove Publishing, 1981.
Zartman, I. William, and Maureen R. Berman. *The Practical Negotiator*. New Haven: Yale University Press, 1982.

ARTICLES

Alker, Hayward Jr. "Dialectical Thinking about World Order: Ten World Hypotheses That Have Made My Day." Paper presented at the annual meeting of the International Studies Association, Anaheim, California, March 1986.
Aly, Abd Al-Monein Said and Manfred W. Wenner. "Modern Islamic Reform Movements: The Muslim Brotherhood in Contemporary Egypt." *Middle East Journal* 36 (3), Summer 1982.
Arian, Asher. "The Electorate: Israel 1977." In *Israel at the Polls: The Knesset Elections of 1977*, Howard Penniman, ed., pp. 59–89. Washington DC: American Enterprise Institute for Public Policy Research, 1979.
Aronson, Shlomo. "Israeli View of the Brookings Report." *Middle East Review* 10 (1), Fall 1977.
Aronoff, Myron J. "Political Polarization: Contradictory Interpretations of Israeli Reality." In *The Begin Era: Issues in Contemporary Israel*, Steven Heydmann, ed., pp. 53–77. Boulder, CO: Westview Press, 1984.
——"The Decline of the Israeli Labor Party." In *Israel at the Polls: The Knesset Elections of 1977*, Howard Penniman, ed., pp. 115–145. Washington DC: American Enterprise Institute for Public Policy Research, 1979.
Ayubi, Nazih, N.M. "The Political Revival of Islam: The Case of Egypt." *International Journal of Middle East Studies* 12, 1980.

Avineri, Shlomo. "Beyond Camp David." *Foreign Policy* 46, Spring 1982.
Avnery, Uri. "Menachem Begin: The Reality." *Worldview* 21, May 1978.
Ben-Zvi, Abraham. "Full-Circle on the Road to Peace? American Preconceptions of Peace in the Middle East: 1973–1978." *Middle East Review* 11 (2), Winter 1978–9.
Bierstecker, Thomas. "Dialectical Thinking About the World." Paper presented at the annual meeting of the International Studies Association, Anaheim, California, March 1986.
Brzezinski, Zbigniew, Francois Duchene, and Saeki Kiichi. "Peace in the International Framework." *Foreign Policy* 19, Summer 1975.
Bruzonsky, Mark. "Interview with Mohamed Ibrahim Kamel." *Middle East Journal* 38 (1), Winter 1984.
——"Interview with Ismail Fahmy." *The Middle East*, July, 1979.
Dawisha, Adeed. "Syria and the Sadat Initiative." *The World Today* 34 (5), May 1978.
Dhani, Mahmud. "The Egyptian White Paper on the Autonomy Negotiations." *Rus al-Yusuf* 57 (issue 2754), March 23, 1981.
Dessouki, Ali E. Hillal. "Policymaking in Egypt: A Case Study of the Open Door Economic Policy." *Social Problems* 28 (4), April 1981.
——"The Transformation of the Party System in Egypt, 1952–1977." In *Democracy in Egypt: Problems and Prospects*, Cairo Papers in Social Sciences, vol. 1 no. 2, Ali E. Hillal Dessouki, ed., pp. 7–24. Cairo: American University in Cairo, 1978.
——"The New Arab Political Order: Implications for the 1980s." In *Rich and Poor States in the Middle East: Egypt and the New Arab Order*, Malcolm Kerr and El Sayed Yassin, eds., pp. 318–347. Boulder, CO: Westview Press, 1982.
Edwards, Paul, William P. Alston, and A. N. Prior. "Russell, Bertrand Arthur Edward." In *Encyclopedia of Philosophy*, Volume 7, Paul Edwards, chief ed. New York: The Macmillan Company, 1967.
Eilts, Hermann Frederick. "Improve the Framework." *Foreign Policy* 41, Winter 1980.
Elazar, Daniel J. "Israel's Compound Polity." In *Israel at the Polls: The Knesset Elections of 1977*, Howard Penniman, ed., pp. 1–38. Washington DC: American Enterprise Institute for Public Policy Research, 1979.
Etheredge, Lloyd S. "Personality Effects on American Foreign Policy: 1898–1968: A Test of Interpersonal Generalization Theory." *American Political Science Review* 72, June 1978, pp. 434–451.
"The Failure of Camp David." *Palestine* 8 (7), April 1, 1982.
Feldman, Shai. "Peacemaking in the Middle East: The Next Step." *Foreign Affairs* 59 (4), Spring 1981.
Goodman, Leo. "Some Alternatives to Ecological Correlation." *American Journal of Sociology* 64, 1959.
Halabi, Usamah, Aron Turner, and Meron Benvenisti. "Land Alienation in

the West Bank: A Legal and Spatial Analysis." Jerusalem: The West Bank Data Base Project. April 1985.

Harik, Ilyia F. "Mobilization Policy and Political Change in Rural Egypt." In *Rural Politics and Social Change in the Middle East*, Richard Antoun and Ilyia Harik, eds., pp. 287–314. Bloomington: Indiana University Press, 1972.

Hinnebusch, Raymond A. "Egypt Under Sadat: Elites, Power Structure, and Political Change in a Post-Populist State." *Social Problems* 28 (4), April 1981.

Ibrahim, Saad Eddin. "Anatomy of Egypt's Militant Islamic Groups: Methodological Note and Preliminary Findings." *International Journal of Middle East Studies* 12, 1980.

Ikenberry, G. John. "The Irony of State Strength: Comparative Responses to the Oil Shocks in the 1970s." *International Organization* 40 (1), Winter 1986.

Imam, Zafar. "Soviet Treaties With Third World Countries." *Soviet Studies* 35 (1), January 1983.

Isaac, Rael and Jean. "The Impact of Jabotinsky on Likud's Policies." *Middle East Review* 10 (1), Fall 1977.

Jervis, Robert. "Cooperation Under the Security Dilemma." *World Politics* 30 (2), January 1978.

Keller, Bill. "Jewish Lobby Sensitive About its Image." *Congressional Quarterly Weekly Report* 39 (34), August 22, 1981.

Kenan, Amos. "'The Labor Party is to Blame.' The Zionist Dream Becomes Nightmare." *The Nation* 235 (12), October 16, 1982.

Knapp, Wilfred. "The United States and the Middle East: How Many Special Relationships?" In *The Middle East and the United States*, Haim Shaked and Itamar Rabinovich, eds., pp. 11–27. New Brunswick: Transaction Books, 1980.

Krasner, Stephen D. "Regimes and the Limits of Realism: Regimes as Autonomous Variables." *International Organization* 36 (2), Spring 1982.

Kreps, David M. and Robert Wilson. "Reputation and Imperfect Information." *Journal of Economic Theory* 27, 1982.

Kurth, James R. "A Widening Gyre: The Logic of American Weapons Procurement." *Public Policy* 19, 1971.

Lake, David A. "The State and American Trade Strategy in the Pre-Hegemonic Era." *International Organization* 42 (1), Winter 1988.

Maxfield, David. "Summit: First Euphoria, Then the Problems." *Congressional Quarterly Weekly Report* 36, September 23, 1978.

McKeown, Timothy J. "Firms and Tariff Regime Change: Explaining the Demand for Protection." *World Politics* 36 (2), January 1984.

Nash, John. "The Bargaining Problem." *Econometrica* 18, 1950.

Perlmutter, Amos. "Begin's Strategy and Dayan's Tactics: The Conduct of Israeli Foreign Policy." *Foreign Affairs* 56 (2), January 1978.

Pierre, Andrew J. "Beyond the 'Plane Package': Arms and Politics in the Middle East." *International Security* 3 (1), Summer 1978.

Putnam, Robert D. "Diplomacy and Domestic Politics: The Logic of Two-

Level Games." *International Organization*, 42, no. 3, pp. 427–460, Summer 1988.

Quandt, William B. "Reagan's Lebanon Policy: Trial and Error." *Middle East Journal* 38, Spring 1984.

Raiffa, Howard. "Arbitration Schemes for Generalized Two-Person Games." In *Contributions to the Theory of Games*, vol. 2, H. W. Kuhn and A. W. Tucker, eds., pp. 361–387. Princeton: Princeton University Press, 1953.

Robinson, W. S. "Ecological Correlations and the Behavior of Individuals." *American Sociological Review* 15 (3), June 1950.

Rosenau, James N. "National Interest." *International Encyclopedia of the Social Sciences*, vol. 11, David L. Sills, ed. New York: The Macmillan Company, 1968.

Sayegh, Fayez "The Camp David 'framework for peace': An Agreement on Procedures — or a Declaration of Principles? A Critical Examination of Some American and Egyptian Theses." *Search* 1, Winter 1980.

Searle, John R. "How to Derive 'Ought' From 'Is.' " *Philosophical Review* 73, 1964.

Selten, R. "The Chain-Store Paradox." *Theory and Decision* 9, 1978.

Simes, Dimitri K. "Disciplining Soviet Power." *Foreign Policy* 43 (Summer), 1981.

Simon, Herbert. "The Architecture of Complexity." *Proceedings of the American Philosophical Society* 106, 1962.

Spiegel, Steven A. "The Carter Approach to the Arab-Israel Dispute." In *The Middle East and the United States: Perceptions and Politics*, Haim Shaked and Itamar Rabinovich, eds., pp. 93–117. New Brunswick: Transaction Books, 1980.

Springborg, Robert. "Patterns of Association in the Egyptian Political Elite." In *Political Elites in the Middle East*, George Lenczowski, ed., pp. 83–107. Washington DC: American Enterprise Institute for Public Policy Research, 1975.

Stein, Arthur A. "Coordination and Collaboration: Regimes in an Anarchic World." *International Organization* 36 (2), Spring 1982.

Stork, Joe. "Israel as a Strategic Asset." In *Reagan and the Middle East*, pp. 17–48, Nasser Aruri, Fouad Moughrabi, and Joe Stork, eds. Belmont, MA: Association of Arab-American University Graduates, Inc., 1983.

Sullivan, Earl. "The U.S. and Egypt: The Potential Crisis." *Worldview* 22, December 1979.

Telhami, Shibley. "International Bargaining and the Level of Analysis Problem: The Case of Camp David." Ph.D. dissertation, University of California at Berkeley, 1986.

——"Israel's Invasion of Lebanon: The Effect on Palestinian Nationalism." Paper presented at the annual meeting of the International Studies Association - West, Berkeley, California, March 25–27, 1983.

——"American Foreign Policy: The Lessons of Beirut." Paper presented at the Center for International Affairs, Harvard University, Fall 1982.

Torgovnik, Efraim. "Accepting Camp David: The Role of Party Factions in Israeli Policy-Making." *Middle East Review* 11 (2), Winter 1978–9.
Tucker, Robert. "Behind Camp David." *Commentary* 66, November 1978.
Ulam, Adam. "Russian Nationalism." In *The Domestic Context of Soviet Foreign Policy*, Seweryn Bialer, ed. Boulder: Westview Press, 1981.
Warburg, Gabriel. "Islam and Politics in Egypt: 1952–1980." *Middle Eastern Studies* 18 (2), April 1982.
Whiting, Allen S. "Foreign Policy of China." In *Foreign Policy in World Politics*, 6th ed., Roy C. Macridis, ed., pp. 246–290. Englewood Cliffs, NJ: Prentice-Hall, Inc., 1985.
Yaniv, Avner and Yael Yishai. "Israeli Settlements in the West Bank: The Politics of Intransigence." *Journal of Politics* 43 (4), November 1981.
Young, Oran R. "Regime Dynamics: the Rise and Fall of International Regimes." *International Organization* 36 (2), Spring 1982.
Zahid, Mahmood. "Sadat and Camp David Reappraised." *Journal of Palestine Studies* 15, Autumn 1985.

Personal Interviews

Moshe Arens
Shlomo Avineri
Tahseen Bashir
Ali Dassouqi
Morris Draper
Butrus Ghali
Philip Habib
Ibrahim Kamel

Aleksandr Kislov
Samuel Lewis
Shimon Peres
William Quandt
Harold Saunders
Moshe Shahal
Ezer Weizman
Sayyid Yasin

Index

Abstractive theories, 19, 20; assumption of rationality, 25; bargaining framework and, 35, 36; definition of, 22-24; outcomes and, 16, 38, 41-42, 160, 183-87, 201; positive theories and, 22-24
Actors: objectively derived preferences of, 159-60; rational behavior of, 25, 37-38; utility functions and, 36
Aggarwal, Vinod, 34
Ajami, Fouad, 203
Algeria, trade patterns of, 75t
Ali, Mohammed, 53, 248n8
Alker, Hayward, 28
Allan, Pierre, 152
Allon Plan, 146
Analysis, levels of, 26-30, 33-34
Anarchy, 32-33, 39-40, 85
Anticolonialism, 63
A priori underdetermination, 36
al-Aqqad, Salah, 100, 105
Arab Cold War, 117
Arab-Israeli war (1967), 56, 95, 99, 117, 118
Arab-Israeli war (1973), 7, 36, 68, 101, 110-11, 120, 136
Arab League, 95, 96, 202
Arab Republic of Egypt, *see* Egypt
Arab states: Camp David accords and, 181; distribution of power in, 94-106; Egyptian influence and, 202-3; interdependence of, 248n7; Israeli relations with, 147-48; unity and, 7; *see also* Pan-Arabism; *specific countries*

Armament zones, 224
Aswan Dam, 60
Atavism, 86-87
Atom bomb, 52, 59; *see also* Nuclear weapons
Axelrod, Robert, 24, 25
Axioms: core theory and, 21; rationality and, 184; reasonableness of, 23
Ayineri, Shlomo, 121

Baghdad Pact, 52, 53
Bakdash, Khalid, 59
Bargaining: evaluation criteria, 158-60; framework for, 14; issues in, 16, 200-1; leaders' involvement in, 161; opening positions, 158-59; outcome of, *see* Outcomes; public opinion and, 194; zero sum game, 36, 161, 183-84
Bargaining behavior, 4; bottom line and, 164; deviation from optimal, 167-74; government systems and, 15, 168-74; leaders' personalities and, 174-80; optimal, 38, 160-67; time and, 170-71
Bargaining set, 38, 41, 42
Bargaining team, 161, 175
Bargaining theory, 18; assumptions in, 258-59n94; formal model, 36-38; framework of, 35-38; *see also* Abstractive theories; Positive theories; Prescriptive theory
al-Baz, Usama, 133, 176
Begin, Menachem, 8, 130, 143; bargaining behavior, 165-67, 173, 177-79;

Begin, Menachem (*Continued*)
  Carter and, 13, 166, 179; Egyptian bargaining position and, 163-64; government system and, 172-73; Ismailia visit, 225; Israeli-American relations and, 13, 105, 122, 144; letters to Carter, 232, 233; occupied territories and, 206-7; Palestinian issue and, 210-12; personality of, 5, 15, 158, 166, 172-73, 177-79, 185; Sinai settlements and, 164, 165; U.S. military aid and, 122; U.S. role at Camp David and, 150; West Bank and, 146, 159, 185-86
Behavior: actors' expectations and, 128-31; prediction of, 20, 22, 128-31; theories of, 20-24; *see also* State behavior
Ben-Gurion, David, 113, 114, 116, 139, 173
Binder, Leonard, 142
Britain: Baghdad Pact and, 52, 53; Egypt and, 53; Geneva conference and, 189; Gulf region and, 51; Iranian oil and, 54; Israel and, 112-15, 116; Persian Gulf and, 56; Suez crisis and, 55
Brown, Harold, 237
Brown, L. Carl, 46
Brzezinski, Zbigniew, 175, 179
Burrows, Bernard, 115

Camp David accords (September 17, 1978), 122, 225-30; associated principles, 229-30; framework for, 14-16, 226-30; peace treaty and, 229; preamble, 225-26
Camp David negotiations, 6-9; bargaining behavior and, 163-67; bargaining issues and, 162-63; exchange of letters, 231-37; form of, 151-53; government system and, 171-74; open-ended nature of, 151-53; outcome of, 197-201; peace framework, 206-7; prescriptive theory and, 160-67; tactical preferences and, 149-53; *see also* Egypt; Israel; United States
Capitalism, imperialism and, 86
Carter, Jimmy, 8, 13, 130, 225; bargaining strategy, 179-80; Begin's bargaining tactics and, 166, 179; commitment to Israel, 137; Egypt's opening position and, 163-64; letters to Begin, 232, 236; letters to Sadat, 231, 235; leverage with Israel, 140; Middle East policy and, 57-58, 120, 139-40; personality of, 15, 27, 158, 173, 179-80; public expectations and, 151; Sadat's bargaining strategy

and, 70, 140; Sadat's confidences to, 163, 167, 176; Sadat's threat to leave Camp David and, 70, 140; Sinai settlements and, 165; U.S. role at Camp David and, 149
Case studies: collinearity and, 26-28; cross-level fallacies and, 28; framework for, 18-42, 196-97; levels of analysis and, 26-30
Certainty, decisions under, 134; *see also* Uncertainty
Chain-store paradox, 13, 107, 108-11, 251*n*2
China, *see* People's Republic of China
Cold War, 51-56
Collinearity, 26-28, 29
Communism: in Middle East, 58-59, 60; Soviet Union and, 52
Conflict: bargaining behavior and, 36; binding threats and, 185
Cooperation, bargaining behavior and, 36
Crises: diplomatic time and, 152; structural change and, 68
Cross-level fallacies, 28-29
Cuban missile crisis, 60
Cultural atavism, 86-87
Czechoslovakia, Egyptian arms sale and, 60

Dayan, Moshe, 116, 164, 165, 166, 172, 173, 192
Decisions: domestic structure and, 34-35; risk and, 134-36
Decision theory, 244*n*24
Dekmejian, R. Hrair, 92
Demilitarized zones, 214, 224
Dependence, types of, 89
Descriptive theory, national interest and, 19-20
Détente, 119, 246*n*25; Egypt's neutralism and, 245*n*2; Middle East politics and, 51; Soviet-Egyptian relations and, 61, 64, 67, 245-46*n*6; U.S. public opinion and, 57
Determinate solutions, 200
Diesing, Paul, 36
Diplomatic tin e, 152
Disengagement agreements, 68-69
Domination, state characteristics and, 86-88
Dulles, John Foster, 52, 54

Early warning systems, 224
Eastern Europe, Soviet Union and, 52, 58
Ecological fallacy, 28

Index

Economic development, 224, 226
Economic power, 96, 101, 198; distribution of, 4, 143; Egyptian dependence and, 91; indicators of, 80-82; Pan-Arabism and, 93-94; regional changes in, 12; state behavior and, 33, 196-200; superpower competition and, 40, 45, 72
Egypt: bargaining behavior, 15, 163-64, 200; bargaining issues and, 162-63; bargaining team, 164; Britain and, 53; bureaucratic elites, 142-43; Camp David negotiations and, 8-9, 150, 208-9, 212-17; domestic preferences, 142-43; economic crisis in, 9-10, 198; economic dependence of, 100-5; environmental instability and, 88; food riots and, 9-10, 198; foreign policy, 91-106; Gaza position, 129-30, 163, 208, 214, 215; Geneva conference and, 7-8, 189-95; government system, 158, 170, 171-72, 185; infrastructure, 94-96; international preferences of, 12, 14, 141, 198; Iraq and, 249n20; Israeli bargaining strategy and, 187-95; Israeli-U.S. relations and, 141; military bases in, 61; military commitments of, 91, 95; military expenditures of, 69, 95, 96t, 99t, 101-2; misperceptions and, 131-34; national interests, 131; open door policy and, 10, 17, 86; Pan-Arabism and (*see* Pan-Arabism); policy changes, 6-7, 9-11; political dependence of, 100-5; preferences of, 12, 14, 39, 90-106, 141-43, 198; regional objectives, 8, 12-13, 39, 46, 99-106, 141, 185, 198, 202; Saudi Arabia and, 242n16; security issues, 208-9; Soviet alliance with, 60-61, 63-68, 137; Soviet expulsion from, 67-68, 119-20; Soviet military support and, 64, 66-68, 69, 76, 79, 142; superpower relations, 7, 12, 46, 62-71, 198; Third World relations, 65; trade patterns of, 73, 74t; United Arab Republic and, 249n17; U.S. aid to, 10, 103-4; U.S. alliance with, 46, 63, 68-71, 120-23, 141; U.S. role at Camp David and, 150; West Bank position, 129-30, 163, 208, 214, 215
Egyptian-Soviet Treaty of Friendship, 66, 68, 69, 76, 82
Eisenhower Doctrine, 55
Ends, prescription of, 21-22
European powers, oil and, 51
Evolution of Cooperation, The (Axelrod), 24

Expectations, behavior prediction and, 128-31
Explanatory variables: collinearity and, 26-27; misperception as, 132; social class as, 29-30; state-level characteristics as, 34-35; *see also* Variables

Fahmy, Ismail, 90, 133, 171
Fallacies: cross-level, 28-29; ecological, 28; individual, 28
Feldman, Shai, 121
France, 116; Geneva conference and, 189; Israeli arms sales and, 55, 56

Game theory, 22, 107-11, 183-84, 244-45n24
Gandhi, Indira, 69
Gaza, 8, 9, 201; Camp David accords and, 226-29; Egypt's position on, 129-30, 163, 208, 214, 215; Israel's position on, 16, 122, 129-30, 146, 159, 163, 185-86, 210-12; U.S. proposals and, 220-23; *see also* Palestinian autonomy
Geneva conference, 7-8, 68-69, 137, 189-95
Geography, security issues and, 88
Ghali, Butrus, 14, 65, 70-71, 103-4, 133, 164, 172, 177, 181
Golan Heights, 165, 186, 214
Government systems, 40; bargaining behavior and, 158, 168-74, 187; centralized, 4, 15, 142, 158, 168, 170; decentralized, 4, 138, 158, 168, 170; preferences and, 138, 169; public opinion and, 148; *see also specific countries*
Great Britain, *see* Britain
Groupthink, 175
Gulf of Suez, 220
Gulf Organization for the Development of Egypt, 103
Gur, Motta, 178, 189

Harsanyi, John, 23, 25, 183-84
Haykal, Mohammed, 47, 132, 172, 187
Hobbes, Thomas, 168
Hobson, John, 86
Hussein, King, 64, 118

Imperialism, capitalism and, 86
Independence, 33, 88-90; domination and, 85, 87; regional power and, 90
Indeterminacy problem, 23
India, Egyptian arms and, 69
Individual, as unit of analysis, 32
Individual fallacy, 28

Inference, cross-level, 28-29
International Court of Justice, 215
International relations: domestic variables and, 34-35; framework for study of, 5-6, 18-42; ideological positions and, 186; international preferences and, 127; national preferences and, 169; nesting and, 31-32
International relations theories: contradictory, 32; cross-level fallacies and, 28; empirical cases and, 4-5; level of generality, 30, 32; levels of analysis, 26-30; overlap of, 18-19
International structure, level of analysis and, 32-34
Iran, 119; Arab-Israeli conflict and, 202; Baghdad Pact and, 52; hostages in, 71; Soviet trade with, 72; trade patterns of, 74t; U.S. military build-up of, 57
Iraq: Arab-Israeli conflict and, 202; Baghdad Pact and, 52, 53; Egypt and, 249n20; Israeli attack on nuclear reactor in, 123; Kuwait and, 249n20; military expenditures of, 96t; Soviet Union and, 57, 60, 76, 82; trade patterns of, 75t
Israel, 8-9; air force, 251n7; Arab states' relations with, 147-48; attack on Iraqi nuclear reactor, 123; bargaining issues and, 162-63; bargaining strategy, 15, 16, 159, 164, 187-95, 200; bargaining team, 166; Britain and, 112-15, 116; diplomatic relations with Egypt and, 130; domestic preferences, 13, 14, 145-49; Egyptian-American relations and, 115-17; expectations of, 130; foreign policy, 13, 46, 107-24; French arms sales to, 55, 56; Gaza position, 16, 122, 129-30, 146, 159, 163, 185-86, 210-12; Geneva talks and, 7-8, 189-95; geographic instability and, 88; government system, 148, 170, 172-73; international preferences, 13, 14, 107-24, 144-45, 199; invasion of Lebanon, 89, 111, 123, 139, 202, 253n38; Jordan's relations with, 147-48; Labor party, 145-48; Likud party, 8, 145-48; military of, 51, 144-45, 194, 251n7; oil supply arrangement with U.S., 238-39; public opinion in, 192; regional preferences, 108, 199, 202; security interests, 13, 15, 88, 108, 148, 206-7; Soviet aid to, 112, 113; strategic importance of, 120-21; trade patterns of, 74t; U.S. alliance with, 13, 14, 50, 70, 108-11, 113-22, 140, 144, 199, 203; U.S. military and, 57, 76;

U.S. role at Camp David and, 150; U.S.-Arab ties and, 108, 110; Western Europe and, 51
Israeli, Raphael, 11
Israeli-Egyptian peace treaty, 123

Jalloud, Abdul Salam, 77
al-Jammal, Ali Hamdi, 63-64
Janis, Irving, 171, 175
Jerusalem: Camp David process and, 207, 233-35; Egyptian position on, 215-16, 234-35; Israeli position on, 233; Sadat's visit to, 6, 8, 70, 137, 148, 198, 225; U.S. position on, 223
Jervis, Robert, 25, 88, 128, 131, 174
Johnson, Lyndon B., 119
Jordan, 95; Arab-Israeli conflict and, 162; Camp David accords and, 186, 208, 226-29; Geneva conference and, 189; Israeli relations with, 147-48; PLO attack by, 131; trade patterns of, 75t; U.S. proposals on, 221-23
Judaea (Judea), *see* West Bank
Justice, theories of, 21-22

Kamel, Ibrahim, 71, 103, 133, 176, 177
Kenan, Amos, 110
Kennan, George, 51
Kerr, Malcolm, 131
Khartoum, Arab summit conference in, 100-1
Khruschev, Nikita, 60
Kierkegaard, Soren, 21
Kissinger, Henry, 7, 11, 55, 57, 68, 136-37, 176, 188, 189, 190-94
Knapp, Wilfred, 109
Korean War, 51, 114
Kurth, James, 4, 36
Kuwait: Iraq and, 249n20; trade patterns of, 74t

Lakatos, Imre, 20
Land purchases, West Bank, 207, 211-12
Lavon Affair, 115
Leaders: bargaining role, 15, 161; level of focus, 175; role separation and, 174-75; *see also specific persons*
Leaders' personalities, 31, 40; bargaining behavior and, 4, 158, 174-80; foreign policy and, 27; government system and, 171-72; state behavior and, 11; *see also specific persons*
Lebanon: Israeli invasion of, 89, 111, 123, 139, 202, 253n38; Syria and, 89
Lenin, V. I., 86

Libya, 56, 95; trade patterns of, 72-73, 75t; Soviet Union and, 77

Means, prescription theories and, 22
Media, government-controlled, 171
Meir, Golda, 191-92
Mersa Matrouth, port facilities at, 66, 79
Middle East: balancing tendency of states, 73-77; GNP of, 96-99; "moderate" states in, 72-73; "radical" states in, 72-73; superpower competition in, 51-52, 54-55, 62-71; *see also* Arab states; *specific countries*
Military bases, 61, 62, 76, 79
Military power: distribution of, 4, 51-52, 95; Egyptian dependence and, 91; indicators of, 77-79; Pan-Arabism and, 93-94; state behavior and, 33, 196-200; superpower competition and, 12, 45, 198
Misperceptions: as cause of behavior, 131-34, 167-68; groupthink and, 171; *see also* Perceptions
Morgenthau, Hans, 85
Morocco, trade patterns of, 75t
Mubarak, Husni, 133
Muslim Brotherhood, 249*n*18

Nasser, Gamal, 17, 54; aid from Arab states and, 100-1; Arab-Israeli war (1967) and, 117-18; Britain and, 53; Pan-Arabism and, 28, 53, 64, 92, 131, 143; popularity of, 117; Rabat Conference and, 105; Soviet Union and, 52, 60-61, 64
Natan, Ebi, 17
National interest: defined, 169, 243*n*3; descriptive theory and, 19-20; government system and, 168-69; prescriptive theory and, 20
Naval forces, port visits and, 82-83
Negotiation outcomes, *see* Outcomes
Negotiations, *see* Bargaining
Nesting procedure, 19, 30-35, 38
Nixon, Richard, 57
Normative theories, 21
Nuclear weapons: Egypt's proposal on, 214; superpower competition and, 78

Oil: British-Iranian relations and, 54; embargo on, 8, 14, 57, 70, 120, 136; European powers and, 51; Israeli-U.S. agreement on, 238-39; price of, 57, 101, 104, 190; U.S. interests and, 14, 50, 72; Western dependence on, 136
Ottoman Empire, 53-54, 248*n*8

Outcomes: abstractive theory and, 38, 183-87, 201; assessment of, 180-83; determinate, 23; explanatory variables and, 34-35; objectively derived preferences and, 159-60; opening bargaining positions and, 158-59; parameters for, 38; probabilities of, 134-35

Pahlavi, Mohammad Reza, 54, 57, 71
Pakistan, Baghdad Pact and, 52
Palestine Liberation Organization, 7, 64, 102
Palestinian autonomy, 16; Arab-Israeli conflict and, 162, 163; Camp David negotiations and, 9, 181, 186, 201, 207, 208-9, 226-29; Egypt's advocacy and, 131, 141, 214, 215; Geneva talks and, 7; leaders' personalities and, 15; Likud party and, 146; symbolic, 12; U.S. proposals on, 220-23; *see also* Gaza; West Bank
Pan-Arabism: Egyptian dependence and, 99; Egyptian elites and, 142-43; Egypt's national objectives and, 8, 12, 28, 91, 141; Egypt's regional power and, 12, 91-94, 141, 198-99; as international regime, 93-94; Nasser and, 28, 53, 64, 92, 131, 143; Sadat and, 3; United Arab Republic and, 7
People's Republic of China: Soviet alliance with, 51, 59, 61; U.S. and, 61
Perceptions: government systems and, 170; preferences and, 128; reality and, 132; *see also* Misperceptions
Persian Gulf, Britain and, 56
Pettigrew, Thomas, 175
Pipes, Richard, 87
Plato, 21
Policy makers, behavior prediction and, 128-31
Political philosophy, 21-22
Political power, indicators of, 82-83
Port visits, political power and, 82-83
Positive theories, 135; abstractive theories and, 22-24; acceptability of, 21; assumption of rationality, 24; bargaining framework and, 35, 36, 38; definition of, 20-21; form of, 20-21; identifying preferences and, 39; prescriptive theories and, 22
Post-colonial movements, 59, 60
Power, 36; changing distribution of, 35, 40, 94-106; political indicators, 82-83; realist theory and, 35; state alignments and, 33; state objectives and, 85; sys-

Power (*Continued*)
  temic vs. dynamic, 77-78; uncertainty about, 37; *see also* Economic power; Military power; Regional power
Prediction, positive theories and, 20-21
Preference function, 161
Preferences, 35; defined, 127; distribution of power and, 127; government system and, 138, 169; identifying, 39; levels of, 39; objectively derived, 159-60; perceptions and, 128; power distribution and, 40, 127; regional politics and, 84-106; state behavior and, 169; superpower competition and, 40, 45-83; uncertainty about, 37, 183-85; *see also specific countries*
Prescriptive theory, 38, 180, 200-1; assumption of rationality, 24; bargaining framework and, 35, 36; Camp David negotiations and, 160-67; definition of, 21-22; government systems and, 170; national interest and, 20; outcomes and, 41; positive theories and, 22
Price, Robert, 174
Psychological variables, 31
Public opinion, bargaining and, 194

al-Qaddafi, Muammar, 56, 73, 76, 77, 102, 105
Qasim, Abd al-Kareem, 249*n*20
Quandt, William, 164, 182

Rabat conference (1969), 105
Rabat summit conference (1974), 102
Rational actor theories, 25
Rationality, 36; assumption of, 24-25; imposed axioms of, 184; liberal vs. conservative, 184; risk and, 135; uncertainty about, 161, 183-85
Ray, James Lee, 28
Reagan, Ronald, 71
Realist theory, 4, 18; bargaining parameters and, 36; identifying preferences and, 39; power and, 35
Regime, Pan-Arabism as, 93-94
Regional power: changing distribution of, 94-106, 198-200; independence and, 90; Pan-Arabism and, 12, 91-94, 141, 198-99; preferences and, 127; superpower competition and, 40, 46-47
Risk, decisions and, 134-36
Rogers, William, 65
Rogers Plan, 64, 65, 76, 131
Role separation, leaders' personalities and, 174-75

Russell, Bertrand, 244*n*13
Russell Paradox, 244*n*13

al-Sadat, Muhammad Anwar, 225; Arab leadership and, 104-5; bargaining strategy, 70, 133, 140, 163-64, 176-77; Carter and, 70, 140, 163, 164, 167, 176; expectations of Camp David, 129-30; Geneva conference and, 68-69; government system and, 171-72; Jerusalem visit, 6, 8, 70, 137, 148, 198, 225; Kissinger and, 176; letters to Carter, 233, 234, 235; military establishment, 142; misperceptions and, 131-34; open door policy and, 17, 86; Pan-Arabism and, 3; personality of, 4, 5, 11, 15, 158, 175-77, 201; public expectations of, 151; regional power and, 94; Soviet alliance and, 64-66; threat to leave Camp David and, 70, 140
Samaria, *see* West Bank
Saudi Arabia: AWACS sale to, 121; Egyptian aid from, 102-3; Egyptian economic policy and, 242*n*16; Egyptian-Iraqi relations and, 249*n*20; military expenditures of, 96t; trade patterns of, 74t
Saunders, Harold, 181, 182-83
Schumpeter, Joseph, 86
Security issues, 85, 148; Camp David accords and, 226; domination and, 87, 248*n*8; geographic instability and, 88; state behavior and, 31, 33; superpower competition and, 40; U.S. proposals on, 219
Self-preservation, 33
Shah of Iran, *see* Pahlavi, Mohammad Reza
Sharrett, Moshe, 116, 147
Shazly, Saad el-Din, 176
Simes, Dimitri, 86
Sinai, 162; Begin's proposal to Knesset on, 231-33; Camp David negotiations and, 8, 133, 162, 165-66, 231-33; Egypt's position on, 214, 233; Israeli military situation and, 144-45; oil fields in, 101; return to Egyptian control, 132
Singer, David, 26
Snyder, Glenn, 36
Snyder, Mark, 174-75
Social class, as explanatory variable, 29-30
Socialist parties, in Middle East, 59
Social order, bargaining team and, 175
Social psychology, 174-75

Social setting, game theory and, 244-45n24
Sovereign authority, 168
Soviet Union: Arab-Israeli war (1967) and, 119; Eastern Europe and, 58; Egyptian alliance with, 60-61, 63-68, 137; Egyptian military support and, 64, 66-68, 69, 76, 79, 142; Egyptian-Soviet Treaty of Friendship and, 66, 68, 69, 76, 82; expulsion from Egypt, 67-68, 119-20; Geneva conference and, 189, 190; Iranian trade with, 72; Iraq and, 57, 76, 82; Israeli aid from, 112, 113; Libya and, 77; linkage politics and, 246n25; Middle East policy, 58-62; military expenditures of, 61; military power and, 51, 73-77, 78, 79; Sadat and, 11; Syria and, 56, 76; systemic power and, 77, 78, 80; trade patterns of, 72-73; *see also* Superpower(s); Superpower competition
State(s): balancing tendencies of, 33, 73-77; environmental effects on, 87-88; external objectives of, 85-88; status quo, 85-86
State behavior: cross-level fallacies and, 28-29; economic power and, 33, 196-200; military power and, 196-200; misperceptions as cause of, 131-34; national preferences and, 169; pursuit of independence and, 88-90; *see also* Behavior
Strait of Tiran, *see* Tiran Straits
Strategic Defense Initiative, 110, 123
Suez Canal, U.S. proposal on, 220
Suez crisis (1956), 53, 55
Suez War, 60, 117
Superpower(s): anarchy and, 39-40; dependence on, 89-90; economic disparities, 47, 247n49; strategic parity, 47; trade with, 80-82; *see also* Soviet Union; United States
Superpower competition, 31, 33; distribution of power and, 45-49; economic power and, 40, 45, 72; military power and, 52, 198; security issues and, 40; Soviet policies and, 59-62; state preferences and, 40, 45-83
Surface-to-air missiles, in Egypt, 66
Syria, 186; Arab-Israeli conflict and, 118, 162, 202; Camp David accords and, 229; Communist Party in, 59; Geneva conference and, 189; Lebanon and, 89; military expenditures of, 96t; Ottomans and, 248n8; Soviet Union and, 56, 60, 61, 76; trade patterns of, 74t; United Arab Republic and, 249n17

Third World, Soviet relations with, 60
Threats, binding, 185
Time, bargaining behavior and, 152, 161, 170-71
Tiran Straits, 220, 253nn.35-36
Trade: arms, 81-82; patterns of, 72-73; radical moderate states and, 72-73; with superpowers, 80-82
Treaties, political power and, 82; *see also specific treaties*
Troutbeck, Sir John, 112, 115
Turkey, Baghdad Pact and, 52

Ulam, Adam, 87
Uncertainty, 37, 134, 161-62, 183-85
United Arab Republic, 7, 249n17
United Nations, 188, 213
United Nations Security Council Resolution 242, 218-19, 222, 225, 226, 228
United Nations Security Council Resolution 338, 218-19, 226
United States: Arab-Israeli war (1967) and, 118-19; bargaining strategy, 15, 167, 200; bargaining team, 167, 180; Camp David proposals, 218-24; Camp David role, 149-50, 153; China and, 61; domestic preferences, 14, 138-39, 149, 150, 199; Egyptian aid from, 10, 103-4; Egyptian alliance with, 63, 68-71, 120-23, 141; Egyptian preferences and, 181; foreign policy, 46, 51-52, 190-91; Gaza position, 220-23; Geneva talks and, 7-8, 189-95; government system, 170, 173-74; international preferences, 136-38, 149, 199; Iran and, 57; Israel's alliance with, 13, 14, 50, 70, 108-11, 113-22, 140, 144, 199-203; Jerusalem position, 223; Jewish community in, 113-14, 120, 190; Middle East policy, 14, 50-58, 136-41; military (*see* United States military); oil interests, 14, 50, 72; oil supply arrangement with Israel, 238-39; preferences of, 136-41; Soviet containment and, 51-52; Soviet parity with, 56; systemic power, 77, 78, 80; West Bank settlements and, 182, 220-23; *see also* Superpower(s); Superpower competition
United States military: Israel and, 57, 76, 194; Rapid Deployment Force and, 71,

United States military (*Continued*)
122; regional power, 79; Strategic Defense Initiative and, 110, 123; systemic power, 78
Universal Declaration of Human Rights, 213

Vance, Cyrus, 166, 176, 178, 238
Variables: abstraction of, 244*n*13; internal, 40; level of analysis and, 34; pursuit of dominance, 86-89; relative weight of, 30, 42; separation of, 28, 30; *see also* Explanatory variables
Vatikiotis, P. J., 92
Vietnam War, 56-57, 119

Waltz, Kenneth, 26, 33, 85
War of Attrition (1968-70), 64

Watergate scandal, 190-91
Weizman, Ezer, 105, 119, 121-22, 159, 164, 165, 166, 172, 173, 178, 237
West Bank, 8, 9, 201; Egypt's position on, 129-30, 163, 208, 214, 215; Israel's position on, 16, 122, 129-30, 146-48, 159, 163, 185-86, 210-12; Labor party and, 146-48; Likud party and, 146; U.S. and, 182, 220-23; *see also* Palestinian autonomy
Wishful thinking, bargaining behavior and, 174, 175-76, 179

Yadin, Yigael, 159
Yasin, Sayyid, 132-33
Yemen, 94, 95, 117

Zero sum game, 36, 161, 183-84

GPSR Authorized Representative: Easy Access System Europe, Mustamäe tee
50, 10621 Tallinn, Estonia, gpsr.requests@easproject.com

www.ingramcontent.com/pod-product-compliance
Lightning Source LLC
Chambersburg PA
CBHW072126290426
44111CB00012B/1799